TRACKING THE HOOLIGANS

D1355612

Michael Layton – To the men and women of the British Transport Police, my late father George for his support during the early years of my police career, and my wife Andry for her continuing support and encouragement to write about my life in the police.

Alan Pacey – To my mum Maureen, who is still going strong at eighty-one years, to my wife Carol for being there, and to my former colleagues in the British Transport Police, particularly those that are still keeping us safe.

TRACKING THE HOOLIGANS

HOOLIGANS

A HISTORY OF FOOTBALL VIOLENCE ON THE UK RAIL NETWORK

MICHAEL LAYTON QPM AND ALAN PACEY

AMBERLEY

First published 2016

Amberley Publishing
The Hill, Stroud
Gloucestershire, GL5 4EP

www.amberley-books.com

Copyright © Michael Layton QPM and
Alan Pacey, 2016

The right of Michael Layton QPM and Alan Pacey
to be identified as the Authors of this work has been
asserted in accordance with the Copyrights, Designs
and Patents Act 1988.

ISBN 978 1 4456 5180 4 (print)
ISBN 978 1 4456 5181 1 (ebook)

British Library Cataloguing in Publication Data.
A catalogue record for this book is available
from the British Library.

Typesetting and Origination by Amberley Publishing
Printed in the UK.

CONTENTS

FOREWORD

As a teenage football fan in the late 1960s and early 1970s, I saw violence at football matches fairly frequently. It seems strange to say it now, but there was almost an expectation that certain matches would be accompanied by aggressive behaviour and the wise football fan took steps to try and avoid likely flashpoints, albeit sometimes unsuccessfully.

While there were often news items about the very worst excesses of behaviour, the frequency of almost casual violence, and destruction of property, was not reflected in the reporting of the day.

When I became a police officer in 1976 I quickly learned just how regularly confrontations occurred between rival groups, and the accompanying crimes of not just violence and damage to property, but also theft, drunkenness and fraud. It was apparent that this was a problem on a massive scale that disrupted the lives of not only the immediate victims, but also people just trying to go about their day-to-day lives in towns and cities across the UK.

Now it is easy to forget that, with a few exceptions, all weekend football matches took place on a Saturday and kicked off at 3 p.m. This meant that thousands of people would be on the move travelling to either home or away matches at precisely the same time. At the football grounds the vast majority would be standing on terraces, rather than sitting, and a fair amount of alcohol would have been consumed, not only beforehand but within the ground and during the match as well.

Some of these games, particularly where there was either intense local rivalry or some historical conflict that had been conflated over the years, presented a huge policing challenge for local police forces. For the British Transport Police the task was even greater, for rather than having just one fixture to think about, each Saturday produced forty-plus matches to consider and to evaluate the policing requirement, which might well involve long journeys by train starting many hours before the game and several after it.

Uniquely the BTP had, and still have, to consider not just the two teams playing each other, but also whether fans were likely to meet with rivals travelling to other fixtures but passing along the same route. The possibility of pre-planned or spontaneous disorder was a real risk and ever-present threat, and that remains the case to this day.

The art of policing football fans in transit required a different approach to local policing of an individual fixture. In a town hosting a match, large numbers of officers could be concentrated in and around the stadium, and the same resources used to escort supporters away from the ground. In contrast, British Transport Police officers had to spread themselves across numerous stations and trains conveying fans. One football special might carry 400 fans and be escorted by just a sergeant and four constables. Additionally, some supporters would choose to travel by regular services, adding to the complexity of managing a large movement of people across the country and within cities.

By necessity, British Transport Police officers became experts in planning and resourcing the large-scale movements of sports fans. Before the advent of so-called 'dry trains' many fans would be carrying large quantities of alcohol with them, and their tribal nature meant that they would behave collectively in ways that individually they would not dare to do.

In order to maintain some semblance of good order, BTP officers learnt the art of 'positive engagement' with supporters, and also how to identify influential members of groups to keep them on side. Fans and officers frequently got to know each other well during the course of a football season as they travelled regularly together, and BTP officers were often perceived to be helpful and supportive – in contrast to local officers, who might be seen as treating all fans the same whether they be a hooligan or law-abiding citizen.

This unique set of circumstances allowed the British Transport Police to develop a body of knowledge and understanding about the dynamics of travelling supporters that would become central to the development of the more organised police response to football violence, and in tackling the spread of British football violence in Europe.

This book charts the development of the intelligence systems in which BTP took the lead, and the creation of structures that enabled the force to respond extremely effectively in public order situations, as well as developing significant expertise in post-incident investigation and undercover tactics. The British Transport Police has a proud history of policing travelling football supporters, and I am pleased that so many retired officers have been able to place their stories 'on the record', thus providing a legacy for the future, and that the BTP History Group has been able to support this venture.

While this book tells the story of how violence is confronted by the force week-in, week-out, it also illustrates the important fact that it still polices with the consent of the vast majority of genuine fans, who want nothing more than to enjoy the game that they love and cherish.

Paul Robb QPM
President of BTP History Society

INTRODUCTION

The FA Cup was first held during the 1871/72 season, and the growth of the railway network from 1840 onwards created greater opportunities for football fans to travel to away fixtures across the UK by means of public transport.

In 1881, in a sign of things to come, two railway officials were knocked unconscious at Wigan railway station by a group of supporters travelling to an away match at Newton Heath. In 1886, a violent clash took place between Preston North End fans and Queen's Park fans, from Glasgow, at a railway station.

Three years later, supporters from Nantwich and Crewe confronted each other across the platforms at Middlewich railway station following the Cheshire final. After an initial stand-off, two men, one from each side, then engaged in a fight on the track before a large number of Nantwich fans stormed across the line to engage their opponents. Order was only restored after a train arrived to take them away.

So what has changed ...

In the 1951/52 football season it was estimated that some 40,000,000 people attended Football League games, with up to 53,000 fans attending Arsenal's home games alone. It was by far the most popular sport in Britain.

In April 1952, policewoman 9 M. Bury, of BTP's special branch in Manchester, wrote an article in a BTP journal on the game of football and concluded,

Yes a football match is a healthy institution, affording a welcome break from everyday responsibilities for a while. Grievances and opinions may be aired freely, but without any deep seated ill-feeling, and a handshake in some club at the end of the day mends quarrels as quickly as they were made. It is to be devoutly hoped that the British people will long cherish their national characteristic, the sporting instinct, and may there always be football matches where it can be so freely expressed.

Unfortunately her heartfelt description of the beautiful game, and hopes for the future, did not live up to expectations.

In 1972, looking back at significant policing issues that affected the British Transport Police, Chief Constable Gay raised issues relating to football hooliganism, which was a major demand on manpower resources, particularly on Saturdays, when requirements exceeded available manpower.

He commented,

Early in the season it seemed as if the combined efforts of the civil police, the railway management, and ourselves were beginning to bite but the situation deteriorated as the season advanced. It was prevented from getting completely out of hand, but more trains to be covered, trouble spots where opposing supporters could confront each other, the increasing number of incidents involving missiles thrown at trains by rival supporters, either on the lineside, or in passing trains, all aggravated the problem.

On an average Saturday some thirty trains carried police escorts of between two and eight officers. Officers sometimes reach the destination with their uniforms soiled with spittle, and other filth, burnt with cigarette ends, or slashed.

In his Chief Constable's Report of 1987, K. H. Ogram QPM said,

Police presence on trains conveying football supporters, throughout the rail network, continues to be a major requirement on manpower. Monitoring supporters movements is particularly necessary within the London area in both London Underground and mainline termini, in order to prevent public disorder.

A total of 2,357 trains were escorted during the football season 1986/87. A total of 863 persons were reported for a total of 3,284 offences committed on trains conveying football supporters. Under the provisions of Sporting Events (Control of Alcohol) Act 1985 and the British Railways Board Byelaw 3(a) 1,210 trains were declared 'dry' and escorted by officers of the force.

In his introduction to the 1997/98 BTP annual report, Chief Constable David Williams said,

Social changes are having their effect on policing of the rail system. Policing of large movements of people attending sporting fixtures and other events is putting an increasing strain on resources ... Football related disorder has been on the increase with an emerging trend of confrontation at stations which is deliberate and well organised.

At 7.20 p.m. on Friday 23 August 2013, a man wearing a football shirt was caught on CCTV following a dreadful attack on a seventy-year-old grandfather. The victim was travelling home from a day out in London with his wife and three grandchildren, aged between six and twelve years.

As the train approached Shenfield station, the suspect became abusive towards the wife and grandchildren. The victim asked him to stop, whereupon he was punched three times in the head, leaving him with bruising to his face and arms.

PC Kelly Durant from the BTP said, 'This was a brutal and violent attack on a man who was simply standing up to abusive and antisocial behaviour ...' Was this the actions of a football hooligan, or did it just happen to be the actions of a mindless criminal who just happened to be wearing a football shirt? Either way, the result was the same in terms of the public's perception.

This book tells the true story of football violence on the rail, ferry and tube networks in the UK, and has been written by two former police officers who experienced the violence and culture of groups of frequently organised football hooligans first-hand. These hooligans often used railway stations and trains as their chosen battlegrounds to confront opponents and inflict misery on the innocent. In the main, the identities of the hooligans remain deliberately anonymous – they simply don't deserve glorification.

In what many might see as a staggering figure, incidents of football-related violence occurring within the jurisdiction of the British Transport Police are referred to in the following chapters covering every year between 1967 to 2015 – a forty-eight-year period!

The book is about what the 'good guys and girls' have to put up with – and all in the name of the beautiful game. It is a tribute to the retired men and women of the British Transport Police who, in the main, found a way to keep the lid on football violence during their service, sometimes using quite unconventional methods. A number of them recollect their experiences in this book and, while there are moments of humour, the common theme is one of small numbers of police officers holding the thin blue line to prevent anarchy.

Now that mantel rests squarely with today's modern BTP.

I

THE EARLY YEARS

Even as far back as July 1951, it appears that Scottish fans visiting London for international matches between Scotland and England were leaving an impression. In one case a Scottish fan was arrested at Euston railway station by a BTP officer as he alighted from a train carrying a parcel, which he alleged he had found squeezed between the platform and the train.

When questioned, he informed police that he had consumed a considerable amount of alcohol, and thought that the parcel contained sandwiches which his friends had promised to share with him. As he ripped the contents open it was in fact a pair of shoes.

As he later stood in the dock wearing a hat with a tartan band and a feather, with a matching tartan scarf, the police officer was forced to admit, when giving his evidence, that the defendant might well have been too drunk to know what he was doing. The magistrate at Clerkenwell Court gave him the benefit of the doubt and dismissed the charge to a round of applause from the gallery.

Dennis Temporal MBE joined the BTP in 1958 in Nottingham, where he commenced his police career. More than two decades later he was to become a key figure in the forces approach to combatting football-related hooliganism. His interaction with football fans in those days was predominately peaceful and he generally had good relationships with local football supporters. Any problems that did arise were generally dealt with by using common sense and some stern words of advice. He later moved to Southampton and was involved in policing Southampton, and Portsmouth football clubs, which again was mostly peaceful in those days.

Rob Davison finished his career with BTP as a chief inspector at Waterloo, and describes his early experiences of policing football fans,

While still a probationer constable, I was transferred from Birmingham New Street to Coventry in 1966, after completing my recruit course at Tadworth Training School. Coventry was my home town and its football club, known as 'The Sky Blues' were riding high under Jimmy Hill's leadership. They had gone into the First Division and I believe that, with the exception of Walsall, all the other Midlands football teams were in the First Division when the 1967/68 season started.

One of the many innovations by the club was the 'Sky Blue Special', which was a dedicated rake of railway coaches that the football club had hired from British Rail and was kitted out for their use for away matches. There was a P. A. system throughout the train and I think they had a DJ playing records and making announcements while on the move. A brake van was adapted for use as a buffet car for refreshments. Fortunately no food or drink were kept on the train between outings, although I seem to remember there were a couple of break-ins while the train was stabled in Coventry Carriage Sidings, but there was nothing to steal.

This arrangement was advantageous to BTP at Coventry because it meant that most genuine supporters would take the 'Sky Blue Special' to away games, and I think there were special rates for them. There didn't appear to be any great numbers of the unruly element, so we rarely got any escort duties. However, there were occasional incidents with Coventry fans at the railway station, or in the vicinity.

One Saturday afternoon, when I think it was Birmingham City visiting, there was an altercation between the two sets of supporters on the front yard of the station. There was always needle between Birmingham and Coventry! The Birmingham mob were ushered into the concourse and station staff were able to block off all but one set of glass doors so that the police could supervise who came in and out. The mob charged the doors and one of them shattered. This was the first time I had drawn my truncheon in anger and it was under instruction from the uniform sergeant who had come from Birmingham New Street. This was Stan Jones and he was captured by a photographer from the local paper, the *Coventry Evening Telegraph*, facing the mob with his truncheon being held in a threatening manner!

The most memorable football-related incident in my time at Coventry didn't actually involve any local supporters. Coventry must have been at home as there was a dog handler, Ivor Kerslake, sent from Birmingham to assist the Coventry officers. However, most of the visiting supporters must have left as there was only Ivor and myself left on duty. It was wintertime and dark when we were advised by the station supervisor that there was a Millwall football special on the way from Birmingham. It was intended for the train to run though to London on the Up line adjacent to platform 2, so Ivor, with his dog, and myself made our way over to the platform. Numbers 2 and 3 were actually an island platform and had a traveller's fare buffet and waiting room.

When the train was due to pass through we could see the lights from it in the distance, and then it came to a halt well before it had got to the platform! We suspected that someone had pulled the communication cord which occasionally happened on these football specials, as an act of devilment and stupidity. We swiftly made our way along the platform to the Birmingham end and went down the ramp onto the track. Before we could reach the train, however, it moved off and slowly trundled along and came to a halt alongside platform 2.

We hurried back only to see a lot of the Millwall supporters leave the train and mill about on the platform. We could see police among them. When we reached the sergeant in charge of the train escort he told us that the Millwall mob had raided the buffet and that he, and his officers, had been unable to do anything about it. I think his name was Wally Leake and he was a big man who looked as though he could handle troublesome supporters!

Leaving Ivor and dog to help him and his men to get the supporters back on the train, I went into the buffet to see what the damage was. Fortunately the female member of staff had been able to lock herself into the kitchen/office area behind the counter and she hadn't been hurt. She said that all the food and drink on display on the counter, and behind and under the counter, had been stolen. I think the till had also been forced so the takings were gone!

By the time I got back onto the platform to tell Sergeant Leake what had been stolen, the train was on the move and the jubilant Millwall supporters were hanging out of the doors and shouting abuse. Unfortunately there were no arrests and it was left to me to do the paperwork!

The Coventry 'nuisance element' had a habit of lurking around the approach road (Eaton Road) to the station after home games in the hope of picking off any stray away supporters. If there were sufficient numbers they would descend en masse on the station, usually after the main bulk of away supporters, and police, had left. On one occasion my Coventry City Police colleague had parked his new Hillman Imp Panda car on the station front and we were chatting when we saw the mob coming down Eaton Road. He told me to get in the car and with headlights full on, blue light and two-tones blaring, he accelerated down the road towards the mob. It was a good tactic and they scattered. He stopped the car at the end of the road and we both got out to see who was still around but they'd cleared off into the city.

During the 1968/69 football season, Portsmouth Football Club were at home to Millwall at Fratton Park. Millwall supporters travelled on the 10.50 a.m. train from Waterloo, and just before it departed one of their number snatched two cartons of cigarettes from a refreshment trolley on the platform and jumped on board. The group continued to behave in an antisocial manner towards other passengers, and then turned their attentions to a secure buffet bar carriage, which was broken into and stock stolen.

The police were alerted by the guard, and a detective sergeant from the BTP stationed at Guildford, together with a sergeant and twenty uniform constables from Surrey County Constabulary, made their way to Woking railway station where the train was at a standstill.

Thirty suspects were subsequently arrested and taken in a shuttle service of police vehicles to Woking police station, where they were interviewed by a team of seven detectives. As a result, fourteen adults and fifteen juveniles were charged with offences of damage, theft, receiving stolen property, and disorderly behaviour, as well as ticket fraud and throwing articles from the train. As far as could be established at the time, this was reported as being the largest number of persons prosecuted at any one time for this type of incident. The investigation also revealed the identity of the cigarette thief at Waterloo, who had this offence added to his list of charges.

Following a series of trials the vast majority of the defendants were convicted and, out of a total number of eighty-nine charges preferred against the accused, seventy-two were found proven. All of this was achieved without one witness from the travelling public coming forward to make statements.

Keith Groves retired from the BTP, as a chief inspector, and recalls his first experiences of football policing,

The first football train I went on was on 18 May 1968, as an eighteen-year-old police cadet, travelling with just one PC on a train to Wembley for the FA Cup final. It was actually a First Class dining train and we were escorting West Bromwich Albion fans to Wembley for the match with Everton. We did not expect to have any trouble on the train and the trip down went smoothly.

The game was 0-0 at full time and then three minutes into extra time Jeff Astle scored the winning goal for West Bromwich Albion. It was the first FA Cup final to be televised live in colour. Everyone rushed back after the game to get the train and one passenger had a heart attack and died. We had to take him off the train at Wembley and it was my first experience of being involved in a sudden death.

The following morning I was on duty again at Birmingham New Street, on platform 12, when a train came in with the West Bromwich Albion team on board. As they left the train one of them handed the FA Cup to me to hold for a few seconds!

In 1969 I was a police constable at Birmingham and remember one occasion when I was monitoring fans on the overbridge at Birmingham, which was always a flashpoint, as different sets of fans passed through changing trains. We were trying to control some Tottenham Hotspur fans who were all wearing boots with steel toecaps when a group of West Ham fans came onto the station. Fans were running around everywhere and some went down onto a platform where a train was standing. As I followed them I noticed the football legend Bobby Moore sitting in First Class on the train watching the commotion and as I went past we made eye contact and he shrugged his shoulders.

Michael Layton recalls,

I joined the British Transport Police as a police cadet on 1 September 1968 at the age of sixteen. Little did I know then that I would finally retire from the police service some forty-two years later, in the same force, with not much change having taken place in relation to some things – one of which was the fact that football hooligans were still around.

After a relatively short spell in the area headquarters, I was allowed to work operationally at Birmingham New Street railway station and, although I had no police powers as a cadet, I had a pair of eyes and a 'nose' for trouble which did not always make me popular with some of my colleagues who would have to pick up the work I created.

I tried to work as many Saturdays as they would allow me to. I loved the atmosphere at the station as thousands of people bustled through it constantly, some going shopping, some meeting loved ones, some going home or simply passing through. Saturdays however had a more sinister side to them because this was the day that many so-called 'normal people' behaved like lunatics and descended into fashioned battles all in the name of the sport of football.

It was the norm on such days for the home fans, predominantly Birmingham City at that time, to send out 'spotters' to look for the opposition. They regarded Birmingham city centre as their territory to be defended at all costs. The spotters would report back to the more hardened members who would then determine their tactics for the day.

Often they would filter into the station in small groups to wait for the opposition coming in on scheduled services, or storm in through the glass doors at the front of the station for the traditional post-5 p.m. confrontation, when away fans would be herded by large numbers of the local police onto the station and often just left for a handful of BTP officers to deal with.

This is when we realised the value of police dogs with handlers who routinely placed themselves in harm's way to separate fighting fans. Most of the dogs were long haired, brown and black coated Alsatians, but one dog was actually much lighter in colour. It didn't change the way in which he was able to bite however! Members of the public would often be oblivious to what was going on until they found themselves caught up in the sudden roar of chants like 'Zulu' and the flash of boots and fists punching the air – and other people.

I hated violence and I hated football violence even more, and sometimes could not understand why we tolerated it. By way of example, if five drunks walked through the station shouting and swearing they would immediately be confronted by police officers and told to behave. If five football hooligans did exactly the same thing a number of officers would stand by with arms folded as if this was normal. I determined at an early age that I would not tolerate it and like many of my, mostly younger in service colleagues, we engaged with them at every opportunity.

Being so young I was well able to mingle with the crowds and on occasions would wear a civilian jacket to see what was going on. It was normal in those days for the adult fans to get children under fourteen years of age to go and buy their train ticket for them so that they could get it for half price. Others simply got platform tickets and jumped on the football special trains in the hope that they could hide if there was a ticket check.

I used to stand watching the youngsters at the ticket office windows and then clock who they passed the tickets to. One day I made myself very popular with the fans, and some of the more senior constables, when I managed to point twelve people out on the platform, before a football special departed, all of whom were lined up and had to be processed for ticket fraud offences.

On other occasions I was able to point the CID officers in the right direction as to where the troublemakers were hanging around. Being in plain clothes they were also able to get close to any fights and routinely made arrests.

Saturdays were crazy days but I loved it. These were the days when British Rail routinely had to replace thousands of light bulbs which were unscrewed in train carriages and either thrown out of windows, or thrown at opponents, and seat cushions were made for slashing rather than being sat on. Every Saturday the hooligans went to battle with their opponents, and we went to battle against them in a three-cornered fight.

Little did the BTP know what the Grim Reaper was going to visit upon during them during the next two decades of violence, as football hooligans became 'firms' and honed their violent skills.

2

THE SEVENTIES – TROUBLE IN THE SOUTH WEST

Specially chartered football special trains were a feature of the seventies, and indeed into the eighties, when football violence was at its peak and the British Rail network provided a platform for pitched battles between hooligan groups, many of whom were well organised and determined.

The hooligan group associated with West Ham FC actually took the name 'Inter City Firm' after the Inter City trains they travelled on, and the 'Leeds United Service Crew' named themselves after the regular services they travelled on, due to them being less heavily policed than special trains. They even featured a British Rail symbol on one of their badges. Newcastle United's hooligans were then known as Newcastle Mainline Express (NME) due to their use of the rail network, while Portsmouth's 6.57 Crew hooligan group took its name from the time that the Portsmouth to London Waterloo train left Portsmouth and Southsea station, early on a Saturday morning.

For many genuine fans the experience of travelling on football specials was like being herded like cattle, but for the ardent hooligan it was all part of the buzz – grouped together with their mates, dressed in their own distinctive style with one single purpose in mind as they boarded the trains, and trying to look as if they owned the place when they arrived at their destination.

'Steve', who retired as a sergeant with the BTP in Birmingham and did a stint of undercover work, remembers his first experience of football hooliganism on trains but it was not as a police officer. He recalls,

> In 1970 I was eleven years of age and had been to Wolverhampton to watch a game with Albion. The train stopped at Rolfe Street station in Smethwick where supporters completely wrecked the coach I was in. This skinhead came up to me and told me to get up out of my seat. I was scared and thought he was going to beat me up. He actually just wanted my seat cushion which he wrenched out of its fitting and threw out of the train.

In 1970, Keith Groves worked as a PC at Coventry, and on one occasion found himself escorting a train full of fans from Coventry to Birmingham on his own. At the end of his 20-minute journey he got off the train and found that the back of his tunic was literally covered in spit.

On 3 November 1970 Detective Sergeant Williams, based at Bricklayers Arms, and Detective Constable Keeling from Victoria were commended for 'Courage and perseverance, when hopelessly outnumbered by a disorderly crowd, in effecting the arrest and subsequent conviction of three men for malicious damage on a football special train.'

In 1971, nineteen-year Police Constable 'M' 177 Michael Layton of the British Transport Police, stationed at New Street station in Birmingham, was a regular part of BTP train escorts for travelling football fans. His regular partner was PC 'M' 138 Brian Preece, an ex-serviceman who knew how to handle himself and was fearless. He was a good man to have next to you.

Now retired from the BTP, Brian recalls,

> I was in the Grenadier Guards, before joining the police, and was used to working in difficult situations. My very first train escort was to take some Villa fans up north in 1971. My sergeant, Frank Henson, pointed out some troublemakers to me, and we threw some off the train before we even left Birmingham. It was a zero-tolerance approach, there were so few of us on a train we had to stamp our mark on the fans so as not to lose control.

Mike Layton and I did a number of train escorts together, and often patrolled service trains from Birmingham to Manchester, on match days, to make sure that fans who had travelled down to London behaved themselves on the way back. We used to come down hard on ticket fraud where fans had purchased platform tickets or child's tickets, even though they were adults, and detected a lot of offences.

We were wise to all the tricks and would often find them hiding under tables between the legs of other fans. On one occasion we had to get the train guard to open up a toilet and inside found two people. The walls of the toilet were covered in fresh graffiti which they denied all knowledge of, but when it transpired that the initials on the walls matched their own names they came clean. We even dealt with someone for stealing all the toilet rolls once from the train, which they were going to throw at the ground. The magistrate told them to buy their own in future and the job was actually in the papers! We were relentless but we had to be.

Brian worked with a number of officers at Birmingham and Wolverhampton, and recalls,

We took one Villa train to Portsmouth but their behaviour was so bad that at Bristol we threw an entire coach off the train. We got into trouble because some of them were juveniles and didn't get back home until the Monday. We used to tell fans to pull the blinds down on return trips because it was not unusual for home fans to stone the trains. On one trip to Hull, PC Keith Fleetwood was in the guards van when a brick came through the window and he was hit in the face by flying glass.

On another occasion we had a full-blown fight on a station and the slashed peak on my flat police cap was knocked off. I had to travel back with no hat. On another day, I was on duty at Wolverhampton railway station when I saw a football fan walking into the station who was soaking wet from head to foot. I asked him what had happened and he alleged that he had been shouting at some opposition fans when a van load of local police officers turned up and threw him in the nearby canal. It sounded like a bit of a tall story to me so I told him to behave and sent him on his way.

Brian went on,

You never quite knew what was going to happen; on one occasion Manchester United fans steamed through all the shops above New Street station. Once again I was with Keith Fleetwood and we were taking cameras and all sorts off fans, but as there was literally hundreds of them the local police inspector told us not to take any prisoners as they couldn't afford to lose officers from the streets.

On another occasion Liverpool fans came to Wolverhampton and we were advised to look out for teams of pickpockets. After the fans left for home we found fifteen wallets and purses stuffed into the toilet cisterns on the station.

Keith Fleetwood, who also spent time in the BTP at Birmingham and retired as an inspector, recalls the incident when he was injured,

With New Street being a crossing point for many travelling Manchester United supporters, especially from the Leamington Spa area, a special train was arranged for a replay, at an independent ground, for an FA Cup qualifier against Liverpool. The station we travelled to was Sheffield Wadsley Bridge station. We had several officers travelling in 'civvies' with the supporters, and a sergeant and four in uniform, as we anticipated problems.

The outward journey passed without problem. At the start of the return journey the trains from this station had to pass through an area of track known as 'Bomb Alley.' At this time the supporters were quiet so all the uniform officers moved to the spare brake van to allow the officers in 'civvies' to settle in with the crowd.

I sat in the guards seat and tapped the wall behind me saying 'I'm safe here' as the only window was between the two carriages. The next moment half a paving slab came through the window and struck me in the left side of my head. Remarkably the slab caused no problems, but the shattered glass penetrated the left side of my face slicing across my left eyeball, and embedding in my nose and cheek.

I was taken to Sheffield Royal Infirmary where as many shards of glass were removed from my face and eye as possible.

The remainder came out of their own accord over the next three years. The benefit was that I did get a free fish supper as local radio in Sheffield broadcast the incident and I was recognised as I entered the fish shop with an obvious patch over my eye.

Brian Preece went on,

On one train I got my first complaint against police. Supporters were forever switching the lights out on trains, to try and punch or kick us in the dark. It was a game and on one occasion when it happened someone tried to trip me up. I lashed out with my truncheon and when the lights came back on someone was sitting there holding his knee in pain. One of the fans opposite, who was travelling on a train for the first time, accused me of using too much force and made a complaint. I had to see the superintendent who gave me some advice, with a bit of a smirk on his face, and told me to carry a torch with me in future.

There were some lighter moments though. I remember going to Blackpool with supporters on one occasion, and we went to the Tower Ballroom for refreshments. Two of the officers were twins, and avid dancers, and asked the sergeant if they could do a bit of dancing in the ballroom in the tower while we were there.

During one Saturday in the 1971/72 football season, a three-coach Diesel Multiple Unit left Manchester for Sheffield with sixty Oldham Athletic supporters, known locally as the 'Latics', on board. The train was so crowded that passengers overflowed into the guards compartment, which contained a number of parcel-post mail bags. The guard was required to leave his compartment to check tickets and when he returned he noticed that some of the mailbags had been interfered with. He arranged for the BTP to meet the train at Sheffield railway station.

At Sheffield, two detective constables had just returned to their office with fish and chips when the duty inspector assigned them to deal with the incident, and promised to keep their food warm. On arrival of the train, forty fans were removed and taken into a room on the platform to be interviewed one by one. During the course of their protestations of innocence the name 'Pooh' kept being repeated. The thirteenth fan they spoke to introduced himself as 'Winnik'.

The remaining fans were released and 'Winnik' was duly arrested and taken to the police office, which by now was full of the smell of burnt fish and chips. The inspector clearly did not know how to use the Baby Belling cooker. The officers recovered a wristwatch from the prisoners possession, which had been stolen from a mailbag, and he implicated a second person who had not been among the forty detained.

With some quick driving two BTP officers detained this suspect at Chesterfield railway station, and he admitted his part in stealing an alarm clock from one of the bags, which had then been thrown from the train. Both suspects were charged and the task of recovering items of property, from the lineside, took several days.

On Saturday 27 March 1971, a football excursion train was returning from Bolton to Hull when some disorder took place. Signalman William Macklin, a member of No. 2 Squadron, 11th Signal Regiment, Catterick, who was a passenger in plain clothes, saw a football supporter deliberately tear off the rexine cover from a table and immediately reported it to BTP officers who were on the train. The offender was later fined.

On Friday 9 April 1971 a large amount of damage was caused by Darlington football supporters on a train from York to Darlington. Private David Rose of the Duke of Edinburgh's Royal Regiment, Catterick, saw a supporter in the corridor of the train carrying a toilet seat from one of the cubicles. On arrival at Darlington he reported the matter to BTP officers and the offender was prosecuted and fined.

Retired BTP Sergeant Bill Rogerson recalls some of his experiences,

> The first football train I worked was in September 1971 from Birmingham New Street to Bristol Stapleton Road. I believe it was the occasion of a Bristol Rovers *v.* Birmingham City game. The outward journey was without incident. The return was much livelier. The Bristol fans charged the Birmingham fans outside the station. Being young and keen I was about to jump over a wall to apprehend some fans but, unknown to me at the point, there

is a sheer drop at the other side of the wall, and it was only the Bristol inspector who saved me from jumping. By the time I got further along the platform the fans on the other side of the wall had scarpered.

On another return escort from Bristol to Birmingham we had that many drunken fans on board the train that I ended up arresting fourteen of them. My colleagues also made arrests. The miscreants were taken, with the assistance of the Birmingham City Police, to Digbeth police station, where they were charged and detained for court on the Monday morning.

One incident that sticks out in my mind, although I was not on duty, was when about fifteen supporters ran from one of the platforms at Birmingham New Street into the tunnel onto the Wolverhampton line. They were rounded up and subsequently appeared at the Birmingham City Magistrates Court and were fined 50 pence each.

I was part of an escort to Blackpool North on a train conveying Aston Villa supporters for a Blackpool *v.* Aston Villa, mid-week evening kick-off. On the return journey I was in carriage with a centre aisle, when, in the Preston area, the lights went out and I was jumped on by some fans, and pushed underneath some seats. Fortunately one of the fans came to my rescue. We locked a couple up for assault but my helmet was missing. A few days later a cardboard box arrived at Birmingham addressed to me, containing my helmet. A note inside was from the BTP at Preston which read, 'One helmet, constable, for the use of' which made me smile.

Paul Nicholas QPM, who retired from the BTP as an assistant chief constable in 2006, recalls some of his earlier experiences,

While a youthful sergeant at Birmingham New Street station, between 1970 to 1974, football hooliganism was at quite a high level. Football specials were the norm and Birmingham City, Aston Villa, West Bromwich Albion, and Wolverhampton Wanderers, in particular, were at the forefront among supporters requiring a high level of police attention.

BTP numbers were much less than they are today and it was quite usual for hundreds of highly charged and drink-fuelled supporters to be escorted by just a sergeant and three or four constables. Good humour and chat was rarely successful on these occasions, and more frequently heavy assertive behaviour, accompanied by a certain amount of bravado and bluff from the escorting officers, was the more effective ploy. After all, none of them wanted to miss the game by being detained upon arrival at the destination station, so the threat of that often worked wonders.

However, I recall on one of my early football escort duties with some Aston Villa fans, my small squad of four constables suddenly and inexplicably reduced to just three during the journey. We eventually found that a new young probationer had been grabbed by some supporters and forced underneath their seat, giving him a sound back-heeled kicking every time that he attempted to extract himself. To add insult to injury they had also stolen his helmet as a trophy!

As we were always heavily outnumbered, 'assertive bluff' has saved my bacon on more than one occasion, like the time on New Street station concourse when Constable Maurice Harris, otherwise known as 'Big Mo', and I were surrounded by fifty to a hundred West Bromwich fans intent on doing us some serious bodily harm. We stood back-to-back with truncheons drawn, literally 15 inches of a useless piece of wood, facing off the fans with the threat 'come on then, who wants to go down first' coupled with some inane thrusts and swings of the truncheon until reinforcements arrived. Our success at withstanding this might of course have also had more to do with the fact that Big Mo was 6 feet 2 inches tall and broad shouldered.

Bill Rogerson recalls another incident,

Another escort saw me travelling to Cardiff with Aston Villa fans. For the return we were on platforms 1 and 2, which is an island platform, with our fans, awaiting the arrival of our train. The local Cardiff fans were on platforms 3 and 4, again another island platform, when all of a sudden the Cardiff fans managed to get hold of some shunting poles about 6 foot in length and with a hook on the end of them. They were throwing them across the tracks at the Villa supporters. It was like a scene from the film *Zulu* and all we needed was Ivor Emmanuel on the platform singing 'Men of Harlech.'

During the early years we were left to our own devices for food at the destinations we escorted to, mainly frequenting fish and chip shops and eating them wherever we could. For one mid-week match I was sergeant in charge of an escort to Wembley Central and the force had arranged an open-plan coach in the bay platform for us to relax in, but for food we had to find our own. Three or four of us found ourselves in a kebab house, a couple of streets away from Wembley Central station. The following day we were struck down with food poisoning.

On a couple of occasions I have escorted trains to Brighton from Birmingham. On one occasion we took a dog handler with us. After dispersing the fans at Brighton we travelled in the empty stock to the sidings. The dog handler took his dog for a walk in the sidings and couldn't understand why it kept yelping. The handler hadn't realised we were in 'third rail territory' and the dog kept touching the live rail. He was very lucky.

In the autumn of 1971, a journalist visited the police office at Euston railway station as part of his research into an article he was doing on the force. He met a veteran constable known as Trev, who treated him to the following anecdote,

Of course if it's action you're after, you should come on a Saturday night. Saturday night is football night. When Liverpool, Everton, Leeds, Manchester City, Manchester United, and West Brom are playing, they come via Euston. Hundreds of them. When they go back, Arsenal, Chelsea, and Spurs come to see them off. Hundreds of them, looking for action.

All the police have got to keep them apart is five men and a dog. Constables have been known to turn pale and vanish.

At that point of the interview the handler comes in with the dog, a furry, loveable Alsatian, very quiet and cuddly. Trev goes on, 'Watch this,' and turns to the dog and says 'Chelsea.' The dog suddenly turns savage, growls and strains at the leash. 'Mark you he does the same if you mention my name,' added the officer.

On a more serious note, he recalled the death of a football fan who had leant too far out of a train window and struck his head on a bridge in Hitchin.

Bill Rogerson reflects,

In those early days of the 1970s Manchester United supporters were regarded as the worst troublemakers. It was not uncommon for us to be sent to Crewe on a Saturday for a four-hour rest day working to escort the Midlands-based United fans back to Birmingham. One of my duties on this half rest day working was to travel to Crewe and escort a service train from Manchester back to Birmingham New Street, dressed as a United supporter.

There was I on the train, complete with red and white bobble hat and scarf, along with a wooden rattle. A couple of CID officers from New Street were on the train as well. As the train was approaching Birmingham I was in a compartment with a so-called genuine supporter when one of the CID officers walked past us. He stuck out like a sore thumb, trilby, open-coat and collar and tie. The supporter said 'He's a copper you can tell them anywhere.' He then proceeded to smash up the light bulbs, at which point I identified myself and his reply to the caution is unprintable.

Paul Majster was another member of the uniform BTP team at Birmingham that travelled regularly on football trains throughout the seventies, and recalls,

Every week we would escort at least two special football trains from Birmingham, with anything up to 400 supporters on each train. It was mainly Villa or Birmingham City and we would escort the fans with just a sergeant and four constables, and sometimes a dog handler. We would walk through the carriages as a pair and leave a third officer to follow us through to watch our backs. If we were travelling during the night a regular trick for the fans was to try to switch the lights off as we were walking through and then to try and punch and kick us, in the dark, or to pull the communication cord.

When this happened we would just use our truncheons and when the lights came back on you would see people holding an arm or a leg in pain. It was a game and those were the rules. We used to take any troublemakers to the guards van, at the back of the train, and lock them in the security cage, which was used to keep mailbags in. If they played up the dog handler and his dog went in with them. It usually calmed them down!

When I look back they were frightening times but we trusted each other and got on with it. Fights were frequent and I got a few smacks but nothing to shout about. Arrests were frequent; I once arrested a Villa fan in possession of a hammer for protection, who was taken to a local police station in London to be charged. As railway police we were not always welcomed by local forces who saw us as a bit of a nuisance. I hated some of the trips to places like Newcastle, Sunderland, or Ipswich, which would take us hours to reach and we would be on our feet all of the time.

The highlights for me were the trips we did bringing the 'Jocks' down to London from Preston or Crewe. They used to call themselves 'millionaires for the weekend' and I have never seen so much alcohol. After one game at Wembley, which Scotland won, they smashed the goalposts up and many of them came back to the trains carrying bits of them. They generally caused no trouble and we had great fun. When we got off the train at Birmingham, eventually, one of the PCs was wearing a 'Tam o Shanter' hat, instead of his helmet.

Bert Stonebridge was typical of many ex-servicemen who joined the police service after the Second World War, and for whom dealing with unruly football hooligans was not the most challenging thing that they had dealt with in their lives. His son Andy recalls his late father's experiences and some of the anecdotes he picked up from his family:

My dad was originally an LMS copper from 1946 having spent the previous ten years in the Royal Horse Guards before nationalisation. He finished his career as a PC at Park Royal HQ in the Criminal Records Office, and his number was 'HQ'6. He was Willi Gay's driver for his last few years before retiring in 1977. His recollections of the few football specials he'd been on, and that must have been in the 70s, were that they were pretty good-natured affairs. He did say that the noisiest sporting event he ever attended was at a girls hockey event at the old Wembley where the noise from the crowd was ear piercing.

The other story was with regard to my ex-wife's uncle Jim Condron who, when I knew him, was I think a chief superintendent at Kings Cross. Earlier in his service he was the senior officer on an escort aboard a Dover-bound ferry, returning from the Continent before the advent of the Channel Tunnel. The fans were getting a bit out of hand, so he conferred with the captain who said that he could withdraw the hull stabilisers therefore making the crossing a lot rougher! This did the trick and within a short time calm was restored as quite a few fans turned green.

3

THE SEVENTIES – A FROZEN RABBIT COMES TO THE RESCUE

On Friday 18 February 1972 a message was received from Belfast that, although Manchester United were playing an away game at Leeds, approximately 300 football supporters were on board the *Duke of Argyle* passenger ferry from Northern Ireland, en route to Leeds to watch their iconic idle George Best play. In the eyes of the fanatical Belfast supporters, Manchester United fielded a team of one player and ten assistants.

At 3.15 a.m. on Saturday 19 February 1972, the BTP police officers on duty at Heysham harbour received a wireless message from the master of the vessel as follows,

> Please meet the ship on arrival at Heysham about 5.25 a.m. A gang of youths have wrecked the Fore Peak Bar, and stolen cigarettes, beer and spirits. They have behaved in a drunken and disorderly manner; fighting among themselves and terrorising other passengers.

All of the local off-duty BTP officers were roused from their beds, and at 4.45 a.m. seven uniform officers, and two CID officers, gathered in the police office for a briefing, together with police dog Czar. At 5.23 a.m. the *Duke of Argyle* docked at the quayside and both gangways, and the car ramp, were sealed off by police to prevent anyone from getting off.

A check of the Fore Peak Bar revealed that spirits, cans of beer, and cigarettes had been stolen, and the suspects were a gang of forty youths who had caused ructions throughout the journey. The bar and both lounges were wrecked, and the floors littered with debris, and vomit, with some of the group lying in it. After a complete search of the ship, thirty suspects were taken into custody, and at one point police dog Czar contained four of the group on his own. Given the nature of life in Belfast at the time, no civilian witnesses came forward to make statements, but the chief steward on the ship refused to be bowed and identified a number of the suspects.

Ten of this group of thirty were subsequently charged with causing annoyance to passengers, contrary to Section 287 of the Merchant Shipping Act 1894. Another two were charged with obstructing a ship's officer in the execution of his duty. Two more were charged with theft of bottles of spirits, and one with receiving stolen cigarettes.

All fifteen were charged and taken to Morecambe police station to be kept in custody for court, where they were all later to plead guilty as charged.

Retired BTP Sergeant Walt Girdley, now in his eighties and who worked at Heysham Harbour, describes his experiences in some detail as follows,

Football duty was done entirely by the Heysham Section, and did not include the use of BTP officers from Belfast.

In 1972 George Best was a spent force in respect of football, and those supporters that travelled between Belfast and Heysham, on the Friday departure from Belfast, did so with the sole intention of travelling on to Manchester to see United play at Old Trafford. It would only occur two or three times a football season, when the most important games were played, and a capacity crowd was expected. In such cases a request would be made by the Sealink management for a police escort to be provided and generally one of the uniform sergeants, together with about six uniform constables, sailed from Heysham Harbour at 23.30 hours on a Thursday evening and arrived in Belfast eight hours later.

During the winter time the Irish Sea can be extremely rough, but fortunately all the officers were excellent sailors and none complained of sea sickness. Generally, with one or two exceptions, the same officers seemed to be on most, or all, of the football trips. They were, Michael Walker, Jim Morris, Terry Booth, Vince Seddon, Clive Bennett, Gerry Baines (dog handler) and another officer.

Most of the officers were in the habit of remaining on the vessel until its departure from Donegal Quay at approximately 21.30 hours on the Friday evening.

The passengers who travelled on the vessel were made up almost entirely of Manchester United supporters and generally it was filled to its capacity of approximately 1,000 persons. At the time when this duty was being performed, the troubles of Northern Ireland were at their highest. There were no sprays or stab proof vests etc. in those days and all that we had was a whistle, which was not much use, a truncheon, and a fair degree of common sense. While no fear or real concern was ever shown by any of the officers, it was realised by all that, because of the vulnerable position we were in, self-preservation must be our first priority.

On one occasion an army officer, who was in charge of several soldiers travelling back to the UK from Northern Ireland, offered to 'sort them out' if we had any bother. This was declined in the knowledge that if they had been given a free hand the vessel would probably have been completely wrecked. Drunkenness was rife in the bars of the vessel and arrests were invariably made for public order offences, damage, theft and assaults.

The arrests always took place at a time when we considered we were in our strongest position, and at a time when the offenders were at their weakest. This was generally during the early hours when the sea was at its most turbulent and the captain, upon our request, had taken in the vessels stabilisers. The offenders were then taken to a room allocated, at the bottom of the vessel, and secured and ably guarded by the dog handler. Contact was then made by the ships radio with the BTP at Heysham Harbour giving details of the number arrested.

On the one, and I believe only, occasion when an inspector accompanied us on one of the sea trips, there were a couple of notable events. Some time before the vessel was due to depart from Belfast, a fairly large crowd had been refused entry because of drunkenness. They soon turned violent and attempted to force their way onto the ship, but were repelled by police officers and some left with sore heads before being handed over to the Royal Ulster Constabulary to be dealt with.

The inspector was John Higgins, who was the officer in charge of the Heysham section at this time, and, because Gerry Baines was unavailable, we had taken 'Ginger' Ablard, the dog handler from Preston. Unfortunately the inspector stepped in front of the police dog when it was at its most fierce, at the height of the disturbances, and received a bite on the leg. I believe the inspector obtained an injection because of the bite, but Ginger Ablard never said whether he also had the dog injected!

Upon arrival at approximately 05.30 hours, the remainder of the Heysham Section met the vessel and took charge of any prisoners. After documentation they were charged with any offences and later taken to Morecombe police station to be detained until their appearance before an arranged special court at about 11.00 hours the same day. Assisting with the documentation would be one or more of the following CID officers: Detective Sergeant George Hart, a well-respected and really nice person, Detective Constable Fred Hulme, or Detective Constable Stuart Buck. Sadly, all three are no longer with us.

It should be mentioned that the Irish prisoners were always fully cooperative and on their appearance before the special court pleaded guilty, such was their desire to get to Old Trafford before the start of the match.

Ginger Ablard BEM retired from the BTP as a sergeant in 1998 after many years on the dog section, and has his own recollection of this particular trip,

It was in the 70s and there was that much violence on some of the ferries carrying football fans from Belfast that they were threatening not to sail without a police escort.

I got a phone call from my chief superintendent telling me to make my way to Belfast to bring a ferry back. At the time I had an

Alsatian dog by the name of 'Ben'. As we were waiting to leave, all hell broke loose as some fans were refused entry onto the ship. As they tried to force their way on we were in real trouble for a while as we tried to restore order with the support of the army and the Royal Ulster Constabulary. Ben and I were in the middle of all this and I can tell you it was frightening.

One officer was bitten on the backside by the dog during the fighting and after we regained control I took him to my cabin because he wanted me to have a look at his wound. He bent over the bed with his trousers down to show me at which point Inspector Higgins walked in – it was a bit of an awkward moment!

We policed the ferry back to Heysham as best we could with some fans telling us that we were 'going over the side.' Our only back-up was a frigate that was operating in the area. We made about eight arrests and all got commendations afterwards.

Ginger Ablard recalls another incident with Ben,

I was on duty at Glasgow railway station monitoring Scotland fans at one of the rear entrances with police dog Ben when a disturbance started just as a very senior BTP officer walked through the entrance, on the wrong side, and was bitten under the arm by the dog. Ben was just reacting normally, even though he was close to retirement he was still up for it, and try as I might it took me ages to get the dog off him. Just to make it worse, I heard that the senior officer hated needles!

When I was released to go home I was making my way to get a train when two other officers approached me and asked me for the name of the dog. I thought that I was in trouble when one of them said 'I just wanted to shake your hand' – it had obviously made their day.

Due to the nature of their work, it was not unusual for BTP officers to find themselves with limited support in crowd situations. This could not have been illustrated more effectively when, at 10.30 a.m. on Saturday 16 September 1972, PC Terence Orchard was on duty alone at Victoria Underground station when some 200 rowdy football hooligans entered the northbound platform of the Victoria line. They pressed forward en masse pushing people out of the way, and an elderly lady was pushed to the ground.

The officer forced his way through the crowd to go to the assistance of the lady, being punched and kicked on the way. As several youths tried to restrain him he was forced to draw his truncheon to clear an area around himself and the woman, who somehow managed to get to her feet.

As a train entered the platform the crowd surged forward, carrying the officer with them bodily onto the train. With innocent passengers clearly in fear, the officer prevented the train from moving, and despite the aggression shown towards him, with the help of station staff and several prods from his truncheon, he managed to force them off the train. As assistance arrived they then managed to disperse the group.

Bill Rogerson recalls,

I think it was November 1972 when Nuneaton Borough were drawn to play Torquay United in the first round of the FA Cup at Torquay. There were seven special trains from Nuneaton, each escorted by BTP officers from the Midlands Division. The contingent from Birmingham, of which I was a part, booked on duty at 06.30 hours and travelled in the Ford Transit mini bus to Nuneaton. We duly escorted our train to Torquay.

On arrival at Torquay, we waited until all of the trains had arrived and the fans had left the station. The Devon and Cornwall Constabulary took us in their Black Marias to a Chinese restaurant in the town centre for a pre-booked meal. The sight of all those Bobbies jumping out the Marias was certainly a sight for the early Christmas shoppers to behold. It was like something out of a *Keystone Cops* movie.

The return journey was quiet apart from the fact that, when we left Bristol Temple Meads station, it was discovered that we had no guard and the train had to stop at Swindon while the guard caught us up by taxi.

On arrival at Nuneaton we were the last train to arrive and we went over to the mini bus, only to find that the diesel had been siphoned out of it. Fortunately the Warwickshire Police came to our rescue with a can of diesel. We eventually arrived back at New Street at around 04.15 hours and booked off at 04.30 hours after a 22-hour tour of duty.

On Saturday 2 December 1972, Swindon Town were due to play Cardiff City in a football league match at Swindon. A special football train departed from Cardiff, en route to Swindon with 450 supporters on board, but just prior to arriving there the match was cancelled. Due to disorder that had already taken place in the town, the train was turned around and re-routed back to Cardiff via Bristol due to track flooding.

During the course of the journey to Bristol serious disturbances took place on the train, with small fires lit in the toilets, cushions and light bulbs thrown from compartment windows and fixtures extensively damaged. Near to Stapleton Road railway station, which is a small inner city station, and the nearest station to Bristol Rovers ground, the communication cord was pulled. On that date Bristol Rovers were playing at home and, as the train came to a halt on the main line, 200 Cardiff fans jumped down onto the track, ran across the main line, and rampaged through the streets to make their way to the ground, causing considerable damage to property on the way.

On arrival at the ground they were rounded up by Bristol Constabulary and taken back to Stapleton Road, where the original intention was to put them onto service trains, which at that time of the year were packed with Christmas shoppers. A BTP inspector arrived on the scene, together with six officers, and fearing the consequences of allowing the fans to mingle with ordinary members of the public, eventually managed to persuade the railway control to lay on another special train, which clearly took some time to arrange.

Owing to trouble taking place at the Bristol Rovers match and in the city centre, the local officers were withdrawn, leaving the seven BTP officers to control the Cardiff fans. As they were not allowed to board service trains, the mood among them became uglier and in the growing darkness the officers were bombarded with stones. Bristol Rovers fans also arrived on the scene and further disturbances took place. It was like a scene from every police officer's nightmare and as each service train arrived on the platform the fans made a concerted effort to push past the officers who resolutely held their line. Finally the new special train arrived and they were escorted back to Cardiff.

Subsequently, following an investigation by the BTP, eighteen adults and seventeen juveniles, whose ages ranged from fifteen years to nineteen years, appeared in court on a total of eighty-two offences relating to criminal damage, disorderly behaviour, byelaw offences and trespass, resulting in fines of over £500.

Policing football in the South West by BTP officers brought its own unique challenges, and those unlucky enough to find themselves escorting fans from Penzance to London could find themselves with a road and rail trip of some 250 miles and a 20-hour continuous tour of duty.

Keith Fleetwood recalls an incident in 1972,

Birmingham City had played Liverpool and a cordon of BTP officers was across the front, and shopping centre, entrances to the station. Prior to this a detective sergeant from Wolverhampton had contacted his son, who was a PC at New Street, to see if he still kept ferrets, and could he make use of a frozen rabbit that had been taken possession of after poachers had been caught for 'Trespass in Pursuit of Conies'.

The PC was stationed inside the cordon on the Birmingham New Street concourse when his father arrived from Wolverhampton. He asked his son if he needed assistance as the crowd was building up inside the barrier. As the detective sergeant walked away towards the office, a member of the Birmingham supporters ran towards the barrier and kicked and attacked three Liverpool supporters passing through the ticket barrier. He then ran backwards towards the PC who restrained him in a 'hammerlock and bar'.

As the noise of the crowd increased, the PC's father turned and saw the officer restraining the supporter. He immediately ran across the concourse throwing his right arm in the air with a supermarket bag flying away exposing a frozen rabbit. As the supporter was still struggling he was struck a blow which rendered him unconscious and then other supporters, who were gathering around, were threatened to keep their distance by the man in the suit brandishing a frozen rabbit.

The offender was convicted with no mention of the rabbit being made until conviction. The magistrate did deliberate as to whether they needed reports before sentencing.

In 1973 British Rail introduced a train specially equipped to cater for travelling football supporters called the *League Liner*, which had a 'disco carriage' with flashing lights and was aimed at giving fans something to do. While it was used by a number of clubs, the idea never really caught on and there were still complaints of vandalism.

Tony Thompson retired from the BTP as a superintendent and served in a number of locations in the force area. He recalls his first experience of football policing,

On 3 February 1973 I had a useful learning experience as a young uniform constable based at Hull Paragon station. Hull City had just beaten West Ham United 1-0 in an FA Cup match and I was ensuring that West Ham supporters boarded their charter trains back to London without being attacked by Hull fans. As one of the trains packed with West Ham fans started slowly pulling away from the platform, I made the schoolboy error of standing rather too close to the train. I was within easy spitting range of supporters hanging out of the train windows. I did not make that mistake ever again and, as well as getting a coating of spittle, I almost lost my helmet to an outstretched arm!

In what was just another day at the office, PC 'W' 160 Rogerson recorded an offence of criminal damage on Saturday 3 November 1973, on a Cardiff to Wolverhampton football train. As the train was entering New Street station he found that a large table in one of the, by now empty, compartments had been pulled from the window fittings and damaged. Just another cost to the British Railways Board, London Midland Region, as scant regard was paid by some fans to other people's property. A bit like feral animals leaving their mark.

On 26 January 1974, Tony Thompson was a sergeant based at Lowestoft in Suffolk when he was deployed on escort duties, with four constables, on a football charter train from Ipswich to Manchester. He recalls,

> The train had a mix of Ipswich and Manchester United supporters on board for an FA Cup match. Alcohol was permitted and we left Ipswich with a full train, and a long journey ahead of us. At that time both clubs were in League Division One, and the rival fans were quite boisterous, and we sought to keep them in check as we periodically patrolled up and down the train.
>
> During one of these patrols I was approached by an Ipswich supporter who made me aware that someone had been injured further down the train. I followed him back to where the injured man, who was also an Ipswich fan, was sitting and found that he had sustained minor facial injuries, close to his eyes, which had been caused when a wine glass he was drinking from had been broken.
>
> It was alleged that some Manchester United fans had been sitting across the aisle at another table when some 'banter' had occurred between the two groups resulting in one of the Manchester United fans getting up from his seat and, with his open hand, knocking the glass from the mouth of the victim as he was about to take a drink. The glass had broken and had flown over the back of the seat, where the injured man had been sitting, and landed on a table several rows away. The assailant had then moved further down the train.
>
> Together with a witness I made a search and found the suspect several carriages away. He was taken to the police carriage at the rear and after being cautioned he admitted being responsible for causing the injury, but insisted that he had accidently fallen on the victim when the train jolted as he walked by. I recall his embarrassed, and sheepish response, when I took down his personal details and asked him for details of his employment, at which point he produced a police warrant card and indicated that he was a CID officer in a local force.
>
> I subsequently reported him by way of summons, and the director of public prosecutions approved a prosecution for assault occasioning actual bodily harm. The match was won by Ipswich on the day 1-0.

Many months later the case was heard at crown court and the defendant was acquitted, as he maintained that he had caused the injuries accidentally and witnesses were tested strongly by the defence as to their recollections. The fact that the glass had flown up in the air, and landed some distance way, was not, in my opinion, adequately explored by the prosecution, and I did not feel that this was consistent with someone falling in a downwards motion.

During the same year, Tony Thompson recalls two other football-related incidents,

In 1974 we took Ipswich supporters to Leicester and, not long after leaving, the BTP escort team arrested several supporters for disorderly behaviour. They were handcuffed to the metal grills in the trains parcels van and told that if they behaved for the rest of the journey we would consider letting them go to the match. They did and on arrival we released them with a verbal warning.

At Leicester station, however, the guard told us that one of the toilet cubicles was locked. I was eventually able to get the door open slightly and was met with an overwhelming stench of vomit and excrement. There was a young man inside who was semi-conscious with his lower garments around his ankles. His clothes, hair and everything seemed to be covered in vomit and excrement. He was in such a state through drinking too much that we had to arrest him for his own safety for being drunk and incapable. I was not the most popular BTP officer in Leicester because the young man, the police vehicle and the custody unit at the station all had to be hosed out.

In the second incident, Tony broke up a fight on Norwich railway station between brawling Norwich fans and visiting Millwall supporters on the station concourse. He arrested a Millwall fan while a colleague arrested a local man, who eventually pleaded guilty at court to disorderly conduct under Byelaw 17.
Tony recalls,

My Millwall supporter pleaded 'not guilty' and several months later he came to court clean shaven and in a three-piece suit looking totally different. He explained that he was a Millwall club steward and had witnessed the 'dreadful fight' but was surprised when I arrested him. The prosecution had not called any other witnesses so it was his word against mine. The magistrates retired to reach a verdict and then came back and gave him the benefit of the doubt. They even awarded him his costs for travelling from London – I was gutted. It was a shame that this was before the introduction of closed-circuit television, because I know what the nice Millwall fan was doing.

Bill Rogerson recalls another slightly different incident,

> Back in the early 1970s, a special football train was due to run from Birmingham New Street to York in connection with a York *v.* Aston Villa league match. I was rostered to work this train with a sergeant, possibly Alan Livesley, and two other PCs. Also, on that day, Birmingham City were playing away somewhere and a special train was to run, escorted by another sergeant and three PCs. One of the officers on that train was an avid Villa supporter and tried to swap with us, but we were told not to. He booked sick and turned up on our train in civvies. He didn't last long in the job after going to see Chief Superintendent Brunskill.

Retired BTP Police Constable Stan Wade was posted to Stranraer on 1 April 1974 and, despite the pressure of staff shortages, routinely worked nine days of 12-hour shifts at the ferry port before taking one day off. While his duties were many and varied, he remembers the 'flute bands' crossing over both ways between Larne and Stranraer each summer, and the difficult escorts on ferry ships. To add to the challenges, they also had to contend with Celtic and Ranger fans coming through the ports, as well as Liverpool supporters. At weekends they would often get additional support from BTP officers based in Kilmarnock, Glasgow, Edinburgh and Aberdeen.

Bill Rogerson went on,

> While stationed at Coventry between 1974 and 1976 I escorted a train with Sky Blue fans to London. On arrival at Euston we were

left to our own devices and the escorting officers, in half blues, ended up in Soho. One of the doormen of a strip joint realised who we were and invited us in to watch a show. We stood at the back. The club was full of the 'dirty mackintosh brigade', and it transpired that once the strippers had performed at one club they moved on to another followed by some of their 'fans'.

Soon after our arrival the strippers had finished their act and moved on. Some of their fans followed them and came past us. I stepped back to let them go by, only to fall through a curtain and down a laundry chute and ended up in a laundry basket, to be covered in dirty washing. We all had a good laugh.

Bill Rogerson continued,

At Coventry we worked alone quite a lot of the time and therefore we had a good working relationship with the local police. I remember one Saturday afternoon working by myself, and relying on the escorting officers of the incoming special train to assist, when the local superintendent came up to me and asked where my senior officer was. I looked around and said 'I am he Sir' to which he replied 'Where do you want my men to assist you.'

I worked in the CID in Leicester for eighteen months and most of our work on a Saturday was spotting troublemakers from teams visiting the city. I remember the occasion of Manchester United playing Leicester and, during a fight I was involved in, one of the United fans hit a colleague of mine across the chest. What made it worse was that the supporter had a plaster cast on his right arm.

Ian Murray, now in his eighties and a retired inspector from the BTP in Scotland, recalls some of his early experiences of football-related policing,

When oil was discovered in the North Sea in the early seventies, Aberdeen became known as the oil capital of Europe. Those employed in the oil industry earned good money and this prosperity was also a factor in the success of the football club.

At this time, I was the Aberdeen sub-divisional inspector for the force. As a result of this prosperity, Aberdeen FC attracted a huge away support. Each Saturday, on away days, several thousand supporters journeyed the 300-mile round trip to support their team. It was not uncommon for between five and seven special trains to be laid on to take supporters to fixtures in Edinburgh and Glasgow. They required a police escort and we were hard pressed to muster four officers for trains conveying around 550 fans each.

There was no alcohol ban at the time and cash-rich fans joined trains laden with whisky and other drinks for the journey south. By the time many had reached Dundee, less than an hour into journeys, which sometimes took more than three hours, many of them were bombed out of their minds. In later years, the notorious Aberdeen Soccer Casuals, who numbered around 200, also started to travel on the trains. In the main, the BTP managed to police the special trains without major incident but the Soccer Casuals were dreaded in the major cities.

On Saturday 17 August 1974 an all too familiar scenario was played out as a member of the public boarded the 18.05 service from London Euston to Birmingham New Street station, via Northampton. She was in possession of a First Class ticket and as she entered the First Class section she found it full of Manchester United football supporters. She remonstrated with the guard on the train in an effort to find a seat but appears to have got nowhere.

The train was an Electrical Multiple Unit, which meant that when the train was in motion the guard was completely isolated from passengers in his compartment and, in reality, he was not in a strong position to do anything. On arrival at Northampton the victim tried to complain again to another member of rail staff about the behaviour of the fans, but they all left unimpeded. Yet another innocent victim left with a complete feeling of injustice.

On Saturday 14 September 1974, just over 200 football supporters travelled on the return football excursion train from Stoke-on-Trent to Coventry. On arrival at Coventry the train was checked and twelve small light bulbs were found to be missing, as supporters continued with their habit of committing wanton damage.

On 6 October 1974, football supporters travelling from Ipswich to Lowestoft caused damage to a train. It was met at Halesworth by police who removed sixteen youths from the train, including a sixteen-year-old. A total of forty light bulbs and ten lampshades had been broken and the sixteen-year-old subsequently admitted damaging four of them. Sergeant Tony Thompson prosecuted the case at court and the offender was made the subject of a two-year supervision order and ordered to pay compensation.

On Saturday 9 November 1974 at 5.28 p.m. a member of rail staff was on duty, in the refreshment room at Coventry, when she heard the bell of a cash till, that was not in use, ring. She went to investigate and saw a Leeds United football supporter taking money from the till. The room was full of football supporters and as he slipped away she reported the incident to PC Crossley BTP Leeds, who was on the station waiting to escort a train back to Leeds.

He in turn reported the theft to a local officer Sergeant 'W' 9 Hyslop, but the offender disappeared without trace and could not be found on the return train. Despite his efforts requiring him to place his hands through a counter grill, turn the cash till round and open it by pressing one of the figure keys, his reward amounted to just £1.49 in loose change.

Rob Davison recalls some of his experiences in policing Scottish fans,

I remember an England *v.* Scotland football match at Wembley which must have been some time after 1974, when I was promoted to uniform inspector at Birmingham. A lot of trains from Scotland had to have police escorts and there was a 'no drink' ban on at that time. To make things easier for the Scottish officers, it was arranged that they should work as far as Crewe and then be relieved by England-based officers.

This was to happen during the night as the trains made their way south, and I was tasked to supervise matters at Crewe. One of the Scottish trains had arrived on a centre 'road' track, i.e. not adjacent to a platform, and I was walking along the nearest platform and watching and listening to the hubbub from the train.

Someone shouted something from the train and I felt a sharp pain on my left ankle as something struck it. I looked down and saw a full can of McEwen's lager rolling away toward a nearby bench. Although the pain was intense, I couldn't shout out as

I didn't want whoever it was who had thrown it to think that they had injured me. Could I do anything about this? Was it feasible to attempt to identify the culprit? Then it occurred to me that it might not have been a malicious act, rather the actions of an over-exuberant Scottish fan wishing to share his drink!

I decided it was the latter, and, trying hard not to limp, I went over to the bench and picked up the can, which luckily hadn't split. Then I turned to face the nearest carriage, raised the can and shouted 'Cheers lads', and those on the train responded by shouting and banging on the doors and windows. I took this as acknowledgement on their part! I ducked into a platform office and sat down to inspect my foot. Fortunately nothing serious, just a bad knock, and I enjoyed the can of McEwen's later.

On 11 January 1975, the leading coach of a Luton to Euston service was completely gutted by a fire started by Chelsea fans returning from a fixture at Luton. In a subsequent written Commons reply to a question on the subject, the Under Secretary, Home Office, Shirley Summerskill confirmed that the BTP had descriptions of four suspects that they wished to interview in connection with the arson attack.

The incident prompted Chelsea fans to add another couple of song to their repertoire: 'Chelsea Sing, Chelsea fight, Chelsea set a train alight,' and, 'If we lose, if we fail, take it out on British Rail la la.' One Chelsea fan commented on a social media site in 2007,

> Yep I was on the train that was set alight by Chelsea fans on the way back from drawing 1-1 with Luton. I was at the other end to the fire I hasten to add. The train stopped and we all piled out onto the track before it really took a hold. Eventually they sent another train to pick us up. Still got the press cutting from the *Guardian* showing the burnt-out carriage.

On Wednesday 15 January 1975, Tony Thompson led another escort on a football charter train from Norwich to Manchester for a League Cup match. He recalls,

> Most of the Norwich supporters were family groups and in good humour. The match was played in the evening, and it was

dark when we arrived and when we left. The game was played at Old Trafford and when we arrived we were asked to assist in the ground by Greater Manchester Police, which we duly did. Manchester United scored first, and the sound was absolutely deafening – even louder than at Wembley, but when Norwich equalised you could have heard a pin drop! It finished in a 2-2 draw.

Our charter train stopped, and departed, from a small station close to the Old Trafford ground and at the end of the game my BTP contingent escorted the 300–400 Norwich fans back there, accompanied by a contingent from the Greater Manchester Police mounted section. To my dismay, when we arrived I found that the train was going to be delayed for an hour, which left five BTP officers, plus the GMP officers, with a large number of Norwich supporters wanting to go home and stuck in a dimly lit street with no facilities.

Fortunately I had a loud hailer with me and tried to keep the fans updated, but although the Norwich fans were well behaved they started to get upset as the GMP horses kept moving sideways into the long line of supporters, trying to make sure that they were all on the pavement, despite the fact that there was no passing traffic. Some fans were frightened of the horses, and others angry, and I could see that this was going to stir up trouble for us for the journey home.

I quickly found the police officer in charge of the mounted – a superintendent on a horse! and told him that the use of the horses in this way was unhelpful and asked him to withdraw them. His response was to tell me in very clear terms that if I didn't want their help he was off home and promptly withdrew all of his staff! The situation, however, calmed down and the BTP were seen as the good guys and we had a quiet trip home. I realised the value of police horses, but not on this occasion.

On Saturday 1 March 1975, the BTP had to mount a large-scale operation, involving 200 officers from various parts of the force, to police the movements of fans attending the League Cup final between Aston Villa and Norwich, which saw thousands of fans converge on Wembley. Eleven football special trains at Norwich alone tested police resources, while BTP officers in the Midlands had to contend with trying to police eighteen service trains to London. All this was taking place at the same time that many London-based officers were engaged with the aftermath of the major incident at Moorgate Underground station, in which forty-three people died and a further seventy-four were injured.

Tony Thompson remembers the day well,

My first trip to the old Wembley Stadium was as a newly promoted uniform sergeant based at Lowestoft in Suffolk. I had to escort Norwich fans on a football charter train from Norwich to Liverpool Street station. The crowd were very well behaved and my next task on arrival was to escort several hundred Norwich fans to Wembley Stadium with five other officers.

At Liverpool Street station the Underground train was packed with Norwich fans and, when they had all boarded the train with my officers, I squeezed into it with my back to the supporters. I had to push hard to get in and just managed it before the doors closed. Unfortunately there was not quite enough room to get my head and my helmet in as well. My cork helmet was crushed between the doors and pulled from my head, as all the supporters around me burst into laughter, which continued as I desperately tried to release my helmet. After what seemed an eternity I eventually did so and was amazed to see it pop back into shape as I placed it rather sheepishly back on my head.

On arrival at Wembley we were actually deployed into the ground by a Metropolitan Police inspector and my serial took up positions in the Aston Villa supporters section. It was standing terraces only at the time and shortly after kick-off I became aware of a disturbance a few yards in front of me. I squeezed through the masses very slowly, but as people were packed in so tightly there was no room for fighting and it fizzled out. I stayed where I was and then suddenly realised that people behind me were getting disgruntled. Being 6 foot 2 inches tall and wearing a helmet I had somewhat blocked the view of the game for some of them, so I did the decent thing and took my hat off and made some new friends. Aston Villa won the Cup 1-0 so there was no more trouble in my area!

On Wednesday 25 June 1975, the BBC reported in the news that the British Railways board were entering into discussions with the Football League to formulate a plan for supporters clubs to provide stewards to patrol trains in order to curb football rowdyism.

At the start of the new season, on the evening of Tuesday 19 August 1975, a number of football matches were played in various parts of the country, which resulted in a number of fans being stranded at Crewe station awaiting trains home. Among them was an eighteen-year-old London youth with previous convictions for various crimes, and who was already on bail for a football-related assault.

At about 12.30 a.m. on Wednesday 20 August 1975, he entered the gents toilet on platform 5 at Crewe station and with a crowbar forced open the cashbox on the coin-operated lock in the toilet, removing the cash inside. BTP were informed and after questioning a number of supporters they discovered the name of the culprit, who by this time had caught a train to London Euston.

Fortunately, due to re-routing the train was delayed back into London and the officers had time to notify their colleagues at Euston. The train was met on arrival and three persons, including the suspect for theft, were taken to the police office. He subsequently admitted his part in the theft and one of the others was found to be in possession of crowbars and a flick knife.

The defendant for theft appeared in court on the same day and after all that effort was fined the princely sum of £2 for theft and £15 for damage, to be paid at the rate of 50 pence per week. So much for justice being seen to be done!

Geoff Lowe retired from the BTP in August 2002, holding the rank of inspector at force headquarters, and recalls one of the so-called south coast derbies, also known as Hampshire Derbies, which were games held between Portsmouth and Southampton.

He recalls,

In the mid-70s I was a PC on a train, with another uniform colleague, travelling with football supporters from Portsmouth to Southampton. Also on the train in plain clothes doing a bit of spotting was a young officer Brian Gosden. This was a bit of a risky strategy given the numbers and so it proved to be. As the train was coming in to Cosham there was a fight on the train. Brian was trying to point out to us who was responsible and somebody must have clocked him because the next thing he was literally thrown out of the carriage he was in. He was unhurt but well shook up and lucky not to have been seriously injured. We made three arrests.

Brian Gosden retired from the BTP as a chief inspector, and has his own memories of policing football trains during this period,

I think it was the 1974/75 football season and I was a probationer police constable at Southampton Central railway station. We regularly used to police Portsmouth fans whose hooligan element were known as 'Millwall by the Sea', due to their reputation. A lot of Portsmouth fans came from the Paulsgrove area, although there were times when we even escorted the ferries to the Isle of Wight if there were large numbers of fans on board.

I remember going to Portsmouth for an evening mid-week match and after the game I was at Fratton railway station, with the Inspector Jack Hartley, as fans returned. As a lot of rowdy fans got onto one particular train I was directed by the inspector to escort it on my own. It's just the way it was in those days, we often simply did not have the resources to put many officers on escorts.

We set off with about forty to fifty fans in one carriage. It was a diesel train, with no corridors, and I had no workable radio. I was completely isolated standing in the middle of them in the carriage, while the train guard was also isolated in a van at the end of the train. The train left with the next stop being Cosham ten minutes away, and immediately they became extremely noisy, opening and closing the 'slam doors' and climbing in the luggage racks, and throwing things at each other.

As I went to intervene I was suddenly hit on the back of my head by a seat cushion. Although they were not capable of inflicting a serious injury they were nevertheless quite heavy. I turned and grabbed hold of the person who had hit me, at which point he started to struggle violently and constantly spat at me, as did his immediate friends. This was the signal for everyone around me to start spitting on me as I clung on to him.

After what seemed to be an age the train pulled into Cosham, and I literally fell onto the platform with my prisoner. Fortunately there were some local police officers there waiting to see the train through and they very quickly came to my rescue. I took my prisoner to the local police station where he was charged with assaulting the police. I always remember the incident vividly because the spit was literally dripping from my body and uniform, and I had to have a good wash to get it off me. It was so bad that my uniform was destroyed afterwards.

The fans didn't always get it their own way, and I remember once during the same period that a train came into Southampton loaded with Manchester United fans, who had been engaged in massive disorder and criminal damage. We were waiting for them on the platform, with the local police, and when they arrived the local inspector decided to arrest every single one of them. This resulted in about 100 fans being escorted in vans to Southampton Central police station. Fortunately that was one for the CID to sort out!

In 1976 a Millwall supporter, Ian Pratt, died at New Cross station after falling out of a train during a fight with West Ham fans. After the incident West Ham hooligans constructed the chant, 'West Ham boys, we've got brains, we throw Millwall under trains'. Two years later leaflets were later circulated at another fixture between the two clubs bearing the words, 'A West Ham fan must die to avenge him'.

On 1 May 1976, Southampton played Manchester United in an FA Cup final at Wembley. Geoff Lowe was on board one of about ten football specials travelling to Wembley,

By this time I had about five years' service and was quite experienced in handling football fans. Four of us were on the train with a lot of the hardcore hooligans. We split into two pairs and took one end of the train each. I was with a young PC and we located where the troublesome group were sitting. The train was supposed to be dry but they all had booze with them and packs of cards out ready to play.

I was somewhat taken aback when my colleague started trying to take the alcohol from them and immediately you could cut the atmosphere with a knife, and I knew if I didn't do something quickly we were going to be in deep trouble.

I immediately took my hat off, told my colleague to sit down, and instructed the fans to get their playing cards out to see how good they were. I also said that if they were having a drink then everyone was having a drink, and the alcohol was duly shared around the carriage, making it less likely that one particular group would get drunk.

We were lucky and this rather unconventional approach defused the situation. We stayed with them for the journey, and when a couple of people started messing about some of their peers actually did the job for us and told them to behave.

When we pulled into Wembley there was a reception committee waiting for us, consisting of a chief superintendent and about twenty officers by the ticket barriers.

I got off the train first and started walking towards the exit. As I did so I was amazed to hear a roar behind me as a large section of some 400 fans formed lines and marched behind me chanting 'Geoffrey is our leader, Geoffrey is our leader.' The chief superintendent's face was a picture and to cap it all Southampton won the game in a shock victory 1-0 with a goal in the 83rd minute of the game.

During 1976, a total of 656 football special trains were provided with police escorts on seventy-eight separate days, with escorts ranging from two to eight officers.

Keith Groves was a detective sergeant at Birmingham between 1976 to 1979 and worked most Saturdays, either as part of a 'snatch squad' at New Street, Smethwick Rolfe Street, or Witton, for the games at Aston Villa, or by running the prisoner reception team in the office.

Keith recalls,

On one occasion I remember we had seventeen people handcuffed and lined up waiting to be processed. I remember another incident when I was at Witton and some London fans on a train were taunting Villa fans on the platform. A Villa fan came up and literally punched the window through with his fist. I locked him up and when I checked him out found that he had got a previous conviction for removing the head from a corpse for a bet. There were no hard feelings and whenever he saw me after that he always made a point of speaking to me.

Paul Robb, who retired as an assistant chief constable with BTP, recalls his early experiences in dealing with football traffic,

In 1976 I joined BTP as a uniform constable at Euston and after training went almost immediately onto nights – it would have been around September time, just after the new season started. On football Saturdays, the night shift would come on at 7 p.m. and the major task was meeting in trains, service and football specials with returning fans who had travelled north or to the Midlands. In those days I was a seasoned football fan and had myself travelled around to watch my team but this was the first time I had seen it through police eyes.

A group of us were sent to meet a train full of Chelsea fans and we were told to stand across the ramp that led down to the platforms to control the flow, and to deal with any problems. At the far end of the platform I could see the locomotive as the train entered the station and, before the whole of it had reached the platform, I could see the doors swinging open on the leading coaches, and fans jumping onto the platform, running to try and keep their footing, some falling and being dragged back up.

Before the train had come to a stand just about every door was open, and the fans had disembarked, and the chanting 'Chel-sea' started. In the high ceilings of a terminus station the noise was amplified as this sea of people came towards us. The initial feeling inside me was a mixture of being mesmerised by the noise, the look of what appeared to be an unstoppable force, and a most peculiar feeling in my legs, which although it only lasted seconds, started with a shake, then an inability to move!

Fortunately for me it was literally a few seconds and then I was fine – the noise was incredible, but the fans passed through without incident.

That night we continued to meet trains in and I actually began to enjoy it, and started to spot potential troublemakers, who had probably had too much to drink and needed either a word or instructions to their mates to control them. Over a period of time it became easier to assess the demeanour of a crowd to determine whether they simply wanted to get home, or to the pub, or were looking for trouble.

Paul Robb recalls another incident in 1976,

We had a chap called Joe Cutting, a PC at Euston who I believe was related to a Northamptonshire Chief Constable Frank Cutting. On his last day in the job, which just happened to be a rest day working, we came back on a train with the Crystal Palace fans and the team. This was a regular event and the manager was Malcolm Allison – the club would book a dining car and Joe went up the train and saw Malcolm, who was drinking champagne. Joe announced that it was his last day as a police officer so Malcolm invited him to join him for a glass of champagne. Joe turned up shortly before we arrived in London looking slightly the worse for wear!

On the evening of Easter Monday, in April 1977, Inspector Dennis Temporal had just twenty officers at Charlton to try to control Charlton and Chelsea fans attending a match. Trouble started soon after the end of the game when a train failed to stop at the station. Thousands tried to join the 600–800 fans already stranded on the platform, climbing fences and rushing barriers in a situation which became increasingly volatile.

Despite support from the Metropolitan Police, urgent assistance was called for and BTP officers from all over London converged on the area until there were more than 120 police officers on the station alone. Officers were required to escort trains to Charing Cross, and one was damaged so badly that it had to be taken out of service. Inspector Temporal said, 'Every officer could have had several bodies but that meant fewer police to deal with the remaining hooligans.'

Viv Head, who eventually retired as a detective inspector, recalls,

In 1977, I was a newly promoted sergeant of five months, stationed at Birmingham New Street. Having served as a constable at Cardiff

Docks I was well used to dealing with some of the seamier elements of life but had very little experience of dealing with massed football supporters or indeed of policing the railway network in general. I was a dock copper.

On 21 May that year, the FA Cup final was played at Wembley between Liverpool and Manchester United, two old rivals. As I came to realise, clashes between rival gangs of so-called football supporters could be noisy, vulgar and violent. With so many First Division football clubs in a relatively small part of the country, it was not unusual to have up to eight, or ten, sets of home or away fans passing through New Street station. Then, just as you thought the rush was over, 400 Manchester fans might turn up, changing trains on their way home from a game in London. More than once, a thin blue line stood side by side spread across the concourse with truncheons drawn keeping two sets of baying rival supporters apart. I had already experienced a twelve-hour night shift beginning at 6 p.m. on a busy football Saturday at Birmingham New Street.

On that particular night I spent the entire shift sorting a mass of paperwork, fingerprints and photographs from the thirty-six prisoners who had been arrested at New Street during the day. It was common practice then for an arresting officer to be photographed with his, or her, prisoner with a Polaroid camera to settle any later arguments on just who had arrested who and when. In the course of a busy day an officer might arrest several different people at different times. And, as happened on at least one occasion, one particular yob was arrested for a public order offence before the game, was bailed, and then arrested a second time for a similar offence after the game.

Given the nature of the game on FA Cup day though, the fans were certainly more family orientated than hooligan, and there was little or no trouble on the inward journey to Wembley. And as it turned out, it was a day that saw the best in football supporters rather than the worst.

My serial of five constables took an early train to Liverpool to escort 600 Liverpool fans on board a special train to Wembley. I don't know how many such trains there were, but I would guess six or eight for each of the two teams. There was not even any real trouble when the train stopped on the outskirts of London right alongside a Manchester United special train crowded with fans. A lot of fairly good natured, if occasionally ribald, banter was exchanged through open windows with the fans within touching distance of each other.

Except in the case of a draw, half of 75,000 fans are going to be ecstatic after the game, and half exceptionally downhearted. We were expecting a bit more of a testing time on the return to Liverpool with Manchester United having won the game two goals to one. My serial was initially employed, along with a large number of other officers, sorting a heaving mass of fans crammed onto the giant Wembley overbridge, channelling fans onto the right platforms. It was positively manic. I was rostered to take the first Liverpool train out at 5.25 p.m. and gathered my serial around ten-past-five to get to the platform and onto the train. The platform was a seething mass of humanity and I was not at all sure that all my officers were aboard when the train pulled out.

A quick check once we were underway, and had got everyone sitting down, found that one officer, WPC Glenise Hyslop, was not on board. No real problem though, she could join the serial on the second train, and five of us would be able to manage well enough. Indeed, we had a trouble-free run back to Liverpool. Two Birmingham serials fitted neatly into the Commer minibus for the return journey by road. It was midnight by the time we got back – it had been a long and tiring day.

But WPC Hyslop's return was not quite what I had imagined. In fact, she had been the first of my serial to reach the platform for the first Liverpool train which was loaded and ready to go when she got on board. It left fifteen minutes earlier than the scheduled time of 5.25 p.m. Unbeknown to me, the train I policed was the second train away not the first. So who else was on the first train with Glenise? No-one, she was on her own.

It took Glenise several traverses of the long train to realise that she was the only police officer on board. Having seen the same policewoman pass along the seven or eight packed coaches several times, it took the fans only a short while longer to also realise that she was the only police presence on the train. A good deal of banter was fired off in her direction and, as an attractive young woman, some of it was often quite suggestive, but all of it pretty good natured. Glenise was a competent and worldly-wise officer, however, and it was nothing she couldn't deal with.

Mid-way through the journey the train came to an unscheduled halt in the Staffordshire countryside. The wait dragged on and the fans started to become restless. It was in the nature of football fans, and perhaps the public in general, to get more frustrated and animated when a train was standing still. It was a time for the police to be insistent that everyone remain seated, and not migrate to the vestibule areas to look out of the windows. The next thing would be for a door to be opened, as you could in those days, and for the fans to start spilling down on the track.

Eventually, the train began to move off and the reason for the delay became clear as the guard moved along the train; the driver had suffered a heart attack and had died in his cab. The accurately named dead man's handle device had brought the train safely to a halt.

Word spread throughout the train and the fans became quieter and more respectful as they realised it put their Wembley defeat into perspective. Soon a whip round began and, as the train was pulling into its destination at Liverpool station, Glenise Hyslop was handed a substantial amount of cash to pass onto the driver's family. A gesture perhaps typical of Scouse generosity, and one that certainly showed that not all football supporters were hooligans.

FA Cup final trains, however, were the exception to the rule. Most football special trains were noisy and boisterous and some were downright violent. They required a firm hand from the police, who often numbered only three or four officers, policing a train load of 600 yobs.

For a year or two, there was a trend for some of the more violent thugs to carry small, razor-sharp craft knives which they would spontaneously produce and slash someone, anyone, across the face, for no other reason than they could. Even among unruly football supporters, they were no more than scum. Anyone found in possession of such a craft knife was immediately arrested for possession of an offensive weapon.

On 25 May 1977, Liverpool played Borussia Mönchengladbach in the European Cup Final, and thousands of fans made the trip from Liverpool to see their team play in Rome.

Ginger Ablard recalls,

By this time I had an Alsatian by the name of Kaison. Because of cutbacks in the number of dogs, and being based at Preston, I found myself regularly doing football duties in the North West and did a lot of Liverpool games, as they were running high in the football world at that time. I got a phone call from a senior officer who told me to make my way to Dover to meet returning Liverpool fans. I thought I would be going with loads of officers but it turned out it was just me with the dog, and a probationary constable.

We got to Dover to meet the ferry and were met by an inspector, with thirty PCs, from Kent Police. As we loaded a train up the inspector asked me how many BTP officers would be escorting it and I pointed to the two of us. He was amazed and said that he wouldn't get on with his thirty officers, let alone two! I was younger in those days so off we went and took them direct from Dover to Liverpool Lime Street with no trouble. A lot of clubs had 'bad boys' but if you treated them firm but fair you mostly got respect back from them.

Tony Thompson was a young BTP inspector at Kings Cross railway station by Saturday 4 June 1977. He recalls,

This date will be remembered for the day the Tartan Army from Scotland invaded the pitch at the old Wembley Stadium following their 2-1 defeat of England in the British Home International Championships. It will also be remembered because some of the Scottish fans tore down goalposts and ripped up the hallowed Wembley turf. Several BTP officers detained Scottish fans after the match in possession of pieces of it and handed them over to our Metropolitan Police colleagues.

Paul Robb also recalled, 'I arrested two Scottish fans for theft of a piece of turf from Wembley after the Scots wrecked the pitch.

It was two days after the game and the look on their faces when I found it was priceless!'

Tony Thompson remembers this day for another reason, involving the death of a young Scottish football fan travelling to Wembley,

> I was meeting trains arriving from Scotland at Kings Cross when I received a radio call to the effect that there had been a serious accident on one of the trains as it headed into one of the tunnels in North London. Apparently one of the Scottish supporters had been leaning out of one of the windows and his head had struck the tunnel wall as the train entered at speed.
>
> I suspected that this would be a fatality and my suspicions proved correct. As the train drew slowly to a halt on the platform I could see what looked like a cigar-shaped plume of blood along the complete length of the side of one of the carriages.
>
> I opened the train door and saw a headless corpse laid on the carriage floor. The head had been completely ripped from the body and was nowhere to be seen. We secured the scene and located some witnesses who were understandably very distressed. I remember hearing the Tartan Army singing loudly, and happily, as they headed down the platform – and then suddenly silence as they spotted the grisly exterior of the carriage.
>
> Our investigations revealed that two friends had positioned themselves at either end of the carriage, and were leaning out of the door windows shouting at each other. Sadly, the one at the London end of the carriage had his back towards the rapidly approaching tunnel and would have been oblivious to any danger. Death was instant.

The area around Kings Cross was, and still is, a busy area for football traffic and Tony Thompson recalls an incident in 1977 when things did not quite go according to plan,

> There was fighting between Newcastle United supporters and London-based fans. I came across two men fighting in Euston Road, while I was out on my own, and managed to grab one of them. I walked him in an arm lock towards the BTP detention

facility at the rear of Kings Cross station, but he was very compliant so I never thought to handcuff him. I radioed ahead to say I was coming in with a prisoner but just as I was approaching the office he suddenly broke free, without warning, and dashed off. Wearing jeans and trainers he was much quicker than me and got away.

I had the embarrassment of walking into custody with no prisoner but my officers were actually very understanding. Several of them accompanied me on a search of the area and somehow we managed to track him to a nearby building site. We covered the exits and I judged that he would soon emerge in an effort to get the last train home. Sure enough, after a short while, I got a radio message to say that an officer had detained a man. I went to the location and there was my prisoner, but this time handcuffed and very quiet.

On Saturday 29 October 1977, five BTP Southern Division officers, one a female officer, were injured by football supporters during violent scenes at Norwood Junction station. It began soon after the end of the Crystal Palace *v.* Charlton game, when rival factions converged on the station on their way home. They were already in an angry mood and, as police struggled to keep them apart, they started throwing bricks at each other across opposite platforms.

PC Gary Ancell, aged nineteen and just out of training school, arrested one of the culprits and a violent struggle ensued when he and WPC Elizabeth Cairns, and PC Tony Theobold who had gone to his assistance, were attacked by a mob of some sixty youths.

PC Ancell was knocked to the ground and kicked unconscious, while his two colleagues were thrown onto the track. Other officers who arrived on the scene were also attacked; PC Mike Dorrington was hit on the arms by a flying brick, and PC Mike Real was punched in the stomach and ribs. Still unconscious, Gary Ancell was taken to hospital and detained overnight, while the others, all based at Victoria station, were lucky enough to get away nursing cuts and bruises.

Routinely, the policing of football fans, travelling on the rail networks, presented the BTP with huge manpower challenges as the thin blue line was stretched this way and that. Additional resources created cost and abstraction issues, all of which brought additional pressures.

Willie Baker, however, who retired from the BTP as a superintendent, recalls one occasion in particular when those extra football resources actually saved the day during an unrelated incident.

His recollection is as follows,

It's perhaps not surprising how sometimes in life we are heavily influenced by experiences gathered during our youth. My school was much more focussed on rugby and cricket than football, and when, after a couple of years, the sports master left and a football-mad replacement arrived, the appetite for 'games', which so many of us had previously enjoyed, just evaporated. Gone were the chances of getting even with a rival on the rugby pitch, or bowling a rock-hard leather ball, at the greatest velocity possible, towards someone who had been involved in previous aggravations.

My distain for football remained, and it might therefore be considered something of a surprise that I elected to join, and was lucky enough to be accepted, into the British Transport Police in my home city of Carlisle. This was at a time when football violence was very much in the ascendancy, and the need for the BTP to provide travelling serials of officers to escort fans was a regular major priority.

Carlisle is not generally noted for the prowess of its football team! Few of the young fans of today would believe that Carlisle United ever played Manchester United, let alone that they did so twice! These were momentous times by any standards, it was the third round of the 1978 FA Cup, on 7 January 1978, and emotions in the border city were running sky-high. I was twenty years old and had been a constable for two years.

Every police officer and his dog, quite literally, was on duty. The Cumbria Constabulary, it is fair to say, was not that accustomed to managing football violence, and had turned-out in enormous numbers. I am pretty certain that Cumbria had also loaned some mounted officers from Lancashire – there were certainly horses present on Court Square, at the front of Carlisle Citadel station.

BTP had sent travelling serials up with the visiting fans that, once safely gathered in the hallowed terraces of Brunton Park, totalled a record 21,700.

To put this in perspective, Carlisle United have a regular attendance now that is closer to between three and five thousand, and the maximum capacity is a meagre 18,000.

The match kicked-off and, as was customary, all officers on duty used the down-time to get some refreshments, or grab a rest so as to be ready for the returning fans, whether jubilant or drowning their sorrows. Excessive alcohol was a major contributing factor to football violence in those days, and legislation was not introduced to curb this until thirteen years later. Prior to this, travelling serials of officers frequently faced enormous challenges, often dangerous, sometimes in remote locations, with minimal resources and greatly out-numbered, and with poor, or non-existent communications.

It was during this rest period that we took a call from the booking office supervisor that there was a man at the window behaving very strangely. Evidently, he had his face pressed up against the glass partition and was lapsing between being calm and friendly to being very hostile and aggressive. On the one hand he was repeatedly saying to the booking clerk, 'Thank you very much, I love you, I love you very much' and blowing kisses at him, and then, as if a switch had been flicked in his head, changed to a swearing, spitting tyrant, going crimson in the face, clenching his fists and baring his teeth, calling the poor terrified clerk all the names under the sun and threatening to kill him.

A colleague, who I shall call Danny, and I left our tea and wandered over the footbridge to see what was going on, and upon arrival in the booking hall we got our first glimpse of a man I will never, ever, forget. He was an imposing figure, around 6 feet 8 inches tall, mid-thirties, not carrying an ounce of fat, and with very short cropped hair. He went on to produce what was undoubtedly, at that time in my life, one of the most terrifying encounters I had ever experienced.

We took him to one side and while we were talking to him a taxi driver wandered across to us and explained that he had picked him up on the main Scotland Road north of the city, and that for the whole time in the back of the taxi he had been behaving in the same unpredictable and extreme way. He had paid for his taxi in cash from a huge wad of notes, and the driver wanted to give him his change.

It was at this point that the man flipped.

Suddenly, we were not looking up at someone a good 9 inches taller than me and having a calm chat. My colleague had been thrown across the booking hall by him, using one hand, and had landed on his back. It looked like I was next! Danny managed to get to his feet and rush back to the fray, and together we started grappling with our new-found muscle-man, who was roaring like a banshee and had the strength of a grizzly bear. We were struggling and being totally overwhelmed.

The ensuing brawl progressed from the booking hall to one of the ticket barriers, where Danny and I managed to restrict him by squeezing him into the one-metre-square capsule that was the cabin the barrier staff occupied. While we had him pinned in there one of us radioed for urgent assistance.

I have never seen so many uniform coppers start appearing from so many different places at one time. Cumbria police from Court Square, BTP running over the bridge from the police office and others from all points around, and who had obviously found far better places offering hospitality during the down-time! In the restricted space we managed to handcuff our prisoner's wrists and get him to his feet. The limited force that Danny and I had been able to effect in our attempts to restrain him had produced a cut to his head, which was bleeding but was certainly not diminishing his lunatic behaviour. He was completely and utterly wild.

Obviously feeling that is was now safe to approach us, the taxi driver gingerly came forward and delivered the most terrifying piece of information by saying 'I think he said something about coming from Carstairs.'

In a nut-shell, Carstairs high security hospital was, at that time, the Scottish equivalent of Broadmoor. It housed some of the most dangerous, criminal, and violent people in the UK, many of whom suffered from extreme psychiatric disorders.

Carstairs was then, and for me remains, a genuinely scary place, and it was evidently the spot from which our prisoner had originated. To this day it is equipped with an air-raid sounding siren to alert local residents if an inmate escapes!

We managed to get our man to his feet and began to walk him over the footbridge to a waiting police van to take him into custody. He had his hands behind his back and his wrists were bound with handcuffs, as was the way then. These were the old-fashioned metal ratchet type. He was surrounded by about a dozen police officers and had calmed a little.

I was a couple of paces behind this group as we walked over the bridge and what happened next was like one of those slow-motion events shown in violent films, where you see what is happening but it is slowed down for added effect.

The first conscious thought I had in my brain was, 'How can he have both his hands in the air and free, when he is cuffed?' He was screaming again, at the very top of his voice, and both his hands were above his head. One wrist was completely devoid of any signs of a handcuff, and on the other was the set of handcuffs being flailed around in the air quite lethally, and proving to be a most effective weapon against responding police officers. We later worked out that, such was the strength in his wrists, he had flexed the muscles in his lower arm and had freed the handcuff by actually tearing the metal teeth from one of the ratchets.

This was one of the strongest men imaginable, throwing police officers around as if they were stuffed toys. He yelled at the top of his voice 'I am the son of God' and for a brief second I was beginning to believe him!

Carlisle station was built in 1847 and is a magnificent structure; similar in some respects to other great stations like York insofar that it has an enormous glass roof. Just right for massive amplification of sound, and his high-volume declaration boomed around all the platforms below.

One of the quick-witted wheeltappers down on the platform below offered an appropriate response by shouting up a suggestion as to what we should do with him, and which was similar to the fate of our good Lord while he was nailed upon the cross! The struggle was back on, and more police resources were called for. Any officer in Carlisle that day, who had up to that time thought that aggression and violence would be caused by football fans, swiftly and dramatically, had that preconception eradicated.

We were-grouped around the man in vast numbers as he went totally berserk but, fortunately, because of the FA Cup, we had numbers on our side.

With four police officers to each leg, and three to each arm, he was sufficiently restrained, carried to the waiting police van and taken into protective custody.

I, and many of my colleagues, did not witness the returning Manchester United football fans because we were somewhat otherwise engaged!

Incredibly, the game was a draw, with single goals being scored by Carlisle's Ian McDonald and Manchester's Lou Macari. The rematch, at Old Trafford on 11 January 1978, was an unsurprising 4-2 victory to Manchester.

Our violent man was detained under the Section 136 of the Mental Health Act, which bestows powers on the police to detain people and take them to a 'place of safety' if they are suspected of suffering from a mental disorder.

It is also perhaps no surprise for those who know me that my collar number at that time was in fact '136' – not a typical football day by any means!

On Saturday 25 February 1978, PC Tucker, with police dog Zac, was on duty at Birmingham New Street station in connection with the Birmingham City *v.* Aston Villa and West Bromwich Albion *v.* Coventry City football matches. Approximately 150 Birmingham City supporters approached the station and began to chant 'National Front, National Front' towards sixty Aston Villa supporters, who were coming down the opposite side of the road. Some of the Villa fans were black, and they reacted angrily to the chants. PC Tucker and his dog stood between the two sets of fans and single handedly dispersed them in opposite directions. The two groups met up again shortly afterwards in the city centre and running battles took place.

On Good Friday, 24 March 1978, Paul Robb was involved in another football-related incident,

Watford, under a young up-and-coming manager, were in the Fourth Division but were on the crest of a wave that would lead eventually to promotion to the First Division. Although they were in the bottom tier they started to get a following, due to their success, and Easter games always used to be popular.

A special train was laid on and, on arrival at Watford Junction, it was clear that there had been a lot of alcohol consumed, and the fans had come with supplies to keep them going on the train to Crewe, where Watford were playing that day.

The journey was, to say the least, eventful and there were a number of loud and aggressive people among the travelling supporters who were spoken to on a number of occasions. Eventually, and inevitably, one was arrested for some sort of public order offence and taken back to the police compartment at the rear of the train. In those days the special trains would have at least one coach with the old-style compartment, with a side corridor, where we would base ourselves and place our kit, such as it was, while patrols were carried out.

This arrest was not well received and it became evident that some of his compatriots intended to try and release him from what they saw as an unjust detention. As the train approached our destination a large body of these fans attempted to push through the connecting doors to reach our compartment. Fortunately, as you could only get the width of about two people through a connecting door, we were able to hold them at bay, partially closing the sliding door and drawing truncheons while holding onto our prisoner.

As the train pulled into Crewe we shouted to officers on the platform, who assisted us in getting the prisoner from the train, by which time the other fans had got off and decided that the match was more important than the fate of their mate. Of course in those days of not having CCTV, and a different mind-set, there was no follow up enquiry to apprehend more of those involved. No major harm had come to the police officers, and, while there was some damage to the train, it was reported internally and logged and that was pretty much it.

Looking back, I think that these type of incidents were probably pretty frequent, and provided some arrests were made, and the behaviour did not lead to harm or serious damage, there was no real appetite to pursue such matters further.

On Saturday 25 March 1978, PC Tucker was again on duty with police dog Zac at Wolverhampton for a match with Liverpool. While patrolling the car park at the side of Wolverhampton station, he saw a group of Wolverhampton supporters standing on top of a wall at the rear of the car park. They were holding stones and half bricks.

Meanwhile, Liverpool fans were being escorted down the station approach road by West Midlands Police, and the Wolverhampton fans were intent on some target practice. PC Tucker realised what was about to happen and made his way towards the Wolverhampton fans, who numbered some 200. He commanded his dog to bark and as he moved towards them, from a distance of about 100 yards, he began to come under attack from bricks. One half house brick hit the dog on his hind quarters, while the officer was hit on the shoulder by a large stone. Using a nearby warehouse wall as a shield, he began to disperse the supporters and was relieved to see the cavalry arrive in the form of West Midlands Police mounted police officers, who dispersed the group without further incident.

Viv Head went on,

Throughout the 1978 season I was the sergeant in charge at the small police post at Coventry. At one of the home games we had seen a whole crowd of away supporters arrive wound up and spoiling for trouble; we knew that, win or lose, there would be trouble after the game and we were not disappointed.

After the final whistle, hundreds of so-called supporters were herded along the streets to the railway station. They were chanting obscene songs and in an ugly mood. The whole mob was fenced in by dozens of West Midland Police officers, including three or four on horseback towards the front, and several police dogs along the sides. No-one strayed outside the moving fence cordon, even some of them who had come by bus, and really wanted to get to the bus station rather than the railway station.

We got the first trainload away and I recall being asked by a West Midlands Police sergeant how many officers we would have on each train. He was incredulous when I said we would have four at the most. There were two reasons why we were able to get away with this kind of ratio. Firstly, to some extent, we had a 'captive audience' in that they were sectioned off into smaller groups contained within each carriage. Secondly, and most importantly, it was vital to impose your authority from the start. Any lack of positive police action would be a sign of weakness and the mob would seek to impose their will on you.

Pick on the apparent leaders: Shut up! Sit down. Don't argue. Do as you're told. Don't even think about lighting that cigarette. Keep quiet. I won't be telling you again! The real key was not to let them wander around. Keep them in their seats. They sit, you stand. This was always more difficult on overcrowded trains when the aisles were also crammed. Such situations were much more inclined to get out of hand – pulling the emergency cord was a favourite trick. This would bring the train to a halt and allow some of the yobs to climb down onto the tracks to urinate and generally cause more mayhem.

On one notorious train carrying Chelsea supporters back to London, from a match at Cardiff, the train ground to a halt from the cord being pulled more than a dozen times before it reached the half-way point to Newport just 12 miles away. The train crew refused to take the train any further until more police were put on board.

Sergeant Jack Hagerty and a serial of officers from Cardiff joined the train while it was stopped between stations to support the London officers already aboard. Yet more officers joined at Newport and eventually the train made some sort of orderly progress to London. Some of those extra officers may well have already worked a twelve-hour day before they were unexpectedly extended for a return trip to London.

On a lighter note, after one busy football Saturday at Coventry, I had stood the troops down around 7 p.m. and got ready to go home myself. I took my helmet and tunic off and put on a blazer, 'half blues' as it was known, to catch my train to Birmingham.

Descending the stairs to the central platform I was surprised to find about forty supporters on the platform also waiting for the Birmingham train. They had slipped unnoticed onto the station and were a bit noisy with a bit of larking about but they were not especially unruly. With no time to return to the office to get my uniform, I stood on the half landing overlooking the platform and bellowed out 'Right you lot, you all know who I am. I'll be on the same train as you and anyone messing about will have their collar felt. Understand?'

In the circumstances it was about the best I could come up with. No sooner had I finished my impromptu address though than the chant went up 'We know who you are, we know who you are.' It was no more than I deserved, I suppose, and in the event there was no trouble during the journey and I had no cause to feel anyone's collar.

A year later, I was on an 'up' escalator from platform to overbridge level at Birmingham New Street station on a busy weekday. I was on duty but had since been appointed as a detective sergeant, and was dressed in a suit rather than uniform or even half blues. Crossing on a 'down' escalator among a knot of people was a youth who, as we passed, was singing softly to himself, 'We know who you are, We know who you are!' Cheeky bugger I thought, but I had to smile at still being recognised in a different place and a different time.

4

THE SEVENTIES – A DEATH AND A MURDER HITS THE TARTAN ARMY

Bill Rogerson recalls some of the days working at Heysham Harbour in the late '70s,

> Covering the Bolton Wanderers home matches had its perks. After dealing with the incoming fans we used to go to the Catholic club across the road from the station for pie and chips and a mug of tea. Then we would go to watch the game as the ground, Burden Park, was situated next to the main line to Manchester and the west goal mouth was situated at the rear of the old Bolton to Bury railway line, which can be seen in the film *The Love Match* starring Arthur Askey.
>
> The Permanent Way staff had built a stand on the railway embankment, out of old railway sleepers, and we, along with the rail staff, used to stand on these watching the games. I remember one Saturday afternoon watching a game and BBC were covering the match for *Grandstand*, from in front of where we were standing. Our inspector was effing and blinding at the referee and we had to point this out to him as he was being picked up by the cameras.

Keith Fleetwood recalls further experiences of policing football supporters throughout the '70s,

> West Bromwich FC were playing at home and at the conclusion of the match the majority of the supporters returned to the old

Smethwick Rolfe Street station. The platform to Birmingham city centre was on a sharp bend, and very narrow, and as such the numbers of supporters were restricted so as not to become overcrowded and dangerous.

The supporters were held at the entrance to the station, in the road outside, which was made up of cobblestones. Two of us were located at the station entrance in front of the double doors. As the crowd built up we were joined by a Birmingham City mounted police officer from Ladywood, who positioned himself between us and the supporters.

The crowd started pushing making it very difficult to control them. The mounted officer asked us to go behind the doors, into the entrance hall, and said that he would give us a knock when we could open the doors. After seconds we heard a loud splashing noise and suddenly a very pungent smell of urine was detected through the doors.

After what seemed like a very long time the mounted officer knocked on the door with his baton to signal us to go back out to the station front. Upon opening the doors the supporters had formed a half circle outside the entrance of about 15 feet. Obviously the cobblestones had the desired effect, causing the horse pee to spray in all directions. We had no problems after this but a number of supporters had difficulty in getting rid of the smell.

Another time, I was at a local derby at Wolverhampton, who were playing at home to Birmingham City. The return special train full of supporters travelled to the parcels yard at New Street station. Upon the arrival of the train there were numerous incidents with groups of the supporters causing public order problems.

After they had all left the parcels yard we began to check the train, and in the rear carriage we found a compartment window smashed. Just outside the carriage, in the yard, we found a 10-inch diameter circle of blood, about 1 inch deep. About 15 feet further on we found another large pool of blood. We continued following a trail like this right the way round to the rear of the Bull Ring area, where we found a very large area of blood. This showed that whoever had smashed the window had lost an extremely large amount of blood.

We continued our enquiries at the Birmingham Accident Hospital, where we found our offender, who had slashed through his Achilles tendon on his ankle. The subsequent bleeding had filled his one trainer causing the blood to be squeezed out each time it became full.

Dennis Temporal continues his own story,

On promotion to inspector at Euston in 1977 things had definitely started to change in relation to football policing. Euston was, and still is, a key station for football policing. It serves a number of the top, and biggest, football clubs in the country, and was often a meeting point for the hardcore troublemakers from these clubs. Football was a big thing at Euston and almost all our resources were engaged with football policing every Saturday during the season, and sometimes midweek as well.

I remember one Friday night when a number of Scottish fans from Rangers or Celtic were on the overnight sleeper at Euston intending to travel to Glasgow to watch the match on Saturday afternoon. They were in drink and the staff of the sleeper train refused to take it out, so I had to send two officers with the train to keep the peace and they didn't get back until Sunday morning!

Dennis also recalls the home international fixtures between Scotland and England that used to take place annually at that time. Whether it was England fans travelling back south or Scotland fans travelling down to London, he describes the trains as looking like pigsties due to the amount of rubbish, empty beer cans and bottles that were left on board when the supporters alighted. Dennis recalls the 1977 England *v.* Scotland fixture in particular, 'Some Scottish fans were arriving at Euston from the match with bits of turf and goal post from Wembley with them.'

As a result of being stationed at Euston, Dennis became something of an expert in relation to travelling football fans during the late 1970s and early 1980s, just at the time when football violence was beginning to escalate to a different and wholly unacceptable level. Dennis recalls battles taking place between various sets of fans along the Euston Road, between King's Cross and Euston stations, on Saturday evenings as a regular occurrence.

Ed Thompson, then a police constable with the British Transport Police in London and now an active member of the BTP History Group, recalls,

We all of course have our memories of incidents involving football yobs during the 70s and 80s.

Most of my service was on the Underground, and like all BTP officers you soon learnt to think on your feet, because very often you could not rely on back-up. Those were the days when our radios did not transmit or receive once you were 'down the hole.' We were very reliant on the station staff passing on information to the control room if we encountered problems. Routine updates such as movements of fans were passed on by the officers via platform telephones, it was very much a game of cat-and-mouse with the fans, and we weren't always the cat.

I never arranged to go out on a Saturday evening because I knew that we would all end up at Kings Cross, or Euston, to ensure that the fans travelling north left the capital in an orderly manner. It usually ended up with us chasing shadows up and down Euston Road until they got bored and we would receive those loving words 'Stand Down'. Sometimes we were obliged to travel north with them when they were particularly rowdy. I recall that at many England *versus* Scotland games drunken fans would cause major problems on the transport networks.

Bill Rogerson reflects,

My colleagues regularly escorted the ships to and from Belfast, and the trains to and from Manchester. This was because George Best, who played for Manchester United, was from Belfast and had a large following from the city, and Northern Ireland in general. I am a good sailor and when I escorted the ships over to Ireland we relied on the rough weather and sometimes a good old 'Gale Force 10' to calm the fans down. Unfortunately, some of my officers would also be found to be speaking to Huey on the big white telephone and looking for Ruth. I always told them not to have a curry before we set sail!

Being based at Heysham, we used to go on mutual aid to Preston, Blackburn, Burnley, Bolton, Blackpool and Manchester to cover the home and away supporters using these stations. While performing duty at Manchester Oxford Road one Saturday afternoon, there was a ticket barrier check. One supporter came to the barrier and offered to pay from Deansgate, the previous station, which was closed for the purpose of the ticket check. This supporter gave false details to my colleague. It transpired that he had travelled from Altrincham and was a serving constable with the Greater Manchester Police.

I remember the first Saturday of the 1978 season when we had arrived back at Lancaster after an uneventful day on football duty at Manchester Oxford Road and Victoria stations. The sergeant and I were just ready to go home when the guard of the 19.30 hours train to Barrow in Furness came to our office and asked for a police escort as he had got a number of Manchester United supporters on board. The sergeant decided that we would travel to Barrow. It was extra overtime for me but the sergeant was not too keen about going and he made this clear. He didn't want to spend his Saturday evenings travelling to and from Barrow and he was due to retire shortly.

As the train left Carnforth, I struck gold, there was a young man who was a supporter, persistently annoying the ordinary passengers. I saw my chance as the train stopped at Silverdale station, which was in the middle of nowhere. In accordance with the byelaws I ejected him. Despite his pleadings, and those of his companions, I would not let him back on the train. The train set off, leaving him on the platform. There was not another train from Silverdale until the following Monday morning, and there were no buses until Sunday afternoon. My plan had paid off, we did not have any more trouble from the Barrow-based supporters for the rest of the season and the sergeant was happy.

From Heysham we were also called upon for mutual aid in Scotland, for the Scotland *versus* England matches, and the Glasgow Rangers *versus* Celtic matches. One particular Scotland *v.* England match saw me policing the concourse at Glasgow Central station, queuing the fans to buy their tickets. Again trouble free, but I've never seen as many large whisky bottles in my life; some were two or three litre sizes.

Another visit to Glasgow, the week before Christmas 1978, saw me patrolling the trains to Hampden Park for a Rangers *v.* Celtic match. One train was absolutely crammed, packed with both sets of supporters that were a little noisy to say the least. I boarded the train and shouted 'Can you keep it down lads please' in my best Lancashire accent. All went quiet and I gave myself a mental pat on the back for taming some of Glasgow's finest.

All of a sudden they all started hand clapping and chanting in unison 'Sassenach, Sassenach'. The next thing I knew I was pulled off the train by one of my colleagues from Glasgow who said 'If ye dinna want your heid kicking in get off the train' – lesson learnt.

On the return, I was at Hampden Park waiting to escort one of the last trains to Glasgow. As I looked down to the track, I couldn't see the ballast or the sleepers for whisky bottles and Tennents lager cans.

A slightly more heart-warming story – from Heysham Harbour we covered Barrow in Furness and there was a small local team called Greengate United. In the Barrow area there was a young boy who was suffering from a life-threatening illness, but treatment was only available in America. Greengate United organised a charity evening and they invited Manchester United to send an autographed ball for the raffle. They went one better and sent a team up to play them. Admittedly none of the first team players played, but two or three of them came up and walked onto the pitch. I was acting sergeant at the time and covered Barrow railway station for the game with one constable. There was no trouble whatsoever, in fact it was a carnival atmosphere.

Ian Murray, from Scotland, recalls an incident which took place in the late '70s as follows,

The main concern of the police escorts was the effect that the intake of alcohol had on the supporters. This situation led to the death of a supporter travelling to a cup final at Hampden Park. For a wager, this alcohol-crazed supporter climbed onto the roof of the train and was instantly killed when he was struck by an overhead bridge near Carnoustie.

This death led to the special train being halted at Perth. A superintendent of the local force, along with a contingent of his own force, met the train there and instructed that it would require to be terminated at that point. The action had not been fully thought out as the detraining of over 500 football fans on their way to a cup final could have resulted in major trouble in and around Perth. After a lengthy discussion it was agreed that the train would continue to Glasgow on the understanding that the police escort would obtain statements of evidence relative to the circumstances of this tragic death en route.

In 1978, Liverpool played Bruges at Wembley in the European Cup. As the Liverpool team were boarding a train at Euston after the game, Graham Souness handed the winner's cup to Paul Robb on the platform to hold for a few memorable seconds.

Again in the late seventies, Andy Fidgett, who served as a BTP officer at Harwich Parkeston Quay, recalls an incident when 1,000 Nottingham Forest fans hired the Sealink ferry *St George* to go to the European Cup Final,

> I believe Forest won 1-0 against Malmo in possibly May 1979. We had eight officers on board to escort the ship. There was no trouble but someone stole the ships flag, and a retired sergeant I meet with for a coffee believes that he has seen the flag behind the goal on England away games.

On Friday 25 May 1979, twenty-year-old Scottish fan John Murray, of New Cummock, Ayshire, was stabbed to death on his way to an England *v.* Scotland Home International match at Wembley, to be held in London next day.

Some 500 passengers, of whom 400 were Scottish football fans, were travelling on the 10.10 p.m. Glasgow to Euston express train when disturbances erupted. Witnesses described a great deal of drinking in a carriage where a group of fans attempted to molest a twenty-one-year-old female. As she tried to escape, the deceased tried to help her and was stabbed. As he and other fans tried to escape from the knifeman, windows were smashed, and some even tried to open the train doors to jump out, despite the fact that the train was moving at speed.

Mr Murray eventually collapsed in a pool of blood with a stomach wound, and in the melee five other people were stabbed, one of whom received serious injuries and was later detained in hospital. Other witnesses described a gang from Girvan being on the train, who had a reputation for being troublemakers.

At 3.15 a.m. the communication cord was pulled on the train, which eventually stopped at Bank Quay station in Warrington, where it was met by eighty police officers who had been drafted in from across Cheshire county. The 400 fans were taken off the train in batches to a local police station. Within 6 hours the vast majority of them were allowed to continue their journey, with a relief train laid on to take them to London.

In an unrelated incident, another female had £120 stolen from her after a thief used a knife to cut away a pocket of her jeans without her knowing. During the investigation the money was recovered.

A group of five fans were detained for further questioning in connection with the murder and local police confirmed that they expected to charge someone later in the day.

There was no buffet car on the train but fans had been allowed to take 'reasonable' amounts of alcohol on board. This case was to start the debate about alcohol consumption and the introduction of so-called 'dry trains'. Twelve months later, Byelaw 3A was introduced to give powers to the police, and the rail industry, to ban alcohol on designated trains.

As Scottish fans poured into London, many were wearing kilts and drinking openly, and commuters at Victoria and Euston found themselves being treated to spontaneous sing-songs, but the crowds provided huge challenges for the police. Some were even welcomed by the Prime Minister Margaret Thatcher in Downing Street.

Ed Thompson recalls,

One incident I recall in the late 70s was when a Scottish fan was murdered on the forward traffic. After the game we all returned from Wembley to Euston to await 'stand down' when we got word that the train staff were refusing to take the train back to Scotland without a police escort. The chief inspector asked if there were any volunteers to escort the train back and an old PC, Wally Xerri, looked at me and winked – we had just done a twelve-hour rostered tour of duty and when I blinked I swear I saw pound notes flashing!

Wally and I boarded the train, which was packed to the gun whales, and we were greeted as honoured guests by the Scots as we walked through the train. We were surrounded by the fans who just wanted to put on our helmets, as all the 'polis' in Scotland wore flat caps. They wanted to ply us with drinks which we of course kindly refused! Unfortunately the entertainment came to an abrupt end when we reached Preston and found a contingent of Scottish BTP officers waiting to complete the escort back north.

On 13 October 1979, Geoff Lowe took a football special from Portsmouth to Huddersfield and recalls,

Although the club had experienced some difficult years on the pitch, resulting in several relegations, they still took up to 800 supporters to away games, including members of the hooligan element known as the '6.57 Specials', many of whom were horrible people.

On the way into Huddersfield, we were five minutes away from the station when we passed a large slag heap. Suddenly people appeared from everywhere on top of it and the train was subjected to a barrage of missiles. Thirty to forty windows were smashed and the train had to be taken out of service while a replacement was found.

The return journey was to be my last with this set of fans as I was about to be promoted to sergeant in London. A colleague of mine, Chris Carter, was also being promoted on the same date. On the return trip we were invited into a compartment by a group of the more troublesome fans and I was amazed when one of their leaders presented us both with a watch and thanked us for being fair with them, even when there were times when firm handling was called for. They had actually had a whip round for us, and all totally unexpected.

Tony Thompson has many recollections of football policing in London during the late '70s. In one incident, as an inspector, he responded to a call relating to an assault on a Tube train arriving at the northbound Victoria line at Kings Cross. With several officers he got to the platform just as the train was arriving. It was normal practice in those days for Tube drivers to bring trains to a stop with just the front end of the train poking out onto the platform if there was a police incident. This effectively prevented people from escaping off the train.

Officers boarded through the train door and found a badly injured Pakistani male with facial injuries, who had been attacked by four Tottenham supporters. He had also been racially abused by them and called a black bastard. One of the attackers had removed a fluorescent light tube and hurled it like a javelin at the victim, hitting him in the face, which caused an injury requiring twenty-three stitches. He was also sprayed with a fire extinguisher.

His attackers had been to a match between Tottenham and Leyton Orient and had been drinking after the game.

Descriptions were obtained and Tony and his officers went through the train. He recalls,

> One thing I noticed when walking through Tube trains in uniform was that the passengers always looked at you. I guess it is a natural reaction. When I spotted a man several carriages away from the victim looking straight ahead he attracted my attention. As I got closer I could see that he was sweating. He fitted the description of one of the offenders and, together with two others we found, he was arrested and charged with various offences. Two of them later got sentenced to two years in prison for wounding, while the other two got shorter sentences for affray.

Tony found that practicing the art of good communication was vital in terms of self-preservation and recalls once travelling on the five-minute train journey from London Bridge to South Bermondsey railway station, on his own, with a number of large and disgruntled Millwall fans. The trip was one of the most intimidating of his service and he found himself suddenly becoming an expert on how well the team were playing!

In another incident, he was rescued in the nick of time by a BTP dog handler at Liverpool Street station, as supporters tried to rescue a prisoner that he had arrested and were prevented from doing so by a German Shepherd on a long leash. At Stamford Bridge he recalls being pelted with stones from rival fans while escorting Chelsea supporters on foot with the Metropolitan Police.

Again in the late 1970s, Tony recalls responding to a mass brawl on a Saturday evening in Euston Road between unidentified football supporters,

> When I reached St Pancras railway station most of the supporters had dispersed, but I spotted a young man from Sunderland trying to carve his initials on one of the ornate marble pillars at the west end of the station. He was arrested and cautioned but this pillar later featured in the Spice Girls video supporting their 1996 debut hit single 'Wannabe', which became the best-selling hit single by a female group.

Finally, in a rather unusual incident during the same period, Tony Thompson recalls attending to a report of a woman being found in the roadway between Kings Cross and St Pancras stations,

> We discovered a lady who had received multiple superficial puncture wounds to her body. She was a prostitute operating in the area and claimed to have climbed into a white van allegedly containing a number of Tottenham football supporters, who had assaulted her with a screwdriver, stolen her money and thrown her out as they reached Kings Cross. Fortunately she only had superficial injuries but her assailants were never traced.

5

THE EIGHTIES – MOBILE UNITS ARRIVE

Ed Thompson takes up the story again,

In the early 80s, I had just been made up to an acting sergeant in the plain clothes section at Victoria. One of my first duties, together with two PCs, was to go to Haydon's Road station to police a pre-season 'friendly' game between Wimbledon and Millwall. We travelled down by car and saw very little traffic through the station on the forward.

After the game only a few fans passed through, so I sent one of the PCs back with the car to get the kettle on, leaving a PC and myself to return by train. Some minutes later we heard shouting and a surge of drunken Millwall fans entered the station, accompanied by the Metropolitan Police. The crowd were immediately unruly and within seconds we both had prisoners.

We had not received any warning of disorder at the ground, but when I look back I don't expect the Met even knew we were there and football intelligence was at an early stage at that time. We soon found ourselves separated from our prisoners, as people pressed around us, and they simply melted into the crowd.

A train entered the station and the yobs crammed on followed by the PC and myself. Immediately the fans started to play up and, to my horror, I saw that, as we left, the Met stayed on the station. Windows were smashed, all the lights kicked out, seats thrown out, and the carriage roared with chants of 'Kill, Kill, Kill the Bill.'

I honestly believed that the two of us were going to be thrown out of the train. We drew our sticks and I remember thinking the first one who moves towards us is going to get it. We did manage to put out an urgent assistance call but we had no way of contacting the driver.

At the station before London Bridge, I think it was South Bermondsey, the crowd got off and melted away. When we arrived at London Bridge, some minutes later, the cavalry was there along with some dogs. The train was wrecked but we were untouched apart from spittle on our tunics.

Cheryl Birbeck was a police constable with the BTP in Manchester in the 1980s, and recalls one occasion when she was working at Manchester Victoria station on a very busy football fixture day,

Newcastle United were playing Bury at Gigg Lane. As usual we were pretty stretched, there were so many matches taking place and not enough officers. Our inspector received a call that Greater Manchester Police were requesting officers to attend Bury Exchange. They wanted a large group of Newcastle fans escorted out of town as soon as possible. They had kicked-off big time, and had been trying to wreck the town centre and Interchange, which consisted of a bus and railway station. The GMP Tactical Aid Group had been chasing them around the Interchange and finally managed to corral them at the front of the station, and now wanted rid of them.

A sergeant and I were quickly despatched on the Bury train. As we arrived we could hear the Newcastle fans chanting. We made our way up the stairs where we were met by a GMP inspector, behind him were what appeared to be most of the GMP Tactical Aid officers surrounding a large group of at least 150 Newcastle fans. On seeing us the inspector first appeared relieved, then on looking behind us he looked worried 'Are you it?' he said with a look of horror. The sergeant and I looked around us and he said 'Looks that way.' You could see panic starting to spread across his face 'But there's only two of you, you can't manage this lot with only two of you.'

My sergeant explained to him that we were used to it and declined an offer of support from the inspector to place one of his serials on the train with us. He told us that he would help us to load the train and would then meet us at the other end. By now he clearly thought that we were nuts and fully expected to pick up the bits when we got there.

We put the fans on the train in one carriage, and locked the doors, so that they couldn't get off at any of the stations on the way to Victoria. As soon as everyone was on board one of the Newcastle fans said 'Thank fuck, it's the railway polis, are we glad to see you' and confirmed that they would be on their best behaviour. As we pulled away the inspector gave us a worried look and shot off up the platform. The Newcastle fans gave the GMP the traditional 'V' salute. They chatted to us and sang all the way to Victoria, and were no trouble whatsoever.

At Manchester Victoria station, GMP were waiting in force as we arrived with a bunch of happy singing fans. Their faces were a picture as we handed them over to other BTP officers for the rest of their journey, and they waved us a cheery goodbye.

The moral of the story is never to underestimate the power of the BTP!

On 10 January 1981, Aston Villa played Liverpool at home in Birmingham. In what was later to be billed as a revenge attack, up to a hundred hardcore hooligans, linked to Aston Villa's 'C Crew', gathered in the rail bar at New Street station to await the arrival of Liverpool fans, who had a reputation at that time for arriving early at away venues to avoid police attention. Many of them were carrying concealed weapons, including a monkey wrench and Stanley knives.

Despite efforts by the police on the station to disperse the waiting group, a fight subsequently broke out as a large group of visiting fans arrived. During the frenzied attack a number of people were injured, as people were slashed viciously with Stanley knives. One prominent Villa fan subsequently went to prison for a total of three years for affray and wounding.

Peter McHugh retired from the BTP as a chief superintendent, and initially started his police career as an officer at Fishguard harbour, where there was no engagement with football policing. His first memories of policing football fans was while working on a secondment at Swansea in 1981, when he worked with a long-serving officer whose approach to policing travelling fans was to get them to sing Christmas carols.

Peter recalls policing a special train on 7 February 1981, however on this occasion they were Rugby Union fans,

> We took a train from Carmarthen to Edinburgh, with several hundred rugby fans on board, for a Scotland *versus* Wales international game.
>
> My sergeant was Bill Tee and I was one of four constables. In those days there were no restrictions on alcohol on trains and plenty was taken on board. In contrast to football there was absolutely no trouble on the train. When we arrived they put us up in a railway sleeper carriage to get some rest, which was situated under the main speakers at Waverley railway station. We lasted an hour and gave up. The return train left Edinburgh at 8 p.m. on the Saturday, and we arrived back in Carmarthen for 11 a.m. on the Sunday morning, exhausted.

At a working conference held on 'Violence on Transport Undertakings' on 6 May 1980, which was sponsored by the Home Secretary and the Minister of Transport, the concept of creating Mobile Units within BTP was established.

In February 1981 the Department for Transport provided additional funding of £1 million to establish twelve Mobile Support Units in various parts of the country, which commenced operations on 15 February 1981. The policing of football fans on the network became one of their priorities.

Former ACC Paul Robb recalls,

> I know the events that triggered MSUs because I was night duty CID when they happened. It was a crazy night. I cannot remember all the details but there was a massive fight at Neasden, on the Underground, that spilled onto the tracks and they had to turn the current off. As that was going on there was a series of calls about fights and stabbings on the Northern line Tube that, I think, started around Elephant and Castle, and then there were further incidents at either two or all three of the Clapham stations. It obviously hit the press and Margaret Thatcher agreed to a 'shopping list', which included MSUs for the rail divisions and led to a substantial increase in resources for the Underground area.

Eamonn Carroll, retired as a chief superintendent with BTP and recalls,

> My uniform service was in the early 80s, on the Underground, and I can remember that my deployment nearly every Saturday was to the Euston Road, between Euston and Kings Cross, where BTP and Met colleagues spent time keeping, or trying to keep, opposing fans apart post matches. We didn't really need briefing as you could work out from who was playing in London whether there would be grief. Often we were chasing shadows with fights breaking out on Tubes, but when we arrived they had moved on. The hooligan reputation of certain clubs was well known and the potential for trouble ever present.

The BTP Mobile Units became very familiar with the various hooligan groups around the country and routinely made arrests. By way of example, the unit based at Leeds engaged frequently with the 'Leeds United Service Crew.'

On Saturday 27 November 1982, Leeds United supporters travelled to Barnsley to play in a local derby. The BTP Leeds Mobile Unit was deployed at Sheffield railway station, which had been the scene of several previous confrontations. Shortly after the end of the game, the unit received information from South Yorkshire Police that a number of youths were running amok on a train and causing severe damage. The leader of the youths had stolen the train's emergency hand-axe and was terrifying ordinary passengers. As a result of enquiries, the unit was able to identify and arrest this person, together with a second youth, and both were charged with affray and various other offences.

Keith Groves recalls some of his dealings with the Leeds Service Crew in the first half of the '80s,

> I had not long been a sergeant at Leeds, and really enjoyed working on the Mobile Unit. We had some information one day that the Leeds Service Crew were going to travel en masse to Nottingham. A few years earlier a Leeds fan had been killed there and they were looking for revenge. The information was that they were tooled up with weapons and we put a plan in place to intercept them.

A large group eventually came onto the station and went down a subway, which we blocked off at both ends and searched everyone. I arrested one with a knife hidden in a plastic cigarette which he was holding in a clenched fist. We took all their details and kept adding to our intelligence so that when West Yorkshire Police started their undercover operation they came to us for help in identifying people.

What the hooligans didn't know, though, was that we had an informant among them. They used to meet in a pub across the road from the station, and would then rush the barriers at the last minute for a train, in order to avoid a police escort. The informant, however, made sure that we knew exactly what time they were leaving, and we would be on the train with them.

On another occasion, Leeds fans went down to London for a game with Chelsea. There was no love lost between the two teams and the Chelsea Headhunters ambushed the Leeds Service Crew on the Underground. Leeds fans came off worst from the encounter. The Metropolitan Police arrested most of the Leeds group and we were sent down to London to escort them back.

They were duly escorted back to the station by the Met, many of them with black eyes and sporting other injuries, and put on the train. They were quiet on the return journey, but the only problem was that our first stop was Leeds and the Met had simply herded people together and there were people on the train who came from the West Country, and places like Lancashire.

On yet another escort our train stopped at Todmorden and we were met by the local police. The superintendent in charge asked where a certain prominent hooligan was, who was said to be one of the leaders of the Leeds Service Crew at the time. We pointed him out and he was promptly arrested to prevent a Breach of the Peace. We then escorted the remainder of the group by bus to Burnley and back.

Bill Rogerson was by now a sergeant, posted to Crewe from the end of 1979 until October 1985. He recalls,

Crewe, as we all know, was a very busy junction, and football special trains from all corners of Britain used to converge there, to and from the matches. It was almost a seven day a week operation dealing with football traffic. We had to carefully plan with the railway authorities the position of the trains in Crewe while locomotives and train crews were changed, so that opposing fans did not clash. On the odd occasion they did, and we had fun trying to sort them out and round them up.

On a couple of occasions I have had to escort overnight services up to Carlisle with returning Celtic or Rangers fans on board.

Our busiest moments at Crewe were in the days of the Scotland *v.* England and England *v.* Scotland matches, where almost all the trains would stop for crew and police change over. Fans arriving on ordinary service trains could cause a problem as well with their behaviour. I remember one Saturday morning I was on duty on Crewe station by myself, such was the nature of staffing levels. I ended up arresting a Portsmouth supporter en route to Liverpool for criminal damage to a door in the gent's toilet – he'd ripped it off its hinges completely.

In my time at Crewe, among the many passenger trains that used the station was 1M10, an overnight sleeping car service from Glasgow Central to London Euston, via Kilmarnock and Dumfries. It would arrive in Crewe around 02.00 hours and would have to be met by the police nearly every night due to problems. One evening I received a telephone call from BTP in Glasgow to say that it was full of Celtic supporters on their way to the Continent. Subsequent messages were received stating that the police had to be called at Kilmarnock, Dumfries, and Carlisle and Preston stations due to disorderly behaviour.

By the time it arrived in Crewe it was well over two hours late. I boarded the train with a couple of constables to find that it was very quiet and that the fans were fast asleep. The whole train stunk like a distillery and brewery, and vomit was all over the floor.

On another occasion involving Celtic supporters on this train, we were called to it on arrival at Crewe, in the early hours of a Saturday morning. An elderly couple and their friend, en route to a holiday in Jersey, had suffered verbal and physical abuse from three supporters in particular. Fortunately, I had two constables on duty that night. The assailants were quickly identified and arrested. They were taken to our office in Crewe along with the witnesses. We had them in separate rooms and we then started documenting the assailants, prior to taking them to the local police station.

While I was documenting my prisoner, one of the constables came in, white as a sheet, and asked if he could have a word with me. It transpired that his prisoner was a serving Strathclyde Police officer. The three prisoners were bailed pending further enquiries. On the Tuesday afternoon, after doubling back off nights, I received a call from one of the Strathclyde assistant chief constables regarding the officer who had been arrested. I assured him that everything had been dealt with properly. He was happy and it turned out that the officer was already on bail for other matters.

Travelling fans on ordinary service trains would regularly leave the trains at Crewe, while waiting for connecting services, and go onto Nantwich Road outside the station and fight between themselves. This caused no end of problems for the Cheshire Police.

One duty as sergeant at Crewe was to escort a train of Crewe Alexandra fans to London Euston, with a female police officer, for a Millwall *versus* Crewe mid-week evening kick-off. On arrival at Euston we walked down to Soho and bought a bag of fish and chips, and stood in a doorway eating them. While we were there, in half blues, a number of men approached the door and on seeing us quickly turned away. It transpired that we were stood in a doorway of a massage parlour.

From Crewe we covered the two teams in the Potteries, Stoke-on-Trent, and Port Vale. One Saturday, Stoke was playing at home to Brentford, and their sixty-or-so fans travelled up unescorted. On the return, the guard of the train refused to take the train without a police escort, and as I was the only officer left I travelled on the train to London Euston without incident. On arrival at Euston I have never seen as many Met or BTP officers in my life. It transpired that the station supervisor at Stoke had told our control that the fans were rioting. I spoke to one of our senior officers and he asked where the rest of my men were, to which I informed him that I was by myself. His face was a complete picture of bewilderment. I was the talk of Euston concourse for the evening. 'The Skip's by himself'!

In the late 1970s and early 1980s there was an 18.05 train from Birmingham New Street to Glasgow Central, arriving in Crewe at 19.05 hours. It was usual on a Saturday night for northern-based supporters who had been watching their teams in the Midlands to return on this train. The Manchester, and Liverpool area, based supporters had to change trains at Crewe. For the Manchester fans there was no problem as they had a local train at 19.16 hours. The buffet car on the 18.05 hours from Birmingham was regularly the target of fans thieving goods from the counter. One evening, while returning from Birmingham on this train with a dog handler, I put the dog and handler in the buffet and it was the first time that the steward reported a profit on a Saturday.

Shrewsbury was part of the Crewe District and Shrewsbury Town FC spent some time in the dizzy heights of the old First Division in those years. Playing teams such as Chelsea, Manchester United, Liverpool, and Leeds etc. was a novelty for them, but a headache for us and the West Mercia Police, finding extra resources. I attended a home game against Chelsea, which was a big match for Shrewsbury. West Mercia Police had drafted officers from every corner of the three counties (Worcestershire, Shropshire and Herefordshire). Some of these officers had never had any experience of football traffic in their careers; it was a wakeup call for them, seeing the fans from the big cities whose behaviour they had only seen on the news bulletins.

Leeds supporters were the most troublesome and they usually travelled on the overnight York to Aberystwyth mail train which came via Leeds and Crewe, arriving in Shrewsbury around 03.50 hours. On their first encounter the supporters wreaked absolute havoc in the town, as the local police were totally unprepared for them. On subsequent meetings the local police had the ground opened up for their arrival. On one occasion we even had the military police from Catterick, in Yorkshire, on Shrewsbury station to assist with the returning fans.

On a sad note concerning Leeds fans, I booked on duty at Crewe at 09.00 hours on a Sunday following a Shrewsbury *v.* Leeds match only to be informed that there had been a very serious assault on a local person at Shrewsbury station, just before midnight, and could I go to Shrewsbury with a DC from Crewe to start the investigation off. On arrival at Shrewsbury I reported to the local superintendent and visited the hospital to see the victim. Enquiries were commenced and I handed the case over to our detective sergeant on the Monday morning. A Leeds fan was arrested and charged with GBH, but sadly the victim died exactly one year and one day later following the assault.

Tony Thompson recalls his experiences working as a chief inspector at BTP's force headquarters, with responsibility for coordinating the movement of fans travelling abroad,

Around 1982 I was sent to a key meeting chaired by Bert Millichip at the FA headquarters in Lancaster Gate, in London. I was the BTP representative, and the Association of Chief Police Officers were represented by James Anderton, who was then the chief constable of Greater Manchester Police.

At the meeting I challenged some of his views on policing football, as a result of which I later found myself accompanying the FA's security advisor, a former deputy assistant commissioner, to some European countries to advise them on how to deal with England supporters. They were trying to qualify for the 1984 UEFA Euro Championship at the time, but England failed to reach the championship so our theories were not tested!

In the 1980s, Paul Majster was a detective constable with the BTP at Birmingham and he recalls,

On big match days we used to have all of the CID officers working in scruffs as snatch squads on the station. We mingled with the fans, who sometimes got involved in horrendous fights on the concourse. We would jump in and grab prisoners and get them away as quickly as possible. The West Midlands Police would routinely escort fans in through the glass doors, and sometimes leave them with us once they were on our jurisdiction. On one occasion a colleague, Ian Mabbett, was rolling around on the floor, in plain clothes, with a prisoner when a West Midlands officer rushed up and kicked him in the chest thinking he was a hooligan.

Keith Fleetwood recalls other incidents, which took place between 1980 and 1985, during his time at Southampton,

After a Southampton home match a number of Southampton supporters chased an opposition fan off the end of the platform and into the mouth of the tunnel. All trains were stopped and the away supporter was found and escorted, shocked and limping, from the track to the police office.

When being spoken to by officers he complained that his ankle was hurting. Luckily, officers noticed and stopped him touching his ankle. He had received an electrical burn that had gone into a 'V' nearly reaching the bone. It was believed that when being chased his ankle had touched the third rail and electricity had passed through his foot killing the nerves around the wound so that he was unaware of his injury.

After a Southampton match at Southampton Central station, two home supporters began fighting in the buffet car prior to the train's departure. Both were seen to commence fighting, stop and then start again. Both were 6 foot 2 inches-plus. I arrested the one and as I escorted him away I indicated the other one to a sergeant for him to be arrested. Both were charged with an offence under the Public Order Act, commonly known as a 'Section 5'.

The only thing strange at the time was that the one stated he was unemployed, even though his manner and appearance seemed to indicate against this. The other one pleaded guilty at the first hearing, but the 'unemployed' one went 'not guilty' all the way to an appeal at the Crown Court, which he lost. He also lost his job and career as a trainee barrister.

Prior to an England *versus* Scotland match at Wembley, there was some sort of failure on the London Transport system with either power or signals. Trains were stopped overground on the approach to Wembley. Supporters left the trains and began walking along the tracks causing even more delays.

Between Willesden and Neasden, a bus depot abuts the line and all the coaches and buses had their windscreens smashed. Because of the delays it was expected that there would not be enough trains in position for the return traffic. Consequently, Wembley Central station was fully crowded and closed to traffic almost immediately after the game.

Supporters who were aware of the London Transport system immediately made their way to Neasden LT station. I was posted to police the booking hall and station entrance with three PCs, with other officers covering the platforms. We had a number to dial in case of emergency which was passed to all section commanders.

In a very short space of time all of the platforms were full, and we were required to close the station, and all of the concertina gates were closed. The crowd built up quickly, with bottles and bricks being thrown against the gates with more injuries being caused to the first four rows than to us. The officers on the platforms were further committed with supporters coming over the roof and lines.

The concertina gates at the station front were forced out of the runner on the floor, and with the crowd pressure had any supporters laid down they could have rolled underneath, further committing us. Supporters were further antagonised as the only way to stop them ripping the gates open was with a swift crack across the knuckles. One of the gates to the platform was unlocked and partially opened to provide us with a point to escape to, if the main gates failed.

The emergency number was called and assistance was promised. The crowd continued to pull at the gates, and one of the officers was sent to maintain position at the gate, which was to become our refuge. Some of the supporters had acquired some road pins and with these being stabbed through the gates, we were committed to trying to remove them, allowing other supporters to pull at the gates.

Just as I was about to withdraw my officers to the refuge point, the officer there shouted that a train was coming into the platform. When the train stopped the doors opened and the passengers disembarked, and every single one was a police officer. The train had been held at a nearby depot awaiting the call. The officers made their way to the booking hall, and at almost the same time Metropolitan mounted officers and Police Support Units arrived in the road leading to the station.

When the station was declared open the entrance gates had to be ripped from their mounting as there was no way of opening them. I dread to think what the outcome would have been if they had managed to force the gates.

Kevin Shanahan, who retired as a detective chief inspector with the BTP, recounts his experiences of a typical train escort, describing in some detail the fragility of small numbers of police officers trying to control large numbers of fans, often in confined spaces,

In April 1983, I was a uniform sergeant leading a serial of five PCs on escort duties taking Arsenal fans to Manchester for a game with Manchester United. It was an evening match on a Wednesday, at a time when football was played twice a week. The train was a scheduled Inter City service to Manchester Piccadilly with a journey time of two hours forty minutes, and we left at about 3.30 p.m. We travelled without major incident, apart from making a couple of supporters pay their fare, and I think I ejected one person at Watford Junction.

The game was scheduled to kick-off at 7.45 p.m. and in those days relations with our colleagues in Manchester were not what they should have been. This arose from their practice of expecting London officers to escort fans right to the ground. This was not a reciprocal arrangement and non-London officers would never escort fans across London.

On arrival at Manchester Piccadilly I was aware of disorder as we were alighting from the train, and saw to my amazement a Greater Manchester Police officer, on a motorbike, riding among the fans. This caused the supporters, who were generally good natured, and many of whom were at the mature age range, to charge at the officer and out into the city centre. Thus GMP lost control of the bulk of the fans who finished up going to the ground unescorted.

As we waited at the station to do the return escort we were made aware of sporadic disorder taking place in the city centre. One train was scheduled to go out at 21.55 and we were supposed to be supported part-way by a compliment of officers from Crewe. In any event, they finished up going on the train without any fans on the authority of the duty inspector.

The next train to London was the overnight sleeper due to leave at 22.45, and in due course Arsenal fans arrived under GMP escort, who were upset because they were all loudly cheering the fact that they had won. I knew at this stage that we were going to be up against it, and had our work cut out for the return. The train left and we tried to contain the fans in the bar area to keep them away from the occupied sleeping compartments.

Fire extinguishers were set off, the night steward wanted support, and many sleeper passengers were complaining about the noise. We managed to calm a number of fans down who were extremely angry at police for delaying them in the ground, and the resulting scheduled train leaving without them. We arrived at Crewe and discovered that a train containing Liverpool fans, travelling back from Birmingham, was on another platform. Sporadic conflict broke out on the platforms with fans running between the trains with us trying to keep them apart. It was only when the London train was about to depart that we were able to get most of the Arsenal fans back on the train.

At this point we were starting to struggle to cope in containing the fans to the one section of the train. With the night steward I locked a lot of the train corridors and managed to arrange for support at Stafford railway station where, at my instigation, six difficult fans were ejected from the train and escorted off the station by Staffordshire Police. This had a sobering effect on the rest who realised that if they played up they would never get home to London at a reasonable hour. The overnight train was due to arrive in London at 5 a.m. and it was now 2.30 a.m.

Many of the fans decided to try to get some sleep, and while they were not impressed by the way GMP had treated them, they seemed to understand that we were just trying to get them back to London. Eventually the train arrived at Euston some time after 7 a.m. I reported back to the station and stood my serial of officers down.

This was the most negative football escort I had involvement in. I understand that some form of complaint was made by British Rail to BTP, but we were supported by the on-train crew and some of the supporters. It was a very long and stressful day. My team were magnificent and worked really hard. Making arrests was an impossibility and our communications non-existent. We were reliant on landline telephones and the support of rail staff.

Subsequently we developed a rapport with some of the regular Arsenal 'away' supporters. Happy days, but when I look back we as a force were very adaptable, and able to work as a team in difficult and often dangerous situations. I was also glad the following year to be back in the CID!

6

THE EIGHTIES – AFFRAY AT ST PANCRAS AND THE 'TEMPORAL' YEARS

In March 1984 it was announced that a further 100 extra BTP officers would be recruited to help police the London Underground following an incident relating to an Arsenal game that resulted in fourteen people being taken to hospital after a tear gas grenade was thrown onto a train. Chief Inspector Tom Baker said at the time, 'We are finding that hooligan minorities are well organised and knowledgeable about police movements. We search fans regularly and find weapons including Stanley knives, which are sharp and deadly, and even keys with razor blades.'

Outside London, BTP Mobile Support Units were trying to tackle the problem and arrests were routine, such as two reported at Cardiff, one involving a nineteen-year-old leaning out of a train window and shaking his fist at the opposition, and another involving an eighteen-year-old who opened the door of a crowded train while it was travelling between Newport and Cardiff.

On 31 March 1984 two youths were arrested for theft, assault and public order offences at Newport railway station during serious public order involving football fans. They subsequently received custodial sentences and five BTP officers were commended for their bravery.

The Leeds Mobile Unit were still very active in relation to football policing, and again Keith Groves recalls incidents in 1984,

We escorted Manchester United fans on a few occasions, and on one occasion were sent to the mainline station at Sheffield to take a train back to Manchester, after a game with Sheffield Wednesday. There was fighting on the platforms and we put GPO mailbag cages between the fans to try to stop them getting at each other. During the course of the fighting I actually got hit accidentally by an officer wielding his truncheon.

We took the train back but on arrival were told that another train had been abandoned by the train crew at Marsden because of rioting on board. We were sent back by road to escort it. When we got there it had been completely wrecked. We finally made our way back to Leeds and, just as we got to the station, we had a call to say that there was a mass fight going on in City Square just outside.

We rushed there and found a fight involving up to 100 people, and members of the Garforth Youth League, who were part of the junior 'risk' group of the Leeds Service Crew. We managed to arrest two as Stanley knives were being openly brandished. We were keen to make some more arrests and after liaising with the local police we found that a number of the people we wanted were playing football in a Sunday league. Next day we went to a football pitch, walked on, and arrested half of their team for wounding and affray.

On another occasion I was again at Sheffield for a game with Newcastle. There was a pub called the Howard opposite the station, where the local hooligans would gather before attacking the opposition on the station. There was some fighting on the station and I arrested a Newcastle fan and processed him at the local police station. I found out later that he had given completely false details, because he was already wanted, and was released before this was discovered. I never forget a face and two years later I was on York railway station when I spotted him again and arrested him despite his protestations that he had never been to Sheffield.

On 2 April 1984, a twenty-one-year-old English Celtic fan, Alan Preston, died after falling under a train during a fight between Glasgow Rangers and Celtic fans at Partick station. The game itself had attracted trouble, with twenty-two arrests made at Celtic Park.

Detective Sergeant Alistair Cumming, from the BTP CID in Glasgow, was seconded onto the investigation, which was led by Strathclyde Police. Three teenagers were subsequently charged with murder after it was alleged in court that he had been pushed from the train after being punched, kicked and spat upon.

Cheryl Birbeck joined the BTP in 1979 and worked at Manchester throughout her career. As a result of being stationed in a city with one of the most famous football clubs in the world on her doorstep, she had lots of experience of policing football fans, either at Manchester Piccadilly station or on the move across the country. She was able to recognise potential trouble when she saw it!

Cheryl recalls one incident in particular when football fans came to her aid rather than causing her trouble. She recalls,

It was the day of Lou Macari's testimonial match at Old Trafford on Sunday 13 May 1984. Celtic were coming down to play Manchester United as Macari had played for them prior to joining the Manchester club in 1973. Everyone was expecting problems due to past trouble with Scottish fans on their travels south of the border. It is estimated that as many as 15,000 Celtic supporters travelled that day. As it turned out, the fans were extremely well behaved, and a small group of them even helped me out in with an incident at the bar on the station!

The day started quietly, and most of the officers on duty had either been sent out on mobile patrol, around the Greater Manchester area, or were doing paperwork in the office. Two of us were on patrol at Manchester Piccadilly station trying to spot any fans travelling to the match and doing the usual general policing of our patch.

It was a beautiful spring day and I was enjoying some sunshine at the front of the station. I was just thinking how peaceful it was, a phrase that should never be uttered in police circles, when a group of Celtic fans appeared from up the approach road to where I was at the station front. They greeted me with 'How ya doin hen?', followed by a lot of banter and laughter, and sign language. I finally figured out they were in search of a drink and wanted to know where they could get one while keeping out of trouble.

I figured the best place for this was the station bar, where we could keep an eye on them. The bar manager was quite happy for their custom, provided they behaved, and we would be nearby to deal with them if there were any problems. I told them they could stay if they promised to behave and with cries of 'thanks hen' and 'you're alright' ringing in my ears, I left them to it and went off to advise control and my colleague what I had done. As I wandered back across the booking hall, leaving my colleague to keep an eye on the fans from the side of the booking office, I got a cheer and a wave from the fans as I walked past the bar.

Everyone in the station was smiling and seemed to be enjoying the party atmosphere, apart from one man sat on a bench opposite the bar, drinking a pint. I hadn't noticed him earlier, but I had a feeling if trouble was going to kick-off it would be coming from that direction.

I went over and suggested to him that it might be a good time to drink up and leave. All I got for my friendly advice was to be told to 'Fuck off, or get my face rearranged.' In hindsight, maybe I should have listened to him. I told him it was time to leave, and looked over towards my colleague to signal him to come over and give me a hand.

As I took my eye off him, for that moment, he suddenly shot up from the bench and punched me in the face. Everything then seemed to go into slow motion. I went backwards and tried to regain my balance, and as I did he punched me on the nose. I remember seeing my colleague running towards me as I fell backwards, I also remember hearing what sounded like a roar.

I hit the floor with the back of my head. The next thing I remember was someone asking me if I was alright, then being dragged backwards and out of the booking hall. I then remember being held up against the office door while they unlocked it, and then being sat in an office and examined by a first aid instructor. He said I needed to go to hospital, as he suspected I was concussed. Everything was a little foggy. As I sat there trying to get my head straight, one of the officers, who must have attended to give assistance, came in with my hat with a bunch of blue flowers in it.

The Celtic fans had collected up my hat, as well as the hats of the officers who had attended to assist me. They had then gone back into the bar and removed all the flowers from the tables, found an officer and given him the hats, including mine, decorated with the bunch of flowers. They had said to the officer, 'Give these to the lassie and tell her we hope she feels better soon. He shouldn't have done that to a woman.' That was the point I finally cracked and started to cry. I was overwhelmed by their act of kindness.

I was later told that the fans had seen the man hit me and all came running out of the bar and jumped on him as he was about to stick the boot in. As they were restraining him, my colleague helped me and called for assistance.

After I was dragged to safety, my colleagues then arrested the man and thanked the fans for their assistance. I believe the man who assaulted me might have received some summary justice from the Celtic fans while he was being restrained, but I am certain they only used as much force as was absolutely necessary! I was treated for a broken nose, a large lump on my head, and concussion, and sent home to recover. The man that assaulted me was treated at a different hospital for cuts and bruises. He was then charged and sent to the central detention centre overnight and taken to court the following day, where he was remanded to Strangeways prison.

He then applied to a judge in chambers to be released on bail, but this was refused. After psychiatric evaluation he was found to be mentally unstable and was sentenced to be held in a psychiatric hospital. The reason he gave for attacking me was that I had 'evicted him from his flat the week before.' It certainly wasn't me! I heard that six months later he had escaped from the hospital, but thankfully I never saw him again.

In the autumn of 1984, three football fans who sprayed passengers, including women and children, with beer and threw lighted paper about on a Cumbrian Coast train were fined, while seven fans who committed public order offences and criminal damage at York railway station were fined. The problems were definitely not going away.

On Wednesday 13 March 1985, Luton Town played Millwall in the sixth round of the FA Cup at Luton's Kenilworth Road stadium. A number of fans from opposing London clubs decided to join forces and travelled to Luton. At least 200–300 Millwall supporters gathered at St Pancras railway station more than 4 hours before the kick-off was due and intimidated ordinary passengers.

BTP advised Bedfordshire Police that they would require horses at the match as the temperature rose by the hour. Mass disorder took place at the ground, and forty-seven people ended up in hospital, while just thirty-one arrests were made, including some Chelsea and West Ham fans. British Rail described the damage done to one train as 'like a bomb had exploded inside some of the carriages,' as a football special was taken out of service, with its ceiling pulled down and the inside gutted.

John Owen, who retired as an inspector with BTP in 2000, recalls the day's events well,

As a police officer with the British Transport Police (BTP) for thirty years, and having spent a great deal of time in uniform dealing with football hooligans, I recall that one of the most notorious football clubs renowned for violence and disorder throughout the 1980s was Millwall FC.

One particular incident which still sticks in my memory, thirty years on, involved Millwall playing at Luton on 13 March 1985. First Division Luton Town were hosts to Third Division Millwall in the FA Cup sixth round at the Kenilworth ground in Luton. It was a midweek evening kick-off match that attracted hundreds of supporters from the south London club.

Travel by public transport was relatively quick and easy for Millwall supporters, who could travel by London Underground trains from south London to St Pancras station in north London. British Rail, as it was in those days, laid on football specials to convey fans the half-hour journey to Luton station. Special ticket rates were in operation for Millwall supporters to segregate them from the general travelling public travelling on normal service trains.

Despite recommendations, the game was not 'all ticket', which resulted in travelling fans far exceeding their allocation.

BTP, as was normal practice, and in conjunction with their British Rail colleagues, supervised the safe loading of hundreds of fans onto the football specials and then serials of officers escorted the trains the short journey to Luton station.

Press reports said that there had been a disproportionately large following that day and described it as being twice the size of Millwall's average home gate. It later transpired other London clubs' fans had gone along for the game.

On arrival at Luton station, the local Bedfordshire Police was on hand to escort fans the short distance through narrow urban streets to the Kenilworth ground. The route to the stadium passed many residential homes, shops and pubs, in car-lined streets.

I was BTP's late-turn duty inspector covering north London and I recall that we had a large contingent of officers, some with dogs, drawn from across London to assist policing St Pancras and Luton stations and to escort the trains.

Chief Superintendent John Parker, now deceased, was the overall commander for BTP's operation and our officers assisted Bedfordshire Police in escorting fans to the stadium. The scene then was extremely noisy and volatile, and it was no surprise that even before the match had started there was trouble from the visiting fans.

Pubs, shops and parked cars had their windows smashed by visiting fans en route to the stadium. Before kick-off, Bedfordshire Police at the stadium were struggling to keep order as hundreds of the visitors scaled the fences, in front of the stands, to rush towards the Luton supporters at the other end of the ground. Missiles of bottles, cans, nails and coins were thrown at the home supporters. Police dogs were deployed on the pitch and, miraculously, the game started on time although it was halted on a couple of occasions because of pitch invasions.

The BTP control room at Tavistock Place was soon receiving reports from Bedfordshire Police that all mayhem had broken out inside the stadium and that additional police resources were being requested from neighbouring forces, including Hertfordshire, Cambridgeshire and Thames Valley. There were no mounted officers at the scene and it was probably too late at that stage to seek horses from the City of London or Metropolitan forces.

BTP were also asked to deploy officers to the ground to assist with escorting the return traffic to Luton station. Some of our officers were caught up in the ugly scenes within the stadium. Meanwhile in London, Chief Superintendent John Parker was out 'on the ground' calling for BTP resources from across London and the south east. Additional travelling serials were mustered and sent straight out by train to Luton.

The Metropolitan and City of London police provided us with an army of officers along with mounted officers to have a welcoming party at St Pancras for when the fans arrived back by the special trains and to help in escorting them back by London Underground to South London. Mounted police in those days were able to ride straight onto the station concourse and they proved to be a very useful part of our armoury.

After the match had finished, the carnage continued through the streets of Luton to the railway station.

The stadium and streets suffered its worst bout of damage and violence Luton had ever seen. Thirty-three police officers were injured in what the local press dubbed as the 'Kenilworth Ground Riot.'

It was a very noisy and ugly journey escorting the supporters back from Luton. We had very limited resources and were overwhelmed by the sheer numbers travelling. Obviously Bedfordshire Police wanted to round up as many Millwall fans as possible and to get rid of them quickly as possible.

Considerable damage was caused to the British Rail rolling stock, and it was estimated that the cost at the time was in the region of £45,000.

The game, which saw a 1-0 victory for Luton, led to a ban on away supporters travelling to the town for four seasons.

On 17 March 1985 BTP commenced an investigation into an arson attack on a train packed with football supporters. A BTP officer, on board the train carrying 360 Aberdeen fans, looked out of a window as it was arriving back at 7.15 p.m. at Aberdeen, after returning from Dundee. He noticed smoke coming from the third coach from the rear and alerted two other colleagues. On searching the train they found that papers, crisp packets and cigarettes had been lined up on a seat and set alight. Fortunately they were able to extinguish the fire themselves.

On 22 March 1985, the media reported that London Transport had asked the Football League to order Chelsea to play some matches behind closed doors after the ambush of a Tube train carrying West Ham supporters. Chelsea fans blocked the track to force the train to come to a stop at Parsons Green.

The train should have run non-stop taking West Ham supporters back from a match at Wimbledon on the night that Chelsea played Sunderland. Chelsea supporters hurled missiles at the train in a premeditated attack that left three police officers injured, and damage caused to five of the six coaches. Police had been standing by at Fulham Broadway in an effort to head-off a confrontation, but the hooligans made their way one stop up the line to avoid them.

On 2 April 1985, football hooligans overpowered a train steward and ransacked the buffet bar of a train taking them to Brighton & Hove Albion's match at Crystal Palace. 200 cans of beer and several cases of spirits were stolen, with some of the fans pouring it over each other, on the 5.17 p.m. train from Littlehampton to Victoria station. 150 fans left the train at Croydon, with many of them clutching their ill-gotten gains. There was no police presence on the train.

In April 1985 BTP officers on board a train with Bolton fans, returning from a local derby at Preston, had to call for urgent assistance as fans went on a rampage and caused extensive damage to the eight-coach train with toilets, seats and light fittings smashed. The communication cord was pulled repeatedly and a further twenty officers from Greater Manchester Police were needed to restore order.

In the spring of 1985, following a number of football-related incidents that had occurred during the previous season, a working party set up by the government published its findings in a report entitled 'Football Spectator Violence.' It was agreed that the BTP would continue to act as the coordinating body for collating information, and disseminating it, in relation to the movements of football fans to, and from, the UK.

Working to the ACC Operations, Inspector Dennis Temporal was the BTP 'football officer' with responsibility for dealing with other forces and agencies at a national and international level. On Saturdays he often based himself, along with Sergeant Bill Taylor, in the Metropolitan Police control command centre, at New Scotland Yard, to monitor the movement of fans in the capital. Five years later Dennis was awarded an MBE for his services to policing in relation to football, and received letters of congratulations from several influential individuals, including Graham Kelly, who was chief executive of the Football Association at the time.

Dennis, who retired in 1992, recalls,

> English fans in particular were causing mayhem in European cities, and on transport to and from Holland, France, Spain and Germany. Large-scale disorder was taking place on ferries taking fans from English ports to places such as Calais and the Hook of Holland. British Transport Police officers began to send escorts on these ferries as the force had jurisdiction on the ferries in those days.
>
> The conduct of the English fans abroad, and on their European travels, caused the government to convene a working party to find ways of dealing with this problem. One of the recommendations was the requirement for a Central Intelligence Unit to collate information on the movement of fans following British clubs, and national teams, travelling abroad. Assistant Chief Constable Ian McGregor from BTP was involved in these discussions and it was accepted that the force was in a strong position to lead the proposed central intelligence function for the police service across the country.

As a result of his expertise, Dennis was asked by ACC McGregor to lead the unit and the BTP Football Intelligence Unit was created with Dennis at the helm. The unit was based at force headquarters and quickly became a critical hub of information, and intelligence, for forces across the country and for BTP officers. The unit collated and disseminated information on fans travelling around the country, as well as abroad for international and European fixtures.

Dennis describes the establishment and operation of the unit in the following terms,

> Relationships were formed with a number of different government departments and the Football Trust, who were funding the initiative by paying my salary. I was able to get into places and talk to people that would not have been possible a few months earlier.
>
> The telex machines were rattling non-stop as a result of the amount of intelligence being created and disseminated. Computerised systems were just coming in and intelligence was being collated on a mixture of paper and computer. I travelled across Europe to build information-sharing and operational

relationships. Various policing and enforcement agencies were involved including the Marechausée from Holland, the Belgian Gendarmerie, the French police, de L'Air et des Frontières, and other national police forces where fans were due to travel, for example Italy and Spain.

I was so busy that, after a while, I had needed the support of another officer and I was joined in the unit by PC Andy Douglas, who was a superb assistant to have. The unit went from strength to strength in terms of reputation and football fans themselves began to contact us with information about some of their own supporters who were potential troublemakers. We managed to prevent a tremendous amount of crime and disorder as a result of the intelligence provided by normal supporters who were as fed up as everybody else with the violence that was regularly taking place at that time. Our officers and mobile support units were often at the right place at the right time on the rail network, to the surprise of those fans intent on causing trouble!

Keith Groves recalls,

I also policed Leeds on that fateful day at Birmingham, when there was rioting at St Andrews football ground, and we never had a problem on the train. It was Saturday 11 May 1985 and after we arrived at Birmingham New Street station we escorted the Leeds fans out of the rear of the station towards Hill Street. When we got there we were suddenly attacked by Birmingham City's Zulu Warrior hooligan group. There was just my serial there, plus PC Alan Morecock and his dog. Myself and an officer called Frazer Sampson made two arrests, before dispersing the crowds, and then made our way back to the BTP office. On arrival, instead of getting thanked for our efforts, I got told off by the superintendent for causing trouble and he told us to stay in the office until it was time to take the Leeds fans back!

They weren't the only group of Leeds fans attacked outside the station that day. On a social media blog years later, 'Parf' said,

Me and a few mates went to that game, we are Leeds fans from Somerset. Our train from Bristol got into Birmingham about lunchtime and we met up with other Leeds fans on the train, and at New Street soon as we got out of the station we were sussed and for the next half hour got chased all around the Bull Ring and the surrounding area. I am sure the Blues were that mean if they had caught any of us they would have killed us, I think the speed of my running proved this. Crazy day.

On 29 May 1985, the Heysel Stadium disaster in Brussels led to the deaths of thirty-nine Italian and Belgian supporters, with hundreds being injured, during the European Cup final. 1 hour before kick-off a large group of Liverpool fans breached a fence and advanced towards Juventus fans, who retreated towards a concrete retaining wall, which collapsed and crushed fans. BTP spotters were at the ground at the time of the incident, including the Force Football Officer Inspector Dennis Temporal.

Dennis recalls,

I was involved in the preparations for the match at the Heysel Stadium, in May 1985, where, sadly, thirty-nine people lost their lives. Liverpool football club had reached the European Cup final and were due to play Juventus in Brussels. About a week before the match, a meeting was held at the BTP Training School in Surrey, which was attended by representatives from the Belgian Gendarmerie, PAF Calais, Calais Town Police, Dutch Railway Police, Kent Constabulary, Dover and Harbour Board Police and officials from the Department of Environment [Sports] and the Department of Transport.

It was agreed, following a request from the chief of Brussels City Police, that BTP would send eight Liverpool-based officers to Brussels. In addition to the BTP officers, a large body of senior stewards from Liverpool Football Club and the Merseyside police football liaison inspector would travel with fans to Brussels.

The journey to Brussels was generally uneventful, but tragically things changed in the lead up to the match and things in the stadium went completely out of control. It was as a result of this lack of control that the thirty-nine individuals lost their lives.

ACC McGregor attended several meetings in the immediate aftermath of the incident and arrangements were made to get the Liverpool supporters back to Ostend then Dover. Everyone was stunned and the atmosphere was eerie as hardly anyone was talking.

As a result of this incident the unit became even more high profile, and officers from other forces began to be seconded into the team. As a result the unit had to move into premises utilised by the Metropolitan police, and PC Andy Douglas moved with the team to Tintagel House. I remained at FHQ and continued running the BTP side of the unit.

Retired ACC Paul Robb recalls,

> I remember being at Tadworth Training School as an inspector and taking officers down to Dover to supervise Liverpool fans coming back after the Heysel disaster. The ferries returned with armed Belgian police on board, which was probably unnecessary as they were the ordinary fans who had clearly been distressed at what they had witnessed and the behaviour of those responsible.

There is no doubt that the unit headed up by Dennis Temporal was the precursor to the National Football Intelligence Unit that was eventually placed under the command of the National Criminal Intelligence Service. A successor to this unit still operates today, known as the UK Football Policing Unit. The legacy of Dennis Temporal's early work definitely lives on.

In June 1985, as a result of enquiries by BTP Sergeant Malcolm Mackay from Aberdeen, the identity of a seventeen-year-old, who had been circulating hate leaflets to self-styled Aberdeen Soccer Casuals before they left by train for the Aberdeen *v.* Dundee United Scottish Cup semi-final in Edinburgh in April, was established. The group had grown from fifty to 500, over a three-year period, and the leaflets incited violence. He was subsequently sent to a detention centre for three months.

In the middle of August 1985, Everton fans travelling on a late-night Holyhead to Euston express train caused chaos as passengers, including foreign tourists, were threatened and assaulted. One Everton fan was seen running through carriages brandishing a knife and several thefts of luggage occurred. One nineteen-year-old was arrested for theft from an American's luggage, and a twenty-one-year-old for assault on a German tourist, who was punched and kicked. There were no police on the train.

On 12 October 1985, eleven Everton fans, who travelled by special train to watch their side play at Chelsea, made complaints against BTP officers after fans spilled onto the platform at Edgware Road Tube station, where a passenger had pulled the communication cord. They alleged that they were assaulted by police officers and after an investigation, where 117 witness statements were taken, summonses were subsequently issued against seven officers.

Bill Rogerson continues his recollections,

In October 1985, while stationed at Crewe, I was asked if I would like to go to Holyhead for a week as the inspector was on leave, one sergeant was on long-term sick, and the other one had retired.

I duly arrived at Holyhead on the Monday morning, only to look at the roster to find that Bangor City were playing one of the top Greek teams in the European Cup rounds. This was the biggest thing since sliced bread to hit Bangor. All the trains on the North Wales coast were packed with supporters. I had assistance from the Mobile Support Units from Liverpool, and to be fair the inspector gave up his leave to assist. Fortunately, everything passed off with good humour. British Rail even laid on a football special from Abergele and Pensarn to Bangor to ease the overcrowding on the normal passenger trains.

On 31 December 1985 I transferred permanently to Holyhead. Here I was introduced to a different kind of football policing. We policed the ships over to Dun Laoghaire in full uniform. Usually the escort consisted of one sergeant, and two constables, for the thousand-plus fans. We had no jurisdiction at all on the ships and we worked under the authority of the captain. Again, having the right attitude and a good sense of humour assisted us in looking after the fans. Dublin had a large Manchester United, Liverpool, and London-based teams fan base and they regularly travelled together on the ferries without too much incident.

On the occasions of Ireland *v.* England matches we had heavy escorts for the supporters. At the beginning of my time at Holyhead I was living in a guest house. I remember working a night shift and, after dealing with a fan, I went back to my lodgings and used the room and same bed linen as the sergeant who was on day shift!

One of the most despicable acts of football violence I came across was from a group of supporters who had travelled from Ireland overnight and badly assaulted a man in a wheelchair who was travelling in the brake-van of an early morning train. I'm glad to say the supporters were dealt with by the court.

On January 25 1986, a group of football fans were attacked on a train by alleged members of Leicester City's Baby Squad. Nottingham Forest were at home when they played Tottenham Hotspur, and after the match a small group of Tottenham fans went for a meal and then boarded a train home. Four of them were subsequently approached by members of the Leicester firm on board the train, who were carrying a knife and a bottle. They were attacked and injured. As the train pulled into Leicester railway station fighting spilled out onto the platforms and two of the Leicester group were arrested.

On Wednesday 5 March 1986, PC Richard Grantham was on duty at Plaistow station when, at about 7 p.m., a train arrived carrying between 150 and 200 Manchester United fans. For some reason, instead of carrying on to Upton Park, where the FA Cup tie between West Ham and Manchester United was due to be played, they got off and made for the exit.

Outside the station, the same number of West Ham supporters were waiting and they started hurling iron tubes, chisels, hammers, and lumps of wood. The Manchester United fans tried to climb over the barriers to get to them, and at this point the officer became aware that a young fan was lying on the ground bleeding profusely from the mouth. As he fought his way through the crowd to get to him he heard someone in the mob shout 'Let's do the copper as well.' On reaching the injured youth he started to administer first aid, despite being hit in the face with a missile. Another colleague was concussed after being hit on the back of the head by a brick.

Another officer, PC Keith Peacock, one of three other officers on duty at the location, said,

> A large crowd had been hitting and kicking the youth on the ground. Dick intervened and covered him with his own body. He actually shielded the youth as objects were hurled at him, including bricks, bottles and lumps of metal. Dick was hit in the eye with a rock. He deserves all the credit. He is very modest.

The injured youth was a Manchester United fan from London. He had a stab wound in his abdomen, which just missed his heart, and was rushed to hospital for an emergency operation. PC Grantham concluded, 'I have never seen football violence like that before, and hope I never have to face it again. It was sheer hate.'

On Saturday 22 March 1986, the last three carriages on a train carrying up to a hundred Dundee Casuals back to Dundee from a match with Aberdeen were severely damaged. The communication cord had been pulled en route, near to Montrose, as tables were ripped out, upholstery slashed and windows smashed, causing hundreds of pounds worth of damage.

The fans were locked in the carriages by a BTP escort, and were met by a police reception committee on arrival at Dundee railway station, where more than a dozen officers, and a police dog, hemmed them in at one end of the platform while each was searched, and they were released in groups of three. Several potential weapons were confiscated, as well as a leaflet explaining where 'gang meets' would take place. BTP officers detained six of the supporters who were taken away for further enquiries.

In May 1986 the media reported three cases involving football fans. In the first instance, officers arrested a twenty-two-year-old Portsmouth football fan after he was seen challenging a rival group of fans in Albion Square, at the entrance to the railway station. In the second, a youth was arrested by BTP officers escorting football fans to Southampton for opening a train door as two trains were running parallel as they went through Weybridge station at speeds of 80 mph. In the third case, two Portsmouth fans were dealt with for trespassing on the railway lines at Woking station after they tried to avoid fighting on the station.

On Saturday 2 August 1986, a young Glasgow Rangers supporter was killed when he fell from an overnight train while travelling between Scotland and London to attend a friendly match at White Hart Lane between Tottenham and Rangers.

7

THE EIGHTIES – CHAOS ON THE *KONIGIN BEATRIX*

On Thursday 7 August 1986, the ferry *Konigin Beatrix* set sail from Harwich towards the Hook of Holland. The following information has been gleaned from media reports, and the recollections of BTP officers who were later involved in what took place on the ferry that night.

The *Konigin Beatrix* was, at the time, one of the newest car and passenger ferries operating on the route, and was something of a show vessel due to its design and fixtures and fittings. For example, it had several glass showcases on board displaying merchandise that could be purchased by passengers – sadly, as you will learn in the next few pages, the cabinets did not survive their journey that evening! The ferry had nine decks of vehicle and passenger accommodation, and on this particular evening was under the command of a very experienced master, Captain J. Nagel.

The ferry set off from Parkeston Quay, Harwich at 22.40 with around 2,000 passengers on board, including 160 football fans from Manchester United and West Ham United. Both clubs were due to play a number of friendly preseason football matches against continental football clubs in Amsterdam over the next few days.

Prior to sailing, the conduct of the football supporters had not given any particular cause for concern, nor was there any intelligence to anticipate what was later to occur once the vessel was at sea.

It was later established that members of West Ham United's infamous Inter City Firm were among the group of supporters on the ferry. The fans of West Ham United were in possession of First Class tickets, and were in the First Class bar situated on deck number eight, while the Manchester United fans occupied a Second Class bar on deck six.

About an hour after setting off, a relatively minor skirmish broke out between some of the fans from Manchester United and some lorry drivers, who were also on board, in the bar on deck six. As a result, the bar was immediately closed by ship staff and remained closed for around 15 minutes.

When the bar reopened, the Manchester United followers began singing obscene songs and football chants. The small band that had been providing entertainment in the bar decided to stop playing and left the location, and it was at this point that one of the football fans took control of the microphone abandoned by the band and started to incite his fellow football supporters who started to gather around him. It was at this stage, urged on by the man with the microphone, that the fans from Manchester went in search of the supporters from West Ham United, and the outcome was probably inevitable with alcohol playing its part.

At around half past midnight, a massive brawl occurred on a set of stairs between deck numbers seven and eight, as the fans from Manchester United attempted to reach the bar on deck eight housing the West Ham supporters. The West Ham fans, who were heavily outnumbered, grouped at the top of the stairs fighting with the Manchester United fans on the stairs below.

By this time the ferry was in international waters, and this led to some interesting debates around judicial jurisdiction when the authorities were deciding which agency should deal with the investigation that later followed. The battle, as it was described by other passengers and ship staff, lasted for about 45 minutes and was ferocious in its intensity. Fixtures and fittings from the vessel were used as weapons, as well as fire hoses and fire extinguishers. The glass cabinets displaying merchandise as described earlier were smashed and the glass used as weapons; hand knives and Stanley knives were also used during the fight. Much of the merchandise on display was also stolen.

Eventually, the Manchester United fans returned to the Second Class bar and the West Ham fans were contained in the First Class bar, which was locked off to keep them in.

Captain Nagel, on viewing the devastation that had taken place, decided it was unsafe for the vessel to continue its journey and ordered the crew to return the ferry to Parkeston Quay to be met by police.

On receipt of the call for assistance, a large number of BTP officers made their way in a convoy up the A12 from London, London Transport vehicles leading the way as, in those days, they were the only BTP cars with blue lights on.

Superintendent Phil Trendall QPM, who retired from the force in 2014, was a police constable at Liverpool Street station in August 1986, at the time of this incident. Phil Trendall was the first officer to board the vessel when the gangplank was lowered, as dozens of officers followed.

Liverpool Street was a sub-divisional station responsible for police posts and operations at Ipswich, Southend, Stratford and Harwich Parkeston Quay. Harwich was funded by Sealink and was relatively well resourced compared to the other parts of the division, and officers at Liverpool Street viewed the number of constables that paraded for duty at that location with some envy.

Phil recalls that Liverpool Street's district was one of contrasts. The mainline terminus was quiet compared to the other London terminus in the division, King's Cross, except for Friday nights when it took on a rather wild-west aspect with financial sector workers from the City of London, in particular, often causing significant problems after indulging in a night on the tiles!

The night shift at Liverpool Street usually consisted of one sergeant and two or three PCs at most. It was the only 24-hour post in the sub-division, apart from Parkeston Quay, and like all mainline stations there was an emphasis during the dark hours on keeping an eye on the last trains, postal and newspaper traffic.

A couple of hours into the night shift on 8 August 1986, Phil recalls a telephone call being received in the office from the police post at Parkeston Quay reporting that there had been a large fight on a ferry en route to the Hook of Holland and requesting additional officers in case the ferry returned to Harwich. The 'control' function at Liverpool Street in those days consisted of a railway telephone mini switchboard, known as a communicator, and a single BT line with a radio handset that would have looked at home in a 1970s minicab office.

On Phil's shift, the sergeant normally manned the phones and it was the sergeant that took the original call from officers at Parkeston Quay that night. He initially declined the request for assistance on the basis that there were too few officers available at Liverpool Street. In fact, it was later discovered that there was a form of contingency plan for disorder on a ferry at sea, complete with code words, but on the night all of the messages were passed in plain language.

As the extent of the disorder became clearer, force HQ, and the divisional duty inspector, became involved and it was agreed that, as the master of the vessel had decided to return to port, as many officers as possible would be sent from London to support officers from Harwich and Ipswich, some of whom had been recalled to duty.

Essex Police were also requested to assist in the response to the incident. Soon a long convoy of vehicles was heading up the A12 from London with officers coming from all three London divisions of the force being deployed to assist. Only the London Transport Division response vehicles were painted in white livery, with fixed blue lights and two-tones, so the more humble BTP vehicles attempted to ride in their slipstream!

Phil describes what occurred when he arrived with his colleagues at Harwich Parkeston Quay in his own words,

We arrived a little while before the ship docked and a group of us were designated as a serial with the duty of securing the ship when the passenger doors were opened. Arrangements were made in the arrivals hall for separate areas to be set aside for witnesses, suspects and bystanders. A room was allocated for the collection of exhibits and the split of responsibilities was discussed between Essex Police and BTP.

This level of organisation did not actually survive contact with reality. Somebody also asked about the jurisdiction of BTP to deal with offences committed at sea and the reply was, as I recall, a little vague. I think it is fair to say that nobody really knew the answer at that stage. Subsequently during my career, I spent considerable time examining and studying matters relating to the jurisdiction of the force, but I never again came across this issue.

Never having worked at the docks, I was surprised by the size of the ferry as it started to pull in to the port. The *Konigin Beatrix* was the pride of the fleet and was much more luxurious than the cross-channel ferries I had previously travelled on.

As the ship docked we were confronted with what seemed like hundreds of people, many of them clearly very scared and others who had obviously been involved in the disorder, going by their bloodstained clothing and their immediate proclamations that they had been defending themselves. I felt a sharp shove in the back as a colleague propelled me forward onto the vessel. I was lucky not to fall over and found myself in the middle of a chaotic scene. There were large pools of water, the result of the use of fire equipment by the fighting fans. There was also considerable damage to all parts of the vessel, especially the glass display cases, and the fixtures and fittings of the retail outlets.

The crew were very obviously frustrated and angry, and it was clear that they believed they would have lost control of the vessel if they had carried on to the Hook of Holland. I found out that at one point, while the vessel was at sea, the master had ordered the barricading of the bridge, due to his concern at the conduct of the football supporters.

Many of the passengers were distraught but relieved to be safe. The football fans were largely subdued but a few managed some half-hearted chanting. A considerable amount of clothing had been dumped around the ship, much of it wet and blood stained. A number of weapons were recovered, mostly improvised from fittings and fixtures that had been destroyed. It truly was a scene of devastation to be dealt with.

The senior BTP officer present on the night was Acting Superintendent Barrie Reynolds, supported in the early stages by the senior CID officer present, Detective Sergeant Alf Preston. Both were faced with a number of challenges in ascertaining the best response to what had taken place. I think it is true to say that none of the officers present had ever dealt with this particular type of situation before on a vessel that had been at sea.

We were formed into teams consisting of an Essex officer, a BTP officer and a member of the ship's crew. The idea was that we would tour the ship and arrest anybody identified by the crew to have been involved in the disorder. This led to about a dozen arrests but it quickly became clear that understanding the full picture would only come from a detailed and very thorough post-incident investigation. The scale of this incident and the number of people involved made the situation very difficult.

The shipping line were keen to get the ship back on its way to Holland and eventually large numbers of people were taken off the ship to allow it to sail. A serial of BTP officers remained on board to escort the ship, as it set off once again for the Hook of Holland. I was supposed to be in this group but missed the departure by minutes, much to my disappointment, because I was logging exhibits!

Somebody then took the decision that the large number of people, nearly all youngish males, who had been taken off the ferry would be taken to London by a special train. This arrangement was not unheard of at the time but I do wonder now what exact legal provision was being used, especially as many of those taken by train had probably not been involved in the disturbances. Indeed some had cars parked at Harwich and had to travel back to collect them.

I was one of the officers escorting the train back to London. By this time everybody involved, including us, were exhausted and the journey passed without incident.

On arrival at Liverpool Street the train was met by a large contingent of media, who were very keen to talk with the passengers that we had escorted back. Some of the obviously wounded fans gave interviews to both the TV and the press. Their bloodied bandages and tribal declarations made good television.

Once again, in Phil's words,

There followed a most impressive investigation headed by Detective Inspector Michael Barry that was able to bring order from the chaos and resulted in some of the last prosecutions under the 1936 Public Order Act. In the weekly, and now almost daily, experience of the BTP in policing football, this event was unique. This was large-scale disorder that occurred on the high seas, far from any football ground and at a time when resources were at a minimum level. The fact that the force was able to respond on the night, and to subsequently mount a successful investigation, is a tribute to an organisation that is sometimes underestimated in relation to its flexibility and specialist acumen.

By the time of the *Beatrix* incident, BTP was very well versed in managing and, more importantly preventing, football disorder on most occasions. Most officers had a clear picture that football violence was always the work of a minority, and that the vast majority of fans were dedicated followers of sport and needed to be treated with respect. Unlike colleagues from other forces, BTP officers often find themselves heavily outnumbered and detached from any source of help; in my view this has influenced the policing style for the better.

Police Constable Chris Hill was another of the officers who attended the ferry as it arrived back in port. He describes the scene, 'The stairwells were awash with blood, and damaged property, and it was obvious that a serious incident had taken place.'

Chris and other colleagues were busily moving around the ferry trying to establish exactly what had taken place. Chris recalls that around twenty Manchester United fans had to be taken to hospital as a result of their injuries, some with stab wounds, while around eleven fans were arrested at the scene for being involved in the incident. Chris also remembers that a group of Hells Angels on the boat had declined to intervene due to the Inter City Firm from West Ham being 'far too violent.'

A total of seventy-five football supporters were removed from the vessel, with fourteen being immediately identified as being involved in the violence and arrested at the time. The massive task of obtaining details of passengers, and witnesses, took place before the ferry was allowed to set sail again to the Hook of Holland at around 6 a.m. on Friday 8 August.

This time the ferry was escorted by a serial of BTP officers, under the command of an inspector, and during the journey several more witnesses came forward and further evidence was obtained.

Damage caused was eventually estimated as being somewhere in the region of £20,000.

A hundred football fans were put on a train to London with a BTP escort.

According to one newspaper report in the *Daily Record*, some of these boasted on their arrival in London about their part in the violence, with one being quoted as saying, 'We threw everything we could get our hands on. It was great.' The Sports Minister Richard Tracey said that the brawl would probably lead to further years being added to the current ban already in place against English clubs playing in Europe. Meetings between the BTP, Department of Transport and the Home Office were hastily convened, and after considering the legal jurisdiction issues, it was decided that BTP would investigate and report on the incident.

This would lead to a significant post-incident investigation headed by Detective Inspector Michael Barry from Liverpool Street BTP station. In any incident where significant numbers of people are involved, it is a mammoth task for investigators to ascertain who exactly did what, and of course CCTV in those days was nowhere near as readily available as it is today.

Michael Barry was an experienced detective, but he would accept that this was one of the most challenging cases he led during his career. He briefly describes the situation as follows,

I arrived for work at Liverpool Street on Friday 8 August 1986 and on being advised of the incident immediately made my way to Parkeston Quay, arriving about 9.30 a.m. There was a massive amount of work to be done and I needed a lot of resources to assist me. I had a fantastic team working for me, which included officers seconded to the incident room from all over the force. The incident room was set up at Kings Cross BTP station, although I spent a lot of time in Parkeston Quay as this was the only place that we could get regular access to the crew.

In fact, the cell at Parkeston Quay became a regular sleeping place, when it was too late to get home and no local accommodation was available! The captain and the crew were really helpful throughout, which helped with the investigation. I also spent a lot of time in Holland interviewing witnesses and was put up in a local army barracks, where I even had to make my own bed. This is how it was in those days!

Michael also describes being allowed to run the investigation without too much interference from above, despite the obvious high level interest that the incident had caused. In fairness, this was a tongue-in-cheek comment, and he was delighted with the support he received in terms of resources and budget at his disposal to manage the investigation and subsequent court proceedings. Eventually, nine individuals were convicted at Chelmsford Crown Court for serious public disorder in December 1987.

At the end of the trial, His Hon. Judge Watling QC commended several of the BTP officers involved in the following terms,

> I think that the police officers who have mounted and conducted this enquiry are all of them deserving of commendation because the experience of the last four weeks I think has certainly made it clear to me – and of course I do not hold any of this against any of the defendants – the great difficulties they must have experienced, because we have had the not uncommon phenomenon of witnesses who made very clear and full statements to police and then failed totally to come up to proof when called to give evidence against fellow football supporters. It demonstrates only too well the difficulty the police have in prosecuting successfully a case of this kind.

The nine offenders were convicted and given various levels of custodial sentences up to eight years imprisonment and Michael, and the investigation team, were delighted that all their effort and hard work had been recognised by the trial judge.

Sixteen officers, from various stations across the force, in all were commended for their actions.

An interesting spin-off benefit for BTP, as a result of this incident, was that direct access to the National Police Computer system, which was introduced nationwide in 1974 and previously could only be accessed through local Home Office forces, suddenly became available to them. Up to this time, the BTP normally applied for criminal record checks via a 'red phone' in their control rooms linked to local force control rooms. This could be a laborious and time-consuming process, but applications to the Home Office for full access had previously been denied.

It is said that Margaret Thatcher, the prime minister at the time, was briefed on the incident by the then BTP Chief Constable Kenneth Ogram, and the lack of direct PNC access was raised as an issue, in that it hampered both the intelligence gathering and evidence gathering processes. In a matter of weeks BTP were authorised to have full access to the PNC, which was installed and operational by the end of 1986.

On 14 August 1986 a sign was put up at Holyhead saying 'Football Supporters will not be allowed on board Sealink ships' in an effort to dissuade Manchester United fans travelling to a game in Dublin. Extra BTP officers were drafted in to monitor trains from Chester and Crewe but no trouble was reported, even though fifty Manchester United fans did manage to slip through the security measures to board ferries.

In the autumn of 1986, the media reported the case of a football fan who bared his bottom to a young woman on an overnight Newcastle to London express train. He was fined and bound over to keep the peace at York Court.

On 20 September 1986, Keith Groves found himself in Bradford for a game against Leeds at the Odsal Stadium when a mobile fish and chip van was overturned and set alight. Keith recalls, 'It was another busy day escorting Leeds fans by train and there was a lot of fighting. We made arrests and just had time to lodge them at the police station, photograph them with the officer, and deal with them later'.

Keith's final memories of policing fans during the second half of the '80s are recalled here,

We were at Leeds railway station one day when Manchester City were playing Leeds United. There was fighting on the station and a Manchester City fan was arrested by another sergeant. He took hold of him and started to escort him to the police vans we had at the front when he broke free and made a run for it. As we ran after him he leapt over a wall, and I told the officers not to bother chasing him anymore. He had jumped over a wall which had a big drop to a roadway below and we found him lying on the floor with a broken leg.

My unit twice worked in Scotland to police international games, and were sworn in as police officers in Scotland. On one occasion we policed a train in from Arbroath to Glasgow. The fans knew we were English because the Scottish officers wore white shirts, and we were the only ones wearing blue at the time. On another occasion we escorted a train from Edinburgh to Glasgow and then policed Queen Street station. I remember seeing a massive skip on the station full of confiscated alcohol. There was a bit of fighting, and one fan was thrown through a plate-glass window just outside the station. Frazer had a prisoner for a Scottish Breach of the Peace.

On Saturday 4 October 1986, a West Ham supporter was fatally stabbed by a Millwall supporter on the London Underground in a late-night attack at the Embankment station. The Metropolitan Police took the lead with the enquiry and set up an incident room at Cannon Row police station, to which BTP officers were seconded. This merely added to the intense rivalry between the two sets of fans.

In a further case in October 1986, the media reported on a football hooligan, already serving a three-year prison sentence for violence, who had been involved in printing train tickets from a stolen ticket machine. Between August 1985 and May 1986 more than 1,000 tickets, with a face value of nearly £12,000, were printed off and handed to football supporters, of which the twenty-year-old admitted printing off some 300.

On Saturday 25 October 1986, a teenage Middlesbrough fan was beaten unconscious outside Bristol Temple Meads railway station by a gang of ten Bristol City fans. Two of his friends managed to escape but he was punched and kicked to the ground, and had his wallet containing £30 stolen. He was given first aid treatment by a police officer and an off-duty nurse as he lay prone on the ground.

On Saturday 1 November 1986, serious problems were experienced in connection with the Charlton *v.* Arsenal match, and officers suffered serious attacks on the forward and return journeys in the Sydenham and New Cross areas. An affray occurred at New Cross Gate station, in which about forty Millwall fans attacked a train carrying Arsenal and Charlton Athletic fans, hurling benches, bricks and bottles filled with ammonia sprays. Police officers were also attacked, amid chants of 'War, War, War', as some of the group forced their way onto the train using the benches as battering rams.

Twenty passengers who had nothing to do with football were attacked. One man had a bottle smashed over his head as he sheltered his girlfriend, and one woman with a baby and small children could be heard pleading to be left alone. Some passengers actually jumped down onto the live rail to try to reach the other platform to escape. Police officers used truncheons to force the attackers back into the booking hall upstairs, where hooligans continued to attack innocent people and smashed windows before running off.

BTP set up an incident room using the operational name 'Lion', and three weeks later they carried out a series of raids in south-east London and recovered a number of weapons. Six people were detained and later questioned at Lewisham police station.

PC Sean Burke subsequently described events in his evidence at court, stating, 'All hell broke loose as the train was bombarded with bricks, bottles, and lumps of concrete.' The officer chased a number of knife-wielding fans from the station and then returned to comfort a terrified black woman, who had collapsed in the ticket hall. However, when the mob rushed back in they noticed that he was on his own.

The officer went on,

I saw that a large number of these youths had returned to the station and were outside the door. They were chanting 'Kill, Kill, Kill the Old Bill'. A number of them, about fifteen, rushed back into the booking hall and began to attack me. One of them was carrying a knife and he began to slash at me. Others kicked and punched me and a brick hit me in the left eye ...

Two of those arrested were later charged with assaulting the officer, who had required seven stitches to his injuries.

Subsequently, ten Millwall fans were charged with affray, and in due course four Millwall fans, members of Millwall's infamous Bushwackers hooligan group, were sentenced to a total of twenty-nine years in prison. At the conclusion of the trial, screaming friends and relatives had to be dragged from the public gallery, and one of the defendants tried to fight his way out of the dock as he struggled with police and prison officers.

At 1 p.m. on 15 November 1986, a seventeen-year Oxford United football fan was arrested at Edgware Road Underground station for threatening behaviour after shouting abuse and kicking out at a train. When he was searched he was found to have two Stanley knife blades attached to a wooden paintbrush handle. He admitted fashioning the make-shift weapon to protect himself against Queens Park Rangers fans and was subsequently sent to a detention centre for three months.

In the 1986 winter edition of the *British Transport Police Journal*, an update was provided on the effectiveness of Mobile Units, which commented on the fact that the Southern Mobile Unit had been involved with the Metropolitan Police in the arrest of 145 Leeds supporters who had been attacking Chelsea supporters at Piccadilly Circus station.

The Euston Unit, which was subsequently renamed the Paddington Unit, had been involved in the arrest of a group of Tottenham supporters who attacked a group of Arsenal supporters. The leader of the Spurs group was subsequently sent to prison for six months.

At 1.40 p.m. on Saturday 10 January 1987, two BTP officers were assaulted at Kings Cross Underground station in London following an incident involving Cardiff City fans. At the time some 150 were gathered in and around the booking hall. PC Aneurin Johnson and PC Heaton were treated in hospital for their injuries and two Cardiff fans were arrested and charged with affray prior to the FA Cup tie between Cardiff City and Millwall. A third man was arrested and released pending further enquiries.

On the day, some 600 Cardiff City fans travelled to London by train with representatives from such hooligan groups as the City Service Crew, the Ely Trendies, the Barry Crew and the Under Fives.

On 21 March 1987, two football fans returning from a West Ham *v.* Chelsea match embarked on a massive binge-drinking session prior to boarding the 11.25 p.m. train from Euston to Northampton. They immediately started to create a nuisance, throwing things around and abusing passengers. As the train went through Wolverton, the two West Ham fans began placing newspapers under the carriage seats and setting fire to them. The flames caught hold and soon the whole carriage was ablaze. Quick thinking by the train staff averted a disaster and they managed to bring the train to a stop at Northampton and disembark passengers. The entire carriage was burnt out, causing damage estimated at over £145,000. The two were eventually traced by BTP and sentenced to two years in prison at Crown Court.

During the Easter Bank Holiday in April 1987, thousands of pounds worth of damage was done to trains by Crystal Palace fans leaving Brighton after a match which saw their team defeated 2-0. Trouble began when several hundred supporters missed the special train back to London. They were then placed on the next service train escorted by seven BTP officers. A group then proceeded to rip up seat cushions, damage fittings and set off fire extinguishers. 150 got off the train at Hassocks and went back to Brighton, where they were met on the platform by over a hundred police officers. They were put back on another train, which this time was escorted by thirty officers. On another train at least seventy seat cushions were thrown from the windows of a train between Brighton and Gatwick.

On 11 April 1987, a large-scale fight took place on the platforms of one of London's major stations. The affray at St Pancras, which involved QPR fans attacking Luton supporters, was captured on CCTV and became the subject of a major enquiry by the BTP CID at Euston. QPR hooligans plotted during the game to engage Luton, meeting up at Goldhawk Road they made their way round to Euston Square on the Underground, and then went through to St Pancras to avoid the police. At the station, scouts were sent into the station to assess Luton's strength and to entice them off the platform.

During the course of the violence, one person threw a heavy trolley onto a supporter lying prone on the platform after being beaten senseless, in what could only be described as a mass fight. In another case an individual was clearly seen on CCTV stabbing an opponent.

The violence captured on CCTV has been uploaded to the internet and has had thousands of views. Some of those passing comment alleged that the attack by a much larger group of QPR fans was a revenge attack, after some of their fans had been stabbed by Luton supporters at a previous cup match. BTP made twenty-four arrests at the beginning of July 1987.

8

THE EIGHTIES – THE BTP GO UNDERCOVER

On 25 April 1987, Tony Thompson was off duty at Doncaster railway station and recalls an incident that would literally mark him for the rest of his life. He recalls,

I was waiting to catch a train to London and stopped on the platform to speak with some of my former BTP colleagues who were policing travelling football supporters. I was in civilian clothes, and they were in uniform. It was about 7 p.m. and all league matches had finished with fans returning home.

I became aware of a train approaching from the north on the 'fast' line. It was a non-stopper, and my colleagues told me that it was taking Chelsea fans back to London from Newcastle. As the train whizzed through the station I spotted several fans hanging out of the train windows shouting at the police officers on the platform.

I saw something glinting flying from the passing train, and instinctively turned my face away as I was struck on my top lip by what turned out to be a ten pence piece that had fallen at my feet. The coin had split the outer and inner part of the top right hand side of my upper lip, and also cut my gum. I was taken by BTP to Doncaster Royal Infirmary to get the wound stitched, but being a busy Saturday night, and after several hours of waiting, the bleeding stopped and I gave up and caught the last train home to London. I still carry a half inch scar on my lip as a permanent reminder.

On Saturday 9 May 1987, Manchester City visited Upton Park for a game with West Ham in a battle to avoid relegation to the Second Division. A total of 800 City fans travelled by train from Manchester to London. At about 2 p.m. in the afternoon a group of some 130 Manchester City fans appeared in Euston Road, the worse for drink. They became extremely disorderly as they made their way to Kings Cross Underground station accompanied by a BTP escort.

Despite various requests to moderate their behaviour they refused, and such was the level of threat towards police and members of the public that, as they were put onto a Tube train, they were told that they were under arrest. This resulted in eighty Manchester City fans being arrested and documented at Snow Hill and Bishopgate City of London police stations, something of a record for BTP at the time.

On 16 May 1987, a group of youths went to Perth railway station to ambush a train carrying Dundee United supporters on their way home from Glasgow. Missiles were thrown at the train as rail staff were threatened, and one seventeen-year-old was arrested for committing a Breach of the Peace.

On Friday 22 May 1987, Swindon supporters travelled to Gillingham and, as rival gangs baited each other, the police at Gillingham railway station were bombarded with missiles, resulting in two BTP officers being injured.

On Saturday 23 May 1987, England played Scotland in an international game at Hampden Park. Friday night saw two packed Nightrider trains leaving Euston for Glasgow. They contained a sprinkling of Scots fans, but in the main BTP identified those on board as being risk fans from different English clubs. At least fifty of West Ham's Inter City Firm were there, as well as fans from Chelsea and Manchester United's Cockney Reds. Officers on travelling escorts described the situation as volatile and had a difficult trip keeping some semblance of order. On the return trip they were joined by members of Portsmouth's 6.57 Crew.

A mammoth police operation by Strathclyde Police and BTP in Scotland failed to stop large-scale disorder as up to 6,000 English fans made their presence felt in Glasgow. By 11 a.m. on the Saturday they were running amok in the main streets around the railway station in Glasgow city centre, smashing shop windows and assaulting people randomly. In all, police made 237 arrests throughout the day.

Also on Saturday 23 May 1987, Leeds were playing Charlton. About a thousand Leeds fans boarded a lengthy special train at Selhurst bound for Victoria, escorted by a small number of BTP officers. The train was delayed due to the communication cord being pulled, and after it finally left officers watched helplessly as seats, luggage racks and fittings were thrown from the train windows of those carriages which were not interconnecting. The train was eventually met by a large contingent of officers on arrival at Victoria, where a number of fans jumped out of the carriages, onto the track, before being rounded up by dog handlers.

Also in May 1987, a group of some twenty Leeds fans travelling on a TransPennine train threatened a group of black youths. The Leeds fans joined the train at Oldham and soon started shouting 'Let's throw the black bastards out onto the track' and armed themselves with fire extinguishers, sticks and a metal rod. While one train guard locked the intended victims in his guards van, a second, off-duty, train guard bravely barred the way of the hooligans, despite being punched and kicked. As the train approached York the communication cord was pulled and some of the attackers jumped out onto the track. Two persons were subsequently dealt with by the courts.

At the beginning of July 1987, a leading light from the Metropolitan Police TO 20 Public Order Unit paid tribute, following his transfer to other duties, to the British Transport Police,

... The football liaison team Dennis Temporal and Andy Douglas for their invaluable help. To the BTP dog handlers from both the main line and 'L' Division, who are always enthusiastic, professional and knowledgeable. To the BTP men on the ground, especially the lads and lasses from the Euston Division who have been tremendously hospitable and helpful throughout the season.

In July 1987, 'James', a serving police constable with the BTP, was approached by his senior officers following a request for support from Detective Sergeant Mike Layton, who at this point in his service was serving with the West Midlands Police and responsible for the day-to-day management of Operation Red Card. This undercover operation had been running for some months and was targeting Birmingham City's notorious Zulu Warriors.

The operation was in need of another officer to work undercover, and due to Mike's previous connections with the force an approach was made and 'James' was duly enlisted. He had no training, but developed a cover story and changed his appearance, which included the addition of a gold stud in his left ear. Often seen wearing a scruffy Adidas top with 77 on it, or a brown crew neck woollen jumper, he would have won no prizes for fashion – to cap it all he was an avid Aston Villa fan.

James became an integral part of the team, which ultimately gathered evidence against more than sixty individuals and led to numerous successful prosecutions. On one particular train journey from Birmingham New Street to Witton railway station, for a local derby match between Birmingham City and Aston Villa, he witnessed Birmingham fans indiscriminately smashing interior lighting, ceiling panels being torn down and seats slashed with knives. One idiot was actually seen opening the train doors as it sped along at 60 miles per hour. Another covert officer, on the same day, witnessed a lone Villa fan with learning difficulties literally being covered in spittle as he sat isolated on a train. This was normality, and all in the name of sport! The story of this operation is told in full in the book *Hunting the Hooligans*.

Geoff Lowe had by this time taken up a sergeant's post at Birmingham New Street as the officer in charge of the Birmingham Mobile Support Unit One, which consisted of himself and six constables. He recalls another incident during this period,

It was sometime during the Operation Red Card period that I was on duty with my team at New Street. Paul Majster had been watching some football fans on CCTV on the station and was interested in three individuals who he wanted to speak to. He called us on the radio and we made our way down to the ticket barriers to join him.

As we got there, I spotted Paul surrounded by a large group of what seemed like a hundred people and suddenly a huge 'Zulu' roar went up and they started punching and kicking him as he went to the floor. All seven of us drew our truncheons and literally charged at the group, who initially stood their ground but then scattered as we forced our way into the middle of them. It was a very scary moment as we managed to rescue Paul, who was shook up but not seriously injured. There were no arrests but it was one of the few times I have been involved in a full-scale baton charge.

This was not the only scrape that Paul Majster got into, as he again recalls,

In the late Eighties we started using video cameras to film the fans. We started to work the last trains out of London to Birmingham on Saturdays, when Birmingham City were playing away, as they had a troublesome group. I came back on one of these trains, in plain clothes and carrying the camera, with a team of uniform officers.

All of the Blues fans were pissed and trying to get into the First Class carriages without paying, and there was a bit of a stand-off when we refused to let them in. I was wearing a Quick Fit Fitters jacket and thought I looked pretty cool, but this one particular fan kept needling me and saying I looked like a 1970s porn star and that we couldn't touch him because we were only railway police. He carried on threatening us as we headed towards the Midlands and I proved him wrong when we got to Coventry railway station and he was arrested for a public order offence by the reception committee I had arranged.

At 11.30 a.m. on 15 November 1987, Liverpool fans caused chaos among ordinary passengers as they threw fireworks on the concourse area and tried to break through security barriers to board trains at Liverpool Lime Street station. Some 200 fans swarmed across the station throwing thunder flashes, and were intent on boarding unsupervised service trains to Manchester rather than a special train which had been laid on. Eleven fans were ejected from trains by the BTP on return services.

On 21 November 1987, Cardiff supporters travelled the short distance to Newport by rail for a Fourth Division match against Newport County. Cardiff won the match 2-1, and during the evening supporters travelled back to Cardiff by various trains without incident.

Tony Thompson was at this time the BTP superintendent in charge of policing arrangements for this match, and based himself at Cardiff railway station.

Later that evening, however, fans travelling from Newport to Cardiff in the rear coach of a train created complete havoc, smashing lights, windows and fittings as two BTP officers on the train were rendered helpless to act as shouts of 'Kill, Kill, Kill' went up. Even before the train left the platform trouble started as the communication cord was pulled.

They sent a radio message asking for assistance and on arrival were met by reinforcements. Tony Thompson recalls,

I took a contingent of BTP officers, and dog handlers, to the platform at Cardiff to meet the train in. As it pulled in it was in darkness, and I instructed my officers on the platform not to allow anyone off the train. Prior to containing the fans some of them jumped out of the carriage onto the track and escaped. Armed with a loudhailer I entered the train and announced to all on board that they were being arrested on suspicion of criminal damage and public order offences. My initial estimate was that there was about forty to fifty supporters on the train, but as they were led away in groups of ten I realised there were much more. By the time the train was empty we had counted 103 supporters!

They were processed at various police stations in Cardiff and then released on police bail pending further enquiries.

Subsequent enquires revealed that those who had jumped from the train were responsible for the damage and as such there were no prosecutions. However, we gained a lot of information about travelling supporters, and sent a clear message out to them as to what would happen if they caused trouble on trains in the future, with the *South Wales Echo* reporting the 'mass arrest' story.

In November 1987, another BTP officer, 'Steve', who retired as a sergeant in Birmingham, became another willing volunteer when he agreed to act as an undercover officer on Operation GROWTH (Get Rid Of Wolverhampton Town's Hooligans). Apart from being in the right age group and having a Black Country accent, he had little relevant training for the role to speak of but bags of enthusiasm.

Working with officers from three other forces, Steve shaved his moustache off, pierced his ear, and took to wearing an old sheepskin coat while mingling with the hooligan element in pubs, on trains, and in stadiums at home and away fixtures. There were times when the cover of some of the officers was blown and they needed to withdraw from the operation, but Steve was there until the bitter end. On one occasion, while travelling north on a train packed with football supporters, he was once nearly exposed as a uniform colleague inadvertently acknowledged him.

Ultimately, at the conclusion of the operation more than a hundred Wolverhampton hooligans were arrested. Steve gave evidence in a number of trials, and following one hearing he was attacked in a pub near to the courts, in what he firmly believes to have been a revenge attack. Next day he continued giving his evidence sporting a large black eye with some of the defendants giggling and cheering from the dock. The judge witnessed their behaviour and commented 'Laughter can soon turn to tears.' At the end of the day's proceedings he remanded them in custody.

Steve recalls going home in the dark, so that the neighbours wouldn't see what he looked like during the operation, and finding it hard to adjust to normal policing on his return. In essence, he was one of the pathfinders to this approach, which proved to be extremely successful in the West Midlands.

On 1 January 1988, a local derby at Cambridge saw unprecedented scenes of violence at the railway station involving visiting Peterborough fans. A special train carrying sixty supporters was ambushed by local youths. Stones were thrown and as the windows of the train were smashed two BTP officers, escorting the train, were injured and suffered cuts as well as receiving glass splinters in their eyes. Twenty people were subsequently arrested and charged with criminal damage and riot.

On 9 January 1988, a Millwall fan on his way to the FA Cup third round match with Arsenal was arrested after smashing a light fitting against a train at Euston railway station. He later admitted threatening behaviour and was sent to a detention centre for three months and banned from attending football matches for two years.

On 31 January 1988 more than £5,000 worth of damage was caused to a train in the West Midlands when serious disorder broke out among returning Liverpool fans from the FA Cup tie with Aston Villa.

On 3 February 1988, BTP officers supported officers from the Metropolitan Police in executing search warrants in dawn raids in London and the Home Counties, which led to nineteen people being arrested and numerous weapons recovered. The operation, code-named Evild, targeted Arsenal hooligans following violence which occurred at an FA Cup tie against Millwall the previous month, when eight police officers were injured. More than ninety officers were involved in the operation.

At 10 p.m. on Saturday 20 February 1988, a gang of sixty hooligans confronted a group of Manchester United fans as they arrived at Manchester Piccadilly railway station, returning from an FA Cup tie in London with Arsenal. Three BTP officers who had been escorting the fans by train were confronted by the group and were punched and kicked, and knocked to the ground.

PC John Duffy, known by many of his friends and colleagues as Joe, was struck on the head with a claw hammer and subsequently had to have a brain operation at Manchester Royal Infirmary as his skull was fractured. Surgeons had to remove a piece of bone that was pressing into his brain. PC Steven Martin received two black eyes and PC Darren Yates was also hit on the head with a bottle as they tried to make an arrest.

This was obviously a traumatic incident for Joe, who actually does not remember some of what happened, which is probably just as well! Joe had joined the force in May 1985, having previously served in the Corps of Royal Engineers for fifteen years. Joe had experienced a lot of difficult situations and was definitely no shrinking violet. He would not have thought twice about doing his duty to try and protect people and to keep the peace.

Joe tells the story, as far as he can remember himself and from things which colleagues have told him since the incident,

Saturday 20 February 1988 is a day I will never forget as it was the day I was assaulted and received a fractured skull, and a hole in my skull, which caused a depression which is still visible today. Colleagues have since told me that they thought I was going to die as a result of my injuries.

In 1988 I was posted to BTP Manchester and I was working on one of the two MSUs based at that location. The MSU I was posted to comprised of Sergeant Peter Clark, police constables Darren Yates, Steve Martin, Greg Perrin, Mick Murray and myself. We regularly worked football duties and I policed all of the big clubs based in the North West, and had travelled with them all over the country.

On that Saturday we were rostered a rest day working to escort Manchester United fans back from London to Manchester after their fixture against Arsenal in the capital. This was a good duty for us as rest day working attracted a good overtime rate in those days, even though it messed with the weekend. The start of the duty was uneventful, apart from the fact that when we booked on duty our pre-allocated tasks were changed, with two of the team, PCs Perrin and Murray, working separately from the rest of us to escort fans involved in the Lancaster *versus* Barrow-in-Furness match also taking place that day. This left only four of us to travel down to London in preparation to escort the United fans back north. We travelled down to London on the cushions, which meant that the journey south was merely to get us to London, rather than any particular policing duty.

At Euston we monitored the trains heading back to Manchester in order to decide which train we should escort back. In fact, the trains were reasonably quiet until a large group of returning fans turned up to catch the train to Manchester leaving at around 8 p.m. Due to this being the largest group of fans we had seen, the duty inspector agreed that we would escort that particular train as a travelling serial.

The train left London without incident and we took a slow walk through the train to let the fans know that police would be travelling back to Manchester with them. We patrolled the train another couple of times, chatting to people who would bother to chat with us, as this was a good way of keeping everybody in order. After leaving Rugby station the train guard called us to a group of youths who had managed to board without tickets or money. I took their details in my pocket notebook and advised them that I would see them in Manchester. The remainder of the journey was uneventful.

On arrival at Manchester Piccadilly I stood on the platform, waiting for the group of youths from the train to approach the barriers, while the remainder of the serial took themselves back to the police office at Piccadilly station to get changed prior to standing down and going for a deserved pint. As the youths approached me I got into conversation and advised them that I would be visiting them at their homes to speak with them in the presence, and hearing, of their parents, as is required for youngsters of their age. As we were talking we continued to walk along the platform, through the barriers, and out onto the concourse.

On doing so I was slightly behind the youths and I saw a group of fifteen to twenty other young men, some of whom were wearing Manchester City scarves and colours, on the concourse. City that day had been playing a game in Manchester, although I cannot remember who it was against. This group ran at the small group of youths that I had been speaking with, obviously intending to attack them and cause injury. I immediately called for assistance, drew my truncheon, and put myself between the opposing groups from the two Manchester clubs.

The group of City fans then turned and started to leave the concourse through the booking hall, and as they did they started to run down the approach road, just past the underpass, to the rear approach road of the station. I was then joined by Darren Yates and Steve Martin, who had responded to my call for assistance, although neither of them had helmets or tunics on as they were in the process of changing to go home when I called for help.

As we went down the front approach road, about 25 yards past the underpass, the group turned and one of them struck Darren Yates in the face. Darren and Steve took this person to the ground and I tried to stand over them to offer some protection. Unknown to us, however, as we passed the underpass a further group of approximately fifty or more additional City fans came behind us, and when the two groups joined the assaults on us took place.

They crowded into us, eventually pinning my arms down, and turned me towards the shops. It was about this time that I was struck from behind, and the noise was one of the loudest bangs I had ever heard, and I fell to the floor. I am unsure if I lost consciousness but my memory is very hazy about the next twenty-to-thirty minutes, until I remember being placed into an ambulance. I do vaguely remember someone going into my breast anorak pocket for my note book, as it had the details in it of the youths I had been speaking with prior to the incident. I think it was Steve Ingham, the duty inspector, who did this.

I was taken to Manchester Royal Infirmary that night, where I was operated on for a depressed fractured skull. My wife Brenda was told about the incident and the operation by the superintendent, although she was left at home on her own with our two children, which seemed a bit harsh, although this is how things sometimes were in those days.

I was obviously off sick for quite a while, but I was visited regularly by several of the detectives who were involved with the investigation. On one visit from Jim Woodcock and John Harris, they told me that they believed that they were taking a dying statement, commonly known as a dying declaration, from me when I was in the hospital.

During the next couple of weeks I was kept in touch with the investigation and one of the officers told me that they had received a phone call telling them that 'Clanger did it with a hammer.' Their enquiries led them to a youth with that nickname, who was subsequently arrested and charged with Section 18 wounding for the assault on me. He pleaded guilty at court and was given a three year custodial sentence but, having spent nine months on remand in custody, he actually was only in prison for a further nine months.

This incident definitely affected me in a negative way and caused me to lose some memories from the past, particularly from my military service, which is disappointing. My wife Brenda also had to put up with me being a bit intolerant for a while after the attack.

When Mickey Francis, a leading Manchester City hooligan, wrote his book called *Guvnors*, which was all about the Manchester City hooligan group, a whole section was devoted to this incident. He refers to it as the 'Battle of Piccadilly', although he was not involved as he was in custody at the time. The fact that the incident made it into that book makes me realise just how big an issue it was.

One theory that was looked at, following the incident, was whether the attack was in retaliation for Operation Omega, which had targeted Manchester City hooligans ten days previous, with twenty-three persons being arrested and charged with conspiracy to commit riot.

Seventeen youths were subsequently charged in connection with the attacks on the officers, ten of whom were later committed for trial charged with causing grievous bodily harm, conspiracy and violent disorder.

Also on 20 February 1988, the BTP were again dealing with disorderly Cardiff City fans following incidents on four trains from Paddington to Cardiff after the game at Leyton Orient. Six arrests were made, and three others ejected, on the 17.59 train that was forced to stop at Ealing Broadway because of disorderly behaviour and damage to the train.

On the 20.40 train, five officers had to control a hundred Cardiff fans, and one fan was arrested for making death threats. On the 21.20 hours service, twenty of the fifty fans were so drunk, before departure, that they were ejected, and a further three BTP officers had to escort the last train back.

British Rail put the total damage caused by the fans as being more than £5,000. ACC Ian McGregor, from the BTP, was so concerned about a series of incidents involving Cardiff City fans during the season that he wrote to the club and sent copies of his letter to the FA and the government, calling for action.

On Saturday 27 February 1988, to finish off a violent month, a Corby teenager lost part of his leg following a violent clash between rival football fans at Kettering railway station. Gary Johnson fell between the carriages and the platform as a train carrying West Ham fans pulled out of the station. Fire officers called to the scene took 30 minutes to free his right leg, which was later amputated below the knee.

The incident started at 7.25 p.m. when a dispute occurred between the victim and four youths on the train. After he fell, four people jumped from the train and ran off across open ground. Following a police search two people were detained, who were later released on bail pending further enquiries. It was alleged that the victim, an ardent Villa fan, had confronted the four, who had then held onto him as the train started to move off from the platform, resulting in the fall.

A nationwide operation was put into place by the BTP to police the first England *v.* Scotland game to be played on a Saturday since 1981. Scottish BTP Assistant Chief Constable Archie Mackenzie briefed officers, north and south of the border, in an operation which was to run from Thursday until the Sunday after the game. Most of BTP's 2,000 officers were to be involved in some way, and every special football train leaving Scotland was to be escorted by uniform and plain clothes officers, with alcohol bans in place on trains and mainline stations.

The England *v.* Scotland Rous Cup match on 21 May 1988 at Wembley was marred by several serious incidents, most of which were drink related. A young Scots supporter travelling to London lost his life when he fell from an express train in Northamptonshire. There were no suspicious circumstances.

Serious disturbances took place throughout the capital on the rail and Underground networks. A youth was pushed onto the track at Wembley Underground station and suffered head injuries and burns. Damage and disorder took place on an Underground train from Wembley, which had 1,000 supporters on board, as lights and windows were smashed.

Chris Jessup carried out thousands of football policing duties during his career and retired from the BTP as a dog handler, but prior to taking on this role he remembers his last day serving on one of the London-based Mobile Support Units on 21 May 1988, as part of the policing operation for the England *v.* Scotland game,

I remember two incidents in particular that my unit had to deal with during the day. The first was as early as 7 a.m. at the start of my duty. As the van was driving around Trafalgar Square on the way to Victoria station it was bombarded by slices of bread being thrown by Scotland supporters. This was more humorous than serious disorder, but the bread had been stolen from early morning deliveries to the local cafés and sandwich shops.

That was dealt with fairly quickly, but later in the day we were called to a London Underground station north of Baker Street, which I think was Dollis Hill. On arrival, the unit had to deal with a group of impatient Scotland fans who were literally trying to rock a train off the rails in protest at being delayed at the station. Offenders on such occasions sometimes have to be allowed to get away with things that at other times they would not, in order to keep the networks moving for the greater good. This went against the grain for the vast majority of police officers who wanted to see justice done. However, we also recognised the need to stop the small minority spoiling the party for the rest!

Chief Inspector Michael Kiely from BTP's Underground Division summed up the feelings of many in an open letter, which was published in the *Daily Telegraph* on 26 May 1988 as follows,

Sir – Having been heavily involved in the policing arrangements relating to the conveying of football supporters to the England *versus* Scotland match on the London Underground system, I am at a loss to know why Central London, Wembley, and the surrounding areas, have to be subjected to such intolerable behaviour on a regular basis. Regular ordinary passengers going about innocent pursuits become virtual prisoners aboard Underground trains that are left awash with beer and urine. Members of London Underground staff are threatened and verbally abused. Trains are severely damaged which has a knock on effect for commuters when trains have to be taken out of service for repairs. Police leave is cancelled and officers from the British Transport Police and Metropolitan Police are drawn away from their normal duties. The only bodies making any profit from this fixture are the English Football Association and their Scottish counterpart, together with Wembley Stadium. While police costs are met for policing arrangements within the stadium no contribution is made to cover the costs of the massive policing operation outside the stadium. Surely it is time that the government called a halt to this anarchy and banned the fixture, or if it must be played hold the fixture in Scotland or in an empty stadium at Wembley. Three days of mindless violence and mass disorder cannot be justified for what is now a meaningless fixture in the football calendar.

During the course of the 1987/88 football season, some 2,241 trains carrying football supporters were escorted by officers from the British Transport Police, and, although football-related offences were overall lower than previous years, the season was nevertheless marred by the serious incidents previously outlined.

On 3 June 1988, police officers from West Germany, Holland and Belgium met with British colleagues, the British Foreign Office and Football Association, in an event hosted by BTP at their training college in Tadworth, Surrey. The meeting was a precursor to the European Football Championship, due to start the following week in West Germany, and discussions took place regarding the exchange of intelligence, as 8,000 English fans were expected to journey abroad. ACC McGregor chaired the meeting and outlined BTP's proposals to monitor the movement of fans from ferry ports.

In the 1988 autumn edition of the *British Transport Police Journal*, details were given of an incident at Inverkeithing railway station, Scotland, when some 160 rival supporters from Dunfermline and Hibernian football clubs engaged in serious disorder, during which BTP and local officers were attacked with bricks and other missiles. A joint operation with Fife Constabulary resulted in a large number of arrests.

On Saturday 19 November 1988, Middlesbrough were visiting Arsenal, and Newcastle were visiting newly promoted Millwall, at games in London. At about 9.15 a.m. that morning, an officer in the control room at Kings Cross noticed on the CCTV monitor a group of six Newcastle supporters entering the station car park and opening the boot of a hired Rover car. The officer became suspicious and directed other officers to the scene.

On arrival they examined the boot of the car and inside found baseball bats, CS gas, a smoke bomb, snooker cues, two Stanley knife blades taped together and scalpel blades. Two men were arrested immediately but the other four managed to make good their escape. Further enquiries were made and, as a result of liaising with officers in Newcastle, the other four were arrested and a house search resulted in other property being recovered. They were brought back to London and all six charged.

During the weekend of 18/19 February 1989, terrified passengers were trapped on an InterCity express train for almost an hour as fifteen Liverpool fans fought a pitched battle with thirty Tranmere fans on the 8 p.m. train from York to Liverpool. Three coaches were wrecked and damage valued at £10,000 was caused, as fans used broken tables and fire extinguishers as weapons, in what was later described by the BTP as a 'near riot' situation.

The fighting started after the Liverpool fans boarded the train at Manchester Victoria and found themselves in the same carriages as thirty Tranmere fans who were on their way home from a match in York. Violence erupted almost immediately after the train departed, with dozens of windows smashed, sliding interior glass doors kicked in and tables smashed to make wooden staves.

At St Helens junction the train stopped and three injured fans, who were subsequently taken to hospital, were hurled from the train as fighting continued. An emergency message was sent and BTP officers awaited the trains arrival, where even then fighting erupted on the platform as fans disembarked. One person was arrested at the time and BTP commenced a post-incident investigation, which was led by Inspector Bob Brown.

In June 1989, *Railnews* reported the sentencing of four members of a fifty-strong gang of Blackburn Rovers fans who attacked a train carrying 250 Burnley fans as it pulled into Darwen station. They smashed windows with iron bars, wooden staves and stones. BTP officers on the train had to restrain Burnley fans from trying to retaliate and urged other passengers to take cover in what must have been a terrifying incident.

During the 1988/89 football season, a total of 762,460 football fans travelled by train to matches.

The British Transport Police officially stopped policing for Sealink on 31 January 1989, but on 5 September 1989 they found themselves back at Harwich again by invitation from the local police. Football hooligans heading to Sweden for a World Cup match with England started fighting on board the North Sea ferry *Tor Britannia* in the early hours of the previous day.

During the course of the disturbances, a twenty-four-year-old fan, believed to have been under the influence of drugs, panicked when a fire extinguisher was set off and jumped overboard. A search for him failed to find any trace and he was presumed drowned. An off-duty police officer on board warned authorities on the ships radio that passengers were in very real danger and the ship was forced to return to Harwich.

On arrival it was met by scores of police officers, who boarded the ship and removed about 150 fans. Many were put on a train under police escort back to London, while eight were charged with a variety of offences and released on bail.

Chris Hall, an officer with BTP at the time, recalls,

> The ship returned to the quay for police to attend. Mr Whent was the divisional commander for Harwich and Clacton at the time. He called in the BTP Public Order Support Units, who were at Tadworth on a training course at the time. They were all sent to the quay and there were officers from up north and Scotland. I can remember all of the blue transit vans lined up on the quay waiting for the ship to arrive. Myself and PC Steve Noon made several arrests for manslaughter and various other offences. All the arrests were made by BTP officers.

This incident was just a precursor to the violence which was to follow, as the match took place in Stockholm. Swedish police arrested a hundred England fans following a riot in the city centre, as well as a substantial number of local fans. They were eventually given three days to leave Sweden and most made their way back by ferry and train to the UK.

The Home Secretary asked the BTP for urgent assistance to escort fans from the Hook of Holland on 7 and 8 September 1989, and other officers monitored trains from Harwich coming into Liverpool Street in London. One particularly rowdy group of forty fans was monitored by police with dogs and horses, as they shouted obscenities and tried to hide their faces from the waiting press.

On 31 October 1989, clashes occurred between FC Liege and Hibernian fans in Anderlecht and local police made thirty-six arrests. A group of sixty returning Hibs fans boarded the 6 p.m. train from Dover to London Victoria, after coming off a ferry, and were escorted by BTP officers. On the journey, fans began causing extensive damage to three carriages, as seats were torn up and windows smashed. On the trains arrival in London it was met by twenty BTP officers who made sixteen arrests. Other officers worked in relays to escort up to 2,000 Hibernian fans from London to Edinburgh.

At the end of November 1989 a Cambridge United fan needed eleven stitches to face wounds after he was slashed with a broken bottle on a train. His friend needed three stiches after being hit over the head with the same bottle. They had been sat near to a group of ten Aldershot fans who began heckling them, and as the group went to get off the train at Ash Vale one of them turned round and struck the two victims with a bottle in an unprovoked attack.

In the same period, two men were arrested on a Wednesday night when BTP boarded a train at Basingstoke. It happened after mailbags were thrown from the train by football fans returning from a Swindon Town *v*. Southampton game, the bags were believed to have been taken at Reading station.

In the autumn of 1989, BTP announced the end of a three-year investigation where thousands of forged Interrail tickets priced at £145 had been sold, many to football hooligans travelling to European games. Several arrests resulted, but losses to the rail industry were estimated to be in the region of £5 million.

There is a clip on YouTube entitled 'Millwall v West Ham', recorded in 1988/89. There is also a similar clip titled 'British Transport Police Millwall v West Ham', which covers the same incident. They epitomise the risks that officers routinely took, and still do. They also graphically illustrate the problems that existed in football at the time as hooligans engaged routinely in purely tribalistic behaviour.

PC Chris Jessup had by now completed his training with police dog Solo and had been posted to the force headquarters' dog section, where he often worked with fellow dog handler PC John Hucks, with police dog Zero. Chris takes up the story,

In the late 1980s, John and I were posted to be part of the operation policing Millwall *versus* West Ham at the Den in south London. This particular rivalry was one of the fiercest in the country in those days, so it was inevitable that disorder would take place despite massive police efforts to prevent it.

At some stage John and I found ourselves in the Old Kent Road area, intending to travel to New Cross to take up our duties. Just after the Canterbury Arms Pub we encountered large numbers of football fans, which was slightly unusual due to the early time and the fact that they were not being escorted by police. We quickly worked out that they were West Ham fans and advised our control room of what we had seen. We deployed on foot with our dogs and found ourselves in Avonley Road, just down from Deptford ambulance station and just off the Old Kent Road. It was near a pub which is now the Hong Kong City chinese restaurant, and by now we were attempting to keep the two rival sets of supporters apart.

We ended up back to back between two parked cars, one of which was a Mini car. We put a call out for urgent assistance on the radio and would estimate that there were about 100-plus fans fighting or squaring up to each other in the street around us.

Unknown to us at this stage, both the Metropolitan Police helicopter, known as India 99, and two covert BTP officers were monitoring the situation, and had already reported the incident that we were involved in. The two covert officers were working with a team undertaking a documentary on the BTP and it is some of their footage that has now made its way onto YouTube.

The situation was getting very serious and we had nowhere to go as we were trapped between the two cars. After what seemed ages, a section of mounted officers from the Metropolitan Police arrived from the direction of the A2. There were about eight of them, and I have never seen mounted officers travelling at such speed, before, or since. What an awesome sight – the cavalry had arrived! They quickly got stuck in, as we would say, and I will never forget the sight of a police horse scrambling over the bonnet of a Mini motor car! We were eventually joined by further units and the fans were separated into smaller groups and dispersed.

It was one of the many close shaves that I encountered policing football during my career, and undoubtedly every BTP officer will have faced something similar.

BTP continued to support national efforts to combat football hooliganism by covert methods, and during the same period Tony Thompson recalls providing support to one such effort,

As a consequence of continuing hooliganism by Cardiff City football supporters in the early 1990s, while area commander of the South West area I had responsibility for overseeing and financing the setting up of an undercover operation at Cardiff, which was managed on a daily basis by my detective chief inspector.

Two BTP officers from South Wales volunteered for this role, and they rented a flat in Cardiff, assumed new identities, and quickly infiltrated the Cardiff City football fraternity. Their role continued for many months as they became part of the Cardiff supporters who travelled around the country, gathering intelligence, and reporting back on the hooligan element.

9

THE NINETIES –
ANOTHER DEATH

Tony Thompson recalls another incident on 10 January 1990,

> The chant of one Cardiff City supporter as they arrived at Bristol
> Temple Meads railway station was 'Kill the Bill, Kill the Bill.'
> The Cardiff supporters were passing through a subway heading
> towards platform 3, and the exit, and could see BTP officers
> waiting at the far end. What they did not see was me in my
> superintendent's uniform standing watching them from behind a
> pillar in the subway, and the chanting Cardiff fan observed at close
> range was duly arrested and charged with disorder.

On 30 March 1990 a group of drunken Cardiff City fans wrecked
a train, as a friend lay dead, following a massive drinking session,
with bottles of whisky and vodka consumed. They went on the
rampage when the train was stopped at Whitland railway station,
in Wales, as ambulance staff were called to a twenty-nine-year-old
who had collapsed.

As medical staff battled to save his life, his friends ran through
the train terrorising other passengers, hurling fire extinguishers
and seats from the train windows onto the track and causing
damage valued at £1,000. They were returning home after seeing
Wales beaten 1-0 by the Republic of Ireland in Dublin, and were
thought to have started drinking during the ferry crossing from
Ireland.

The Fishguard to Paddington train was halted at the station but a doctor and the ambulance crew were unable to save the deceased, who had apparently drunk a bottle of whisky and a bottle of vodka. Police boarded the train and made nine arrests, two of whom were charged with causing criminal damage, while the others were bailed pending further enquiries. A waste of a life and someone left a widow at the age of just twenty-six years.

On 2 June 1990, ACC Ian McGregor announced the commencement of Operation Umpire, which was BTP's response to policing the movement of fans during the World Cup. A ban on alcohol on all trains from London to the Channel ports was also announced and Sealink paid for BTP officers to help security officers in policing the ferries.

In July 1990 the live rails had to be shut down at Folkestone East station after fans returning from a World Cup game spilled out onto the track as the train arrived at a platform. Some 400 fans were subsequently escorted by the BTP back to London Victoria station.

On 17 August 1990, Hibs played a friendly game with Millwall in London. It turned out to be a far from friendly affair and clashes took place between the two sets of fans in the ground, and at New Cross station.

On Wednesday 15 November 1990, just thirty BTP officers supervised the movements of some 30,000 football fans at Wembley Park Tube station for a match at Wembley Stadium between England and Italy. The officer in charge on the day, Inspector Wayne Clayton-Robb, stressed the importance of good communication between the officers and the fans, as the behaviour of boisterous fans was moderated with some quiet words.

Retired BTP Superintendent Dave Farrelly recalls some of his earlier football exploits,

In 1991, while travelling back to London from Liverpool with a large group of London-based football fans, three of us in the escorting serial were confronted by a large group of fans in a carriage close to the buffet car.

One fan was particularly abusive in front of his drunken friends. He made various personal comments to me in order to wind me up. Staring at me and taking up an aggressive stance he asked me what I was going to do about it. Knowing that we were hugely outnumbered, on a moving train, in the middle of nowhere, I walked up to him and whispered in his ear 'You may be with your mates now but when we get back to Euston station I will be with my mates and we will see what happens then.' I winked at him and walked away and stood in another carriage.

The fans travelling back were very drunk, loud and disorderly, and despite our best efforts it was an unpleasant journey for all concerned, including ordinary passengers who had to endure this. About forty minutes later my tormentor found me again, by which time we were a lot closer to Euston station! He walked up to me and in his hands was a can of coke which he handed to me, 'Look mate I am really sorry about earlier. I was just showing off in front of my mates. I didn't mean any harm. I am really sorry.'

His apology seemed genuine but clearly he was worried about what might happen when we got back to Euston station. I explained to him that I needed to save face as I had contacted Euston station, and arranged for the Met Police Territorial Support Group to meet the train when we arrived. I took him aside and told him very politely that if he managed to keep the noise down in the carriage, and stop the swearing and bad behaviour of his fellow supporters for the rest of the journey, that I would ensure that he would get home that night.

He took me at my word and he kept his friends quiet and orderly until we reached Euston. At the station barrier line, the three of us police officers on the travelling serial, stood alone watching the travelling fans pass on to the concourse. My new friend approached me again and said 'There never was any riot police was there?'. I said 'No there wasn't and neither was there any message asking for support. The point is you will never know when there has been such a request made or not.'

In another incident he recalls his experiences of dealing with fans from abroad,

While policing an Arsenal *versus* Paris Saint-Germain match at the old Highbury Stadium, BTP officers were posted to Arsenal station early before the game. The French fans arrived early by coach and, much to their annoyance, they were taken to the ground very much earlier than anyone had anticipated.

The Met Police had not deployed to the streets around the stadium, and the hooligan element took the opportunity to start exploring, and disobeying the instructions to go straight into the ground. Having quickly encountered the first group of home fans, the PSG hooligan group drew knives and started to fight, encouraged by the absence of police. Seeing the fight on the Highbury control room CCTV, the BTP officers assigned on the ground ran up the hill and, much to the surprise of the French fans, caught them all red handed.

The law on offensive weapons being more permissive in France, they did not even have the good sense to discard or hide their weapons and they were duly arrested.

An Italian side with a strong hardcore of hooligans were visiting London in 1991. There was a great deal of intelligence about the group, their intentions and the tactics they favoured, and we had good quality photographs of the violent hardcore element that were well known to the Italian authorities. They seemed a real nasty group of violent criminals, with some very nasty criminal convictions.

On the forward traffic to the game they were not seen, and similarly after the game not spotted or picked up. At 2 a.m. a group of twenty men was then seen in Euston Road, wandering aimlessly and hailing black cabs unsuccessfully. Myself and two other officers approached the group and it soon became clear to us that this was the hardcore group all together in one place!

They looked a pretty rough, and tough group, and all of them that we had photos of were present in the group. Fortunately, they were tired and wet. We brought them into Euston station, out of the rain, and tried to engage with them positively as we were hopelessly outnumbered if they kicked off.

After much talking in broken English we discovered that they were looking for Gatwick Airport to catch their morning flights home. Explaining that they were a very long way from Victoria station, and even further from Gatwick, we decided that it was probably not in the best interests of public order, or safety, to let this group wonder off into the London night. Eventually we secured the services of two police transit vans with the intention of driving this group directly to Gatwick Airport.

The difficulty in explaining to twenty Italian-football hardcore violent criminals that we were going to put them into two police vans and drive them to Gatwick was difficult to explain with their limited English. After a thirty minute stand-off, in which you could feel the deep level of mistrust, the group eventually got into the vans and we drove them without further incident to Gatwick. On leaving the vehicles the Italian fans were very different towards us, shaking our hands and thanking us.

In another incident, Dave Farrelly recalls,

In the early 1990s Manchester United were playing at Wembley. Euston station, where I was based at the time, was very busy with fans travelling in from Manchester and other parts of the UK.

Two groups of supporters were monitored in and around the station from about 10 a.m. on the morning of the game. We played cat-and-mouse with the two groups all morning, keeping them apart and disrupting their attempts to come together and fight. At several stages the two groups came close together with verbal abuse and gesticulating taking place.

Eventually, the inevitable happened in Eversholt Street next to Euston station. A large fight broke out between the two groups of fans. There was significant disorder and police, both BTP and Met Police, intervened with about a dozen arrests being made for public order offences.

When the dust settled and we were back in the custody suite, we were surprised to discover that both groups were in fact Manchester United fans. It seems they did not know, or bother to find out, who they had been stalking for the best part of two hours. The fans arrested were distraught and apologetic towards each other. They were not wearing any 'colours' shirts, scarfs or other identification as to what team they supported. Adrenalin and the need to fight got the better of them!

On Saturday 25 January 1992, Millwall were travelling to Norwich to play. Retired PC Andy Fidgett takes up the story,

The game got called off due to bad weather. Sergeant Derek Bigmore, who sadly is no longer with us, got on the train at

Ipswich and made an announcement to tell the fans. To everyone's surprise, the fans got off and went into Ipswich rather than go back to London. They ran Suffolk Police ragged all day, causing trouble all over the town. As Ipswich FC were away, Suffolk only had normal strength on duty and couldn't really cope.

Myself and PC Keith Feaviour came on duty in the early evening, as was normal for a Saturday, and I remember, when we arrived fifteen minutes before our start time, I said to Keith 'That train shouldn't be there.' What had happened was that Suffolk Police had marched the Millwall fans down to the station to get rid of them out of the town, and held up a train to put them on.

We hurriedly got into uniform and, together with two other officers, boarded the train. As soon as the train left the Millwall fans broke into the buffet bar and we decided to try and keep them in that area. They smoked, they gambled, they swore, and generally did as they liked. One helmet was taken off someone's head and the trip was hell. In those days there were no mobile phones or pagers, the best you could do was to throw a message out at a manned station asking the station supervisor to phone on ahead. We got to the next station at Colchester and threw a message out asking for help.

As the journey progressed we feared getting a severe kicking. One of the Millwall fans I believe was called Big Frank, and he said that he was a retired mercenary. He was growling all the time and talking about throwing one of us out of the window. When we thought that things could get no worse, the senior conductor came through the train asking for tickets. We urged him not to approach the Millwall fans but he did. He had his son with him on a day out and the poor boy was in tears. As the tension rose, to a point seldom felt by me, a little old Millwall fan got up and said 'We don't scare little kids.' He then showed all the tickets and the tension eased.

On arrival at Liverpool Street, we were met by Chief Inspector Chapman with two support units. When he approached us he said, 'Christ you four have got more service in than all my blokes put together, it probably saved you.' It was time for a cup of tea before we went back to Ipswich.

Above: Photograph of PC Andrew Fidgett and police dog Ned at Stratford railway station in London in January 2005 following disturbances involving up to 100 youths.

Below: Photograph taken at Wellington railway station during an EDL demonstration, which appeared in the *Shropshire Star* on 15 August 2011.

LEG HORROR: FANS SOUGHT

Tragedy after row

POLICE are today hunting several youths after a Corby teenager lost part of his leg following a vicious clash with rival soccer fans at Kettering railway station.

Gary Johnson fell between the carriages and the platform as a train carrying West Ham fans pulled out of the station.

Shocked passengers rushed to help him and firemen, sent on the scene, took 30 minutes to free his mangled right leg.

Surgeons at Kettering General Hospital have amputated below the knee and his condition today is said to be comfortable but not critical.

Four youths who leapt from the train ran off across open ground behind the station and a police dog team was called in to search for them.

Two youths were later questioned by police but were yesterday released without charge pending further inquiries.

Gary's ordeal began when the train pulled into Kettering at about 7.25am on Saturday. Police say there had been an argument between Gary and four youths before he fell.

His mum Irene, of Leighton Road, Corby said today: "Gary was happy because Villa had won.

"Hassle started between him and other fans. When he got off the train at Kettering they shouted abuse about Villa and Gary went to catch to much them.

"The youths then held onto him and the train started to go off with his leg caught between the platform and the train. It's been a traumatic experience for Gary and we have been going into

■ DRAMA . . . police quiz rail travellers soon after the incident

hospital every day to be at his side."

Football fan Gary's bedroom is decorated in Villa colours and is plastered with posters, programmes and pictures of his favourite team.

The 19-year-old, who had watched Villa's game in Birmingham with younger brother Jason, caught a London-bound train after changing at Leicester.

He works as a trainee welder at BEGA Electronics on the Weldon industrial estate and is a former Lodge Park Comprehensive School pupil.

Police sealed off Platform Four while they examined the scene and the train was held up for more than an hour.

Police want to hear from a taxi driver who may have taken three or four youths from Broughton to the Northampton area.

Any other witnesses should contact Kettering officers on 411411 or the British Transport Police on 0633 517618.

Crowded prisons problem

BEDFORD and Lei prisons are am Britain's top five overcrowded jails, a ing to a report out toda

It says the pr population is rising a that to accommodate males properly prisons the size Wormwood Scrubs w have to be opened e three weeks.

In a briefing paper National Association the Care and Resettle of Offenders (NAC gives a "league table of Britain's five overcrowded prisons December 31, 1987:

● Leeds Prison, with places, held 1,307 prison (111 per cent overcrowd

● Leicester Prison, with 200 places, held prisoners (102 per overcrowded).

● Bedford Prison, with places, held 332 prison (69 per cent overcrowded)

● Birmingham Pri with 592 places, held 1 prisoners (88 per overcrowded).

● Reading Prison, with places, held 331 prisons (86 per cent overcrowded)

Above: Photograph of Superintendent Michael Layton on New Street station in Birmingham in the spring of 2009, in the company of a BTP football intelligence officer who wishes to remain anonymous.

Left: Fan loses leg – photo/newspaper cutting at Kettering railway station, *Northamptonshire Telegraph* 29 February 1988.

Above: Photograph taken at Wellington railway station during an EDL demonstration, showing police dogs. This appeared in the *Shropshire Star* on 15 August 2011.

Right: Photograph of Alan Pacey as an assistant chief constable, delivering a pre-event briefing in 2014.

Above: Operators viewing screens inside the BTP Silver Events Room – taken on 19 May 2007. (Courtesy of the British Transport Police Media Centre)

Left: Monitoring football traffic at Wembley Park station in 2014. (Courtesy of the British Transport Police Media Centre)

Above: Escorting Leeds fans at London Bridge railway station in October 2008. (Courtesy of the British Transport Police Media Centre)

Below: BTP officers engaged at the Eurostar in London in connection with the FIFA World Cup 2006, with CI Kenwrick in the foreground. (Courtesy of the British Transport Police Media Centre)

Above: Policing football fans at Kings Cross railway station in October 2008. (Courtesy of the British Transport Police Media Centre)

Below: BTP search dog checking an England sports bag on a railway platform. (Courtesy of the British Transport Police Media Centre)

Above: BTP Police Support Unit escorting fans through the streets for the FA Cup fifth round tie between Luton Town FC and Millwall FC on 16 February 2013. (Courtesy of the British Transport Police Media Centre)

Below: A further picture of BTP officers escorting fans on 16 February 2013. (Courtesy of the British Transport Police Media Centre)

Above: Mounted Police lead the way – an example of joint working with BTP. (Courtesy of the British Transport Police Media Centre)

Below: The BTP monitoring fan activity at Wembley Stadium.

On 9 January 1993, Fulham fans travelling on the rail network were attacked by Swansea fans.

On 1 August 1993, Hibernian fans fought with Leeds supporters in Edinburgh city centre and outside Waverley railway station. During the violence twenty-two arrests were made, and one Leeds fan received serious head injuries.

On 8 October 1994, Hibernian Capital City Service hooligans, armed with coshes and knives, arranged to meet Glasgow Rangers fans, who were armed with claw hammers, at Slateford railway station in the west of Edinburgh before the match. In the ensuing confrontation, seven Glasgow Rangers fans received stab wounds and were hospitalised.

Retired Inspector John Owen again reflects on his experiences with Millwall fans,

Sometime during the mid-nineties, I was the inspector in charge of BTP at Paddington when we had the experience of Millwall supporters at their worst again. It was another mid-week evening kick-off match when large numbers of supporters travelled from South London, via the Underground, to Paddington station, where they boarded ordinary service trains for the hour-long journey to Swindon.

On this occasion there were no football specials so the Millwall supporters travelled on regular service trains. There was a frequent service to the West Country in which many of the trains called at Swindon. On the outward journeys, and where possible, we arranged with the train operator for the fans to travel in designated coaches separated from the general travellers. This enabled us to police the trains more effectively. Because of the frequency of the service to Swindon, however, it meant that the Millwall supporters travelled in smaller numbers on various trains.

We had serials of officers ready to escort the trains and the forward journey passed off relatively peacefully. Further BTP officers were sent to Swindon station in readiness for the return traffic to London.

We had received reports from the local Wiltshire Police that they had encountered problems with the visitors during and after the match. The fans were escorted back to the railway station more or less en bloc, which caused us, and the train operator, problems with loading them onto the regular service trains. The London-bound trains originated their journeys in the West Country and South Wales, and so by the time of their arrival at Swindon they were exceedingly busy with ordinary passengers.

The Millwall supporters boarded one particular train, as I recall, and our resources were extremely stretched to monitor and control them throughout the eight-coach train. Almost immediately they were chanting obscenities and causing alarm among the ordinary travellers. It was a winter's night, during the hours of darkness, and the lights in the coaches were constantly being switched off, plunging passengers into total darkness and putting them in fear of their safety. In those days switches for lighting on the train were easily accessible in the vestibule of each coach.

It was a frightening experience for the many ordinary passengers to have to travel with such an unruly and threatening mob of fans. We were stretched to the limit in trying to keep order. We managed to radio ahead for assistance at Reading, being the next calling station. Thames Valley Police (TVP) had been alerted, and by extending their late-turn officers, and utilising their night duty, were able to provide us with a sizeable number of officers.

Thames Valley Police agreed with me that it was a better option all around for everybody, train operator, police and passengers, for the train to continue the half-hour journey to London with an enhanced police presence, rather than to try and eject a large core of troublemakers onto the streets of Reading late at night.

With the grateful help from TVP, we continued the journey to Paddington with officers positioned strategically throughout the train. I'm sure the genuine passengers appreciated the enhanced police presence and the train arrived into London with only minor incidents to report. A welcoming party of BTP and Met officers was on hand to assist and, along with the TVP officers, the Millwall fans were escorted back to South London by the Underground.

All that remained for us in BTP was to arrange transport by road for the dozen-or-so TVP officers to Reading police station after a job well done.

It was another eventful night by which to remember Millwall Football Club and their notorious unruly following.

On Wednesday 15 February 1995, a friendly international game was played at Lansdowne Road Stadium in Dublin between the Republic of Ireland and England. It was predicted by the UK National Criminal Intelligence Service that trouble would take place, and that's exactly what happened. Members of the neo-Nazi organisation Combat 18 created trouble in the ground and twenty people were injured.

The game attracted hundreds of travelling England fans, but one group didn't even make it past Holyhead railway station when fighting broke out between Huddersfield Town and Stoke City fans. Stena Sealink refused to allow the Huddersfield fans to board a ferry and they were escorted by police back onto a train.

800 English fans who did go to the game subsequently returned to the UK via ferries to Holyhead. The first set of fans came back on the night of the match, with the remainder travelling in smaller groups over a 24-hour period. As fifty officers from the British Transport Police and North Wales Police monitored them through Holyhead, many of them tried to hide their faces while others waved Union Jack flags. It was obvious that many of them had been fighting, with black eyes, bloodstained shirts and surgical dressings all on show.

In the main, the fans departed to other destinations peacefully after a very rough Irish Sea crossing had dampened their spirits, however as someone on the railway concourse shouted 'I thought Sealink had banned the transport of animals on their ships' one fan reacted and punched a photographer.

In 1996, a quarter of a million football fans were expected in the UK for the European Football Championships (Euro 96). With the first game scheduled for 8 June 1996, Chief Superintendent Geoff Griffiths took the lead role in overseeing BTP's planning. Inspector Paul Traies-Roffe was appointed as the force's international liaison officer, and a forward control point was established by BTP in the Police Nationale's premises at Lille Europe station. From there he would be tasked with establishing contact with the French and Belgian authorities in Lille, Paris and Brussels to identify booking travel patterns.

In addition, the Force Intelligence Unit was tasked with liaising with the dedicated football unit within the National Criminal

Intelligence Service, and officers were rostered to escort Eurostar service trains as required. Each of the eight venues for Euro 96 housed a police command centre and intelligence was exchanged via something called EPI, which was a secure electronic mail system. Ten 'photophones' were also provided to each of these centres, plus one to the co-ordinating centre in New Scotland Yard and one to the British Transport Police.

Keith Groves, who by now was a chief inspector in charge of operations for the BTP North East area, coordinated the rail movements of travelling fans from Sheffield, Leeds and Newcastle attending Euro 96 games. At this stage he was also the chair of the Football Intelligence Meeting for the area, which Dennis Temporal attended from time to time.

Dave Farrelly recalls,

During Euro 1996 England played a number of games that were plagued by disorder and violence, most of it taking place away from Wembley where the games were played. During one game I was posted to the West End of London, where large numbers of England fans had gathered outside of a variety of pubs. My serial was sent to Leicester Square Underground station. There was a group of several hundred fans both inside and outside the Porcupine Pub drinking. They were noisy, verbose, and aggressive towards another group of fans who had gathered on the opposite side of the street.

I deployed my resources to the centre of the road to keep both sides apart. I also called for some more reinforcements as it was clear to me there was insufficient resources to keep the groups apart if they decided to fight. We were joined by another BTP serial who reinforced the thin blue line.

There were various unsuccessful attempted incursions by the fans to get at each other. The irony for me was that all these fans were England supporters who, for some reason unknown to me, wanted to fight each other.

We maintained the peace, or near peace, for nearly an hour when we were relieved by the Metropolitan Police Territorial Support Group. We withdrew from the road and returned to the station. Within minutes the situation deteriorated in the street to bloody disorder. I immediately closed the station as running battles erupted. My officers wanted to assist but the Met officers had deployed in full riot gear, and outside bottles and glasses flew.

On re-opening the station the street was quiet and the road, and pavements, were covered in broken glass. The pub was closed and the Met Police and the hundreds of fans had gone. Given the amount of broken glass it was nothing short of miraculous that no one had been seriously injured.

In December 1997, planning for World Cup France 1998 stepped up a gear with an international seminar, which was held at BTP's training school in Tadworth, Surrey. French police officers attended, together with representatives from the Port of Dover Police, Kent Police and the Metropolitan Police, as well as officers from the UK Immigration Service, the National Criminal Intelligence Service and the Football Association.

Colleagues from the French railways, Eurostar and the Gatwick Express also participated in the discussions, as interpreters provided a simultaneous translation of the various presentations.

With plans by Eurostar to run twenty-six service trains a day to Lille, and Paris, there was plenty of scope for Scotland and England fans to reach the various qualifying round matches, and therefore a real prospect of BTP being busy with large-scale movements of supporters.

In February 1998, an opportunity arose for BTP to conduct a dry run when England played France in the Five Nations rugby, and 120 BTP officers escorted trains each day, for three days, with up to forty officers staying overnight in Paris for early return escorts the next day.

By April 1998 a dedicated BTP World Cup 98 Intelligence Unit had been established, which was headed by Detective Sergeant Bob Waller supported by four other police officers. DC Graham Naughton was seconded to the NCIS Football Unit for the duration of the games, and negotiations on a Memorandum of Understanding with French authorities, in relation to British Transport Police operating in France, were at an advanced stage.

Andy Fidgett recalls two other incidents that attracted violence,

I believe that it was in 1998 and Ipswich Town played Charlton at Portman Road. There had been minor trouble between the fans at the ground and we were looking to put the Charlton fans on a train after the match at 17.45 hours. This was a favourite train for BTP and Suffolk police to try to get away fans on. On this occasion I was at the front of what I believe was a nine-coach service, with another colleague, while two officers were at the rear. We had fans in the First Class coaches, which we intended to move as we got underway, but just as the train pulled out of the platform someone threw a fire extinguisher through the closed window of one of the First Class carriages. The person responsible was clearly aiming at an officer on the platform.

The train came to a stop and more officers were put on to escort the train. On arrival at Liverpool Street we were met by a large number of BTP officers and City of London Police, as well as dog units. Two arrests were made by other officers on the train, and I recall one of the prisoners had arms that were so big we couldn't get handcuffs on him, and one of the dog handlers suggested using two pairs!

On another occasion Ipswich Town played Norwich City in a local derby match, and I remember real violence with batons drawn, and used, with loads of fans fighting on the station, outside the station, and on the bridge over the river opposite the station. During the disorder, which we later referred to as the Battle of Burrell Road, a sergeant and myself believed for a time that we were going to finish up getting thrown in the river but decided that our chances were better as the tide was in. In the end we were rescued by a large number of Suffolk officers.

For six weeks from 7 June 1998 to 14 July 1998, the BTP were engaged in a complex policing operation for World Cup 98, with over 100 officers a day, drawn from all parts of the force, deployed to police international trains to France. Eurostar trains were ¼ mile long with two bars on board, which required constant, but sensitive, patrolling.

By this time, with the support of the British and French governments, a Memorandum of Understanding was signed and in place, which defined the role of the BTP for joint policing purposes with French police. BTP command posts were established in Paris by Inspector Bob Kenwrick and in Lille by Inspector Bob Squibb, which linked back to an operations room at Waterloo station.

As part of the overall strategy, Eurostar took the decision to ban passengers carrying alcohol on their trains during the World Cup. Where supporters were refused entry by French police, they were escorted back on trains by BTP officers. Over 450 trains were escorted during this period, with just four arrests being made as officers adopted a high-profile approach to nip antisocial behaviour in the bud at an early stage.

This was a unique policing operation for the BTP.

In September 1998, trouble flared between 200 Manchester United and Coventry fans travelling on the same train to separate fixtures in London, while in October 1998 Coventry supporters inflicted serious head injuries on a man in an unprovoked attack at Euston railway station. In November 1998, major disorder broke out on a train from London to Sheffield involving fans from Sheffield United, Chesterfield and Nottingham Forest, including offences of robbery and assaults on police officers. Serious disorder three months in a row clearly indicated the scale of the ongoing problems.

Retired Chief Superintendent Peter McHugh recalls how, in May 1999, football fans showed how incensed they could easily become,

> The Midland Metro was opened in this month, linking Wolverhampton with Birmingham, and BTP were contracted to provide policing on the new system. One of the tram stops was named The Hawthorns, due to its proximity to West Bromwich Albion's football ground. We received information from the local police that Wolverhampton fans were upset because there was no Molineux tram stop to recognise their club, and that disorder was going to take place as a form of protest. We finished up having to put a load of police officers there for a while until things quietened down.

In 1999 the BTP found themselves facing an increase in the movement of football fans, and sports fans in general, with a trend of increasing disorder. In the Midlands area, BTP officers reported an increase in problems with Leicester City fans. This was borne out on 17 July 1999, when Kettering played Leicester in a preseason friendly game. After the match, Kettering fans went to their local railway station and got involved in a confrontation with Leicester supporters. Fourteen fans were arrested and bailed.

In the North West area, Horwich Parkway station served the Bolton Wanderers ground and, during a visit in September 1999 by Manchester City, 300 fans confronted each other with just six BTP officers successfully keeping them apart.

Preston fans returning from England's game in Scotland in November 1999 turned the town centre into a battlefield. This culminated in a mass fight involving up to a hundred fans at 10.30 p.m. on Preston railway station. The fight was pre-arranged with groups from Preston, Wigan Athletic, Burnley and Manchester United all returning from the north, using mobile phones to arrange the confrontation.

The qualifying stages for Euro 2000 brought together Scotland and England for two games within a week in November 1999. Extensive BTP policing operations were put in place as Scotland played England at Hampden Park on a Saturday, with the return game being played at Wembley the following Wednesday. As part of these preparations, 250 BTP officers from England were sworn in under Scottish law to help escort fans travelling north, and to work on Scottish railway stations.

Dave Farrelly reflects on football policing at the end of this decade,

One of the key London derby matches is the Arsenal *versus* Spurs match. The games were always difficult to police with rival hardcore hooligans organising disorder weeks in advance of any game. All manner of tactics were tried by the football authorities to avert trouble at these matches. Early kick-offs, late kick-offs, all licensed premises being closed, strict segregation, holding away fans back until the home supporters had dispersed and disruption tactics were all attempted. Most games either started, or ended, with disorder or violence, and some had both. The otherwise small number of hooligans were swelled by other supporters at these emotional matches.

In the late 1990s I policed an Arsenal *versus* Spurs match. We had lots of intelligence about organised meetings for fights, and we spent the hours up to, and after, the game chasing shadows and disrupting disorder, some more successfully than others.

At a point in the early evening we were informed that a large group of Arsenal supporters had been cornered by the Metropolitan Police in a pub just outside Manor House Underground station. As the inspector of a serial consisting of ten officers, we went by train to the station and met with our colleagues outside the pub. On arrival, the Met officers had blocked the pubs main doors by backing up a police van to the doors, to stop anyone entering or leaving the pub. The other doors, windows and fire exits were all guarded by uniformed police officers to prevent entry or egress.

According to the Arsenal spotters, there were a couple of hundred organised hooligan elements inside the pub. They were singing, and shouting and drinking, and occasionally they would push forward at a door, or window, in order to challenge the artificial blockade.

We had been there about ten minutes when contact between Arsenal and Spurs police spotters warned us that there were several hundred Spurs hooligans marching towards the tube station and the pub. It would appear that a large-scale fight had been organised. Immediately, we began to call for back up and support on our radios as it was clear we had only a few minutes to avert serious disorder, in which we would be in the middle. The Met Police officers, numbering about eight, held the Arsenal fans in the pub. We began to prepare for the arrival of the Spurs fans.

We were then given the devastating news that the Met Police TSG and the football serials that had policed the game, and the streets around, had all been stood down. This news was compounded by the fact that the traffic had now ceased to run and the information was that the Spurs hooligan fans were moving en masse towards us, blocking the whole road.

We continued to call for assistance but units had been tied up with another event in central London, and it was a busy Saturday evening. I prepared my officers by pairing them up, and pairing the two female officers with my largest and strongest male officer. I told them to keep together and we would do all we could to stop the Spurs fans getting into the pub. The Met officers agreed to keep the Arsenal fans inside as best they could. At this point the Spurs fans could now be seen. I was honestly expecting a blood bath, and believed that we would all be waking up the next day in hospital. I was truly frightened for myself, and all of my colleagues.

At this point two dog vans arrived in answer to our call for assistance. They quickly deployed with four dogs and four handlers. They came to me and asked me what the plan was as I was the senior officer. The honest truth was that my plan was based on survival. I asked them if they were prepared to deploy across the road, with ten of us behind them, and that we would move forward to intercept the fans before they got to the pub. Enthusiasm for my plan was not great but I explained that it would put distance between the two groups of fans, and that we would only have to fight on one front, so long as the Met officers kept the Arsenal fans in the pub.

One dog handler tried to talk me out of this, as it was not a Home Office approved use of police dogs in such a public order situation. I pointed out that no official from the Home Office was present and we were about to be beaten senseless by a mob. Reluctantly, they agreed and we deployed as described with the four dogs on long leashes barking and snapping aggressively, and ten uninformed officer behind them, bearing their truncheons, as we walked towards the mob several hundred in strength.

I was convinced that this tactic would fail but it was better in my mind to try and do something rather than nothing. As we approached the Spurs hooligans, and without warning, every one of them stopped, and to a man they turned and ran back. No one was more surprised than I was. I was clearly not alone and the four dog's handlers and my officers started to chase after them. I was forced to call them back just in case the Spurs hooligans changed their minds. The whole event ended well and quite suddenly. The only casualty was an elderly male who was injured when the hooligans turned and ran. Nobody was after medals for bravery that day. We were all pleased to go home in the same way we had arrived.

Again in the late 1990s, Dave Farrelly recalls another brush with Tottenham fans,

> While policing a Tottenham *versus* West Ham London derby, I was posted with a group of officers to Seven Sisters station. We were called to a mainline train containing West Ham fans. The fans were intent on leaving the train to confront Tottenham fans, and when it arrived we got onto the train and prevented a large number of West Ham fans from getting off. We closed the automatic doors and held the train while I, as the police serial commander, talked to the train driver and his control. My officers were posted to each carriage to prevent disorder. I wanted the train to go non-stop into Liverpool Street station to prevent the hooligans getting into a confrontation with the Spurs hooligan element.
>
> Arranging a non-stop order took several minutes. Once it was agreed the train started to move off, only to be stopped by the application of a passenger alarm in one of the carriages after travelling about ten metres. Police and the train driver started to search the train to detect which emergency passenger alarm had been operated, and as soon as it was found it was reset.
>
> Almost immediately the train came under a hail of missiles from the opposite platform and the windows on the train began to smash and cover the West Ham fans with glass. They started to punch out the broken windows and verbally abuse the Spurs hooligans who were throwing objects at us. Neither the fans on the train nor us police officers on the train were able to escape as the train was partly outside of the station, and the carriages were not wholly aligned with the platform. I got into the drivers cab and convinced the driver that we needed to move now! More passenger emergency alarms were activated, and I told the driver to move the train immediately, and to contact his control to ensure that we could get the train into Liverpool Street station without any delay.
>
> This was done, and as we moved off again the West Ham element on the train became very angry and aggressive. They tried in vain to stop the train by operating passenger alarms, and breaking the already cracked and shattered windows. It felt like a long journey and I called for assistance at Liverpool Street station

to meet and escort these fans out of the station on our arrival. After what seemed like an age we arrived to be greeted by about thirty police officers and police dogs. Despite the police presence the hooligans still kept trying to break away from the police.

The train was a complete mess and it was taken out of service, costing hundreds of pounds to clean and replace the windows. Hostilities continued in north-east London until about 9.30 p.m. that night, such was the animosity and venom between the organised hooligan groups.

Keith Fleetwood also recalls an incident with Millwall during this period,

When policing Millwall at home, one of the stations policed by the BTP is South Bermondsey mainline station, which is in view of the Millwall ground. The station comprised a narrow island platform with stairs and a slope leading down to the street. The position of the platforms gave a view of the ground, and at the conclusion of the game a clear view of home and away supporters could be had, normally under escort.

On one occasion the game finished and the away supporters appeared in the road, closely followed by Millwall supporters, but with no Met Police officers. Effectively a running battle started as soon as all the supporters entered the road. As the fighting drew nearer we knew that once the supporters entered the station there would be no escape routes.

We allowed the platform to fill with the away fans. Four of the six officers then took up position at the narrowest point on the approach to the platform, standing back to back, between the two groups of fans. It was a 'stand-off' that seemed to go on forever. Thankfully the restricted access worked to our advantage in other ways with many of the missiles being thrown by the Millwall supporters actually hitting their own fans at the front.

Suddenly the Millwall supporters disappeared just as though a plug had been pulled when the Met Police officers eventually arrived in the road outside. Since this time, a subway has been built from the ground under the railway line, making the process of managing supporters far easier.

10

A NEW CENTURY – NO CHANGE

Dave Farrelly again takes up the story,

In 2000, Peterborough United played Darlington at the old Wembley Stadium for the Division Three play-offs. The match meant that tens of thousands of fans from both clubs would travel through Kings Cross station. I was the sector commander at that station. The day started badly with early violent and disorderly clashes between rival supporters, and this carried on throughout the build up to the evening kick-off. The return after the game to Kings Cross station, and their train's home, was more controlled. We had deployed officers along the route and officers travelled on trains to Kings Cross station.

Once back at Kings Cross station, the games of cat-and-mouse began with small groups of rival hooligans hiding among genuine supporters and family groups. BTP spotters were in place, monitoring the activities of the small number of hardcore hooligan organisers who orchestrated and organised fights and confrontation. While we were stretched, we managed to contain any disorder.

Until, at one stage, I was standing in the centre of the concourse when I recognised the man standing beside me as being the leader of the Peterborough organised hooligan group. He was alone. I walked up to him and engaged him in conversation calling him by his first name even though I had never met him before.

At this point another male supporter ran up to him and I saw much to my surprise that this was the leader of the Darlington organised hooligan group. I smiled at him and addressed him by his first name and the three of us engaged in a bizarre but civilised conversation about the game and the fact that these hooligan elements had been running us ragged all day.

Both men were not youths but mature males, who were well spoken and intelligent. The conversation ended with a shake of the hands between all three of us and me pointing out to them that this was a better way to behave. They both laughed and walked off to their respective last trains out of Kings Cross. They waved me, the football spotters, and the officers standing on the concourse farewell. It was clear that hooliganism was as much a game to them as the game itself.

Chief Inspector Neil Moffatt retired from the force in 2015, having worked in the north-west of the country for the entirety of his career. When you work in an area that houses Manchester United, Manchester City, Liverpool and Everton, you will have worked hundreds of major football duties throughout your career, and this is certainly true in Neil's case. However, he pointed out on many occasions when discussing football policing that it was not always the supporters from the most famous and fashionable clubs that caused problems.

In the 1999/00 season, Stoke City were playing in the third tier of football but still drew reasonable crowds and had an element within their supporter group that could cause trouble. They were known as the Naughty Forty. That season the club reached the final of the Football League Trophy (Auto Windscreens Shield), with the match being played at Wembley Stadium on 16 April 2000.

Supporters of the big clubs would probably scoff at this particular competition, but those that follow the smaller clubs will know that a day out at Wembley is a big deal! This was actually the last Football League Trophy final to be played at the stadium before it was closed for redevelopment. Their opponents were Bristol City and Stoke City won the match 2-1. BTP were running an operation for the return journey back to Stoke including passenger screening, revenue protection, and travelling football serials, which were all standard tactics for this type of operation.

Neil describes what happened in his own words,

From 6 p.m. onwards, Euston station saw significant numbers of Stoke City supporters who were understandably in a jubilant mood. The trains going back to Staffordshire were loaded up with fans and travelling BTP serials were deployed, in line with the football plan that had been devised for the event. Trains departed direct for Stoke at 6 p.m., 7 p.m. and 8 p.m. and all left without any problems. These return journeys to Stoke were lively but without incident. After 8 p.m., only two services remained that would have been carrying football supporters; the 9 p.m. direct service to Stoke, and the 10 p.m. service that would have involved onward travel from Crewe. BTP resources from the North West area that remained in Euston to cover these last two trains consisted of one sergeant and six constables.

As the 9 p.m. departure was about to leave, I sent three constables to escort the train. This left myself and three constables waiting for the final service from Euston that the fans from Stoke could use. As we patrolled Euston, information was received from colleagues in the Metropolitan Police that around eighty Stoke City supporters were drinking in a pub along Euston Road, and were becoming disorderly and difficult to manage. This group included the self-styled Naughty Forty Stoke City hooligan element.

At 9.55 p.m., or thereabouts, this group entered Euston intent on catching the 10 p.m. train to Crewe. They were drunk, non-compliant, rude, obnoxious, and generally carried a lack of respect for any figure of authority and the public at large. Although the train was a dry service with no alcohol allowed to be carried, this was largely irrelevant as the damage had already done in pubs in London, so to speak. A number of the group were denied access to the train and prevented from travelling due to their behaviour, but this seemed to antagonise the remaining fans and as the train departed the station with me and my three colleagues on board as a travelling serial, officers at Euston arrested two of the supporters who had not been allowed to travel.

I remember BTP had recently issued stab vests and side-handled batons to their uniformed officers and the sight of such items was still something of a novelty. During the journey, myself and my three colleagues suffered a tirade of abuse which included threats to test the new stab vests with knives and guns. Several suggestions were made that involved sexual activity with the officers' partners and cannabis smoke was clearly present in various parts of the train. The supporters also openly boasted about the use of cocaine.

This was turning into a very difficult train escort duty! Our response was to separate the football supporters from the bona-fide passengers in an attempt to minimise the impact of their unacceptable behaviour. We also supported the staff on the train, and closed the buffet, to avoid further confrontation as no alcohol was going to be sold. We searched several of their number for drugs and maintained a constant physical presence in the two carriages where these fans were seated.

During the journey I telephoned control and arranged for a reception committee at Crewe to include prisoner transport as a number of the supporters would be coming in. I briefed the travelling constables to pick one of the worst offenders each and to get the offence and exact details of their conduct clear in their minds for the custody sergeant at Crewe. This is sometimes difficult when a large number of people are involved, and clever defence solicitors can make great play of the fact that very specific detail of the conduct of their individual client was missing.

As the train arrived at Crewe station, BTP and Cheshire Constabulary officers were in attendance on the platform. Having picked one each, four of the main offenders were arrested for drunkenness, disorderly conduct and threatening behaviour offences.

As the prisoners were being escorted to the awaiting transport, the remaining fans attempted to free those who we had arrested. This carried on and they even attempted to overturn the prisoner van outside Crewe station. On arrival at the custody suite and now out of the comfort of the big group, I noticed that two of the arrested supporters had started to cry! I think this demonstrates how the pack mentality of football fans can sometimes make individuals behave, when in a group, in a way that they never would if they were on their own.

Following completion of our lengthy statements, all four were charged and sent before magistrates at Crewe Magistrates Court. The town of Crewe has strong community links with the railways, and many of its populace work, or have a family member who work, for the railway industry. This point was driven home to me weeks later when I rang the BTP prosecutions office for the result of the court hearing and was told ninety days, forty-eight days and two lots of twenty-eight days imprisonment for the four offenders. Justice was done!

On 15 July 2000, seventy Aberdeen fans arrived at Newcastle, by coach, and then travelled by train to Hartlepool for a preseason friendly game. At the railway station fights took place, which continued after the match until BTP and local officers managed to herd them back onto a train.

On 21 July 2000, a group of sixty Dundee fans arrived at Cleethorpes railway station for a game with Grimsby, and disorder occurred with local fans. BTP and Humberside Police intervened to disperse the group, and later fighting involved up to 200 people.

During the summer, the Euro 2000 tournament once again tested BTP planning as officers were engaged in policing across three European countries. Using a video briefing system called Forcelink, BTP were able to take video stills of fans departing Waterloo International and share them with other BTP resources. Thirty-eight people were denied entrance to Belgium as a result of information passed by BTP, which accounted for two thirds of those refused entry.

On 5 August 2000, forty Plymouth fans attended Exeter on the pretext of a birthday party. They were then joined by forty Everton fans, who arrived by train, for a preseason friendly with Exeter, and disturbances took place on the railway station. Shortly afterwards a group of Exeter fans turned up and further fighting ensued, resulting in BTP officers calling for urgent assistance.

Also on 5 August 2000, Leeds fans travelling to Huddersfield were attacked on arrival at the railway station. In a sinister development, the Huddersfield fans made it clear that they would attack BTP officers at every opportunity. It was a day when batons were drawn, and police dogs deployed, at regular intervals to quell disturbances.

On 19 August 2000, seventy Huddersfield Town supporters left Sheffield en route to Huddersfield. The train had to pass through Barnsley railway station, and on arrival a group of Barnsley fans standing on the platform kicked out at train doors. BTP officers travelling on the train kept the two sides apart before the train departed. However, at the next stop thirty of the Huddersfield fans got off and travelled back to Barnsley, where they got involved in fighting, and one of them was knocked unconscious.

On 26 August 2000, two BTP dog handlers found themselves holding the line between two groups of opposing fans numbering more than a hundred. Sergeant Tom Goodyear, with police dog Barney, and his colleague Maurice Stanford, with police dog Jac, were the only thing separating the two factions, who were intent on fighting each other. Despite having missiles thrown at them they stood their ground until help arrived.

On 11 September 2000, 150 Swansea fans travelled by train to London and made their way to London Bridge for a game with Millwall. After the match serious disorder took place outside South Bermondsey station, where Millwall fans threw bricks, bottles, pieces of wood, and scaffold posts at police officers. The Swansea group were escorted to Victoria station, where one of them let off a CS gas canister. They were eventually escorted back to Wales, but on arrival at Cardiff they tried to disembark at the railway station to confront local fans. BTP officers were deployed, with batons drawn, and one arrest was made.

On 23 September 2000, twenty Walsall fans made their way back to Wrexham railway station following a match. Twenty Wrexham fans then ran onto the station and a fight ensued, during which the glass panels to the front doors were smashed. Two BTP officers placed themselves between the two groups and two arrests were made.

On the same day 125 Burnley fans, including five risk supporters, got on a train to Huddersfield. They got off the train at Halifax looking for a confrontation, but police were waiting for them.

On 1 October 2000, 150 Manchester United fans travelled to London by train and, after the game with Arsenal, were involved in violence. They were eventually put back on a train at Euston but fifty of them subsequently got off at Watford, where they caused problems before catching the last train back. On the train passengers were abused, sprayed with fire extinguishers and two females indecently assaulted.

On 7 October 2000, England played Germany at Wembley Stadium in a World Cup qualifier. It was to be the last game at the stadium before renovations began. Ninety BTP officers were on duty to monitor some 50,000 fans passing through Wembley Park station, with a Public Order Support Unit on standby.

Inspector Alex Carson was the officer in charge at the station, with experience of policing twenty-five events at the location in 2000 alone. Up to an hour before kick-off the mood among fans was that of a family atmosphere, but as hardened drinkers left it to the last minute to get to the match the mood changed and the visible police presence was necessary to keep good order.

After the game up to five sets of supporters, from different domestic clubs, tried to fight each other outside St Pancras station, resulting in two arrests. On a train from London to Birmingham, nine BTP officers battled to contain trouble between travelling Aston Villa and Birmingham City fans, and two people were injured. In a further incident there was a minor disturbance on a train at Warrington. Eleven arrests were made in all, of which nine were English, and two German.

On 14 October 2000, thirty Stockport fans returning from their fixture in Burnley made their way to Blackburn to drink until closing time. They then made their way back to the railway station, where they started fighting with passengers. Police attended and arrested four of the group for assault and public order offences.

On 21 October 2000, Millwall played at Stoke and large numbers travelled by train. There was trouble at the ground and the Millwall fans were the subject of a heavy police escort all the way back to the railway station as officers attempted to keep the two factions apart.

On 28 October 2000, a group of West Ham fans tried to attack Newcastle fans while travelling on the Tube network. As police intervened to keep the groups apart they smashed fittings on the train, and four arrests were made.

On the same date, Millwall fans attacked other youths at London Bridge station, resulting in one of them being thrown onto the track, which had a live rail.

On 18 November 2000, a group of thirty Burton fans were escorted to Kidderminster railway station, where they were attacked on the station platforms by local fans, resulting in two arrests.

On the same date thirty-five Oxford fans, some of whom already had banning orders, travelled by train to Macclesfield for their FA Cup match. On the return journey they got off at Stoke and were drinking in the station buffet when they were attacked by fifty Stoke fans. Serious damage was caused in the attack, and one BTP officer badly assaulted.

On 9 December 2000, a group of Newcastle fans travelling back from London attacked a male passenger and his two children, one of whom was threatened with a broken bottle. One of the group was subsequently arrested.

On 30 December 2000 more than 200 Manchester United fans travelled on the rail network for a game at Newcastle. At Huddersfield and Castleford stations, twenty-two fans were ejected from trains for disorderly behaviour and ticket offences. On the return, at 7.25 p.m., fifteen Manchester United fans entered the buffet on York station and stole a quantity of alcohol.

In 2001, Peter McHugh got promoted to chief inspector and recalls,

I got posted from Birmingham, where football was manic, especially during games between Birmingham, West Bromwich, Villa and Wolverhampton, to Cardiff. I quietly congratulated myself that I would now only have to worry about Cardiff and Swansea when I discovered that the Millennium Stadium had signed a contract with the English FA to hold all their events there while Wembley was being rebuilt.

Suddenly I was facing the prospect of policing travelling fans for football, rugby, and speedway in a 74,500 seated stadium which was no more than a few hundred yards from the railway station. It was not unusual for us to get 35,000 people travelling to the venue by train, due to its close proximity, and I soon became an expert on crowd control.

On 20 January 2001 a group of Newcastle fans got off a train at Leeds railway station and went into the bar on the concourse.

The bar was then attacked by a group of Leeds fans, and a fire extinguisher and bar table were thrown through the bar windows before police restored order.

On 7 February 2001, a disturbance took place on the platforms at Huddersfield railway station between local supporters and Nottingham Forest supporters, as missiles were thrown.

On 17 February 2001 a group of Nottingham Forest fans, travelling back on a train from London after their game with Fulham, began abusing passengers on the train. They then began damaging fittings, and during the disturbances a serious indecent assault was made on the female train manager. Police met the train at Loughborough and five people were arrested for public order offences and indecent assault.

On 20 February 2001, after the match between Bury and Stoke City was called off thirty drunken Stoke fans boarded a train at Manchester Piccadilly. The group became aggressive towards police officers at Macclesfield station and officers needed to draw batons to control them.

On 16 May 2001, two men were arrested at Edinburgh Waverley station in possession of £700 in forged banknotes. This followed a testimonial game in Scotland when large amounts of forged notes were circulated in Glasgow.

On Saturday 14 July 2001, five people needed hospital treatment after violence erupted, involving up to forty football fans at Chorley railway station between Blackburn and Bolton supporters. One group of twenty started throwing stones and bricks across the platforms at another group before engaging in close-quarters fighting, raining punches and kicks on each other. The five people were taken to Chorley hospital with various injuries, including a broken nose and a fractured skull. BTP officers made four arrests.

On 4 August 2001, prior to a game with Tottenham Hotspur, members of Millwall's hooligan group gathered near to Bermondsey station to engage in the ritual spotting exercise, looking for members of the opposition.

Retired Sergeant Bill Rogerson reflects on his last train escort,

On Sunday 12 August 2001, the Charity Shield was played in Cardiff between Liverpool and Manchester United. I escorted a train from Holyhead to Cardiff and return. This was to be my last football duty as I was going on leave the following week, prior to retirement in September.

On the return leg there was a fan who was an absolute nuisance. He was dealt with for disorderly conduct and ejected at Hereford. On the station platform he told me that he would be reporting me and said that he would have my job. I had great pleasure informing him that he could have it as I was retiring. That shut him up.

Wales & West Trains, and Central Trains, circulated a leaflet before that match saying, 'Customers are reminded that rowdiness, the singing of adult songs, or the over indulgence of alcohol can be frightening and offensive to others ...' Clearly this fan had not got the message.

On 19 August 2001, a large police operation was mounted in Birmingham for the arrival of visiting Millwall fans. Intelligence suggested that a pre-arranged confrontation had been arranged with Birmingham City's Zulu Warriors.

The sheer scale of police numbers prevented disorder on the journey to Birmingham City's ground from New Street station, but on their return to the station the Millwall fans were attacked and running battles took place. The situation was complicated by the arrival of Wolverhampton's hooligan group, who arrived back at New Street station at the same time, on their way back from a match with Coventry.

On 22 September 2001, fighting broke out at a station when a train carrying Everton fans pulled into a platform where Liverpool and Tottenham supporters were queuing, and police had to draw batons to separate opposing fans.

On 31 October 2001, some 250 Millwall fans went by train to Wolverhampton. On arrival at the railway station they broke through police lines and attacked a nearby pub occupied by members of the Wolverhampton hooligan element known as the Subway Army.

On 3 November 2001, Luton Town fans, known as the Migs, made their way back from Mansfield after a match. A group of them left a train at Leicester and ambushed thirty members of Leicester City's Baby Squad at the station. Police had to draw batons to break up the fight.

On 17 November 2001, a police officer was injured while trying to separate fans at Sheffield Midland railway station when fighting broke out between West Bromwich fans returning from Rotherham and Birmingham fans on one of the platforms.

On 24 November 2001, a train carrying Brighton & Hove Albion fans to Swindon was vandalised to such an extent that it had to be taken out of service. The fans were put on a replacement train, which in turn was also vandalised.

Peter McHugh recalls a match on Sunday 6 January 2002,

It was an FA Cup game at Ninian Park in Cardiff between Cardiff City and Leeds United. We were not expecting any fans from Leeds by train, but 200 went by coach to Hereford railway station at 9 a.m. in the morning, and then caught a train into Cardiff. They were escorted to the ground as Cardiff fans constantly tried to ambush them. Sam Hammam was the chairman of Cardiff FC at the time and he went round the touchline encouraging the Cardiff team and fans. This did not go down well with the Leeds fans.

At the end of the game there was a pitch invasion and police in riot gear, and police dogs, were deployed to keep the two sides apart. BTP provided support at the ground and in the media the next day was a picture of BTP dog handler Paul Morse with his dog on the pitch. Eventually, with BTP support, the Leeds fans were 'bubbled' all the way back to Cardiff railway station and put on a train.

On 9 January 2002, one man was stabbed in a fight between Chelsea and Tottenham fans outside Kensington Tube station in London and, subsequently, a small group of Tottenham fans attacked Chelsea fans at Victoria railway station, in what was believed to be a revenge attack.

On 9 February 2002, a small group of Aston Villa fans attacked Chelsea fans at a station in Birmingham, and later in the day a racially motivated attack was carried out by Chelsea fans returning by train to London.

Keith Fleetwood recalls another Millwall game,

On 9 March 2002, for the first time in many years, Portsmouth and Millwall met, both having reputations to live up to. The outward journey passed without incident but from the very start of the game Hampshire Police were under a great deal of pressure, with problems in the ground and in the city centre. BTP had three sections led by Chief Inspector Randy Otter, Inspector Carl Foulkes, and myself.

We each allocated officers to remain at Fratton railway station and at the conclusion of the game posted them between the stadium and station using our dog handlers and officers to separate and control the supporters approach to the station. I policed the main approach from the ground to the station and, upon receiving information with regard to the numbers at the station, used my section to hold the Millwall supporters away in the main road, using dog handlers to hold the Portsmouth supporters away in the side streets.

The Millwall supporters were addressed in the most basic of terms as to what would happen if they moved further towards the station. I was aware of a Hampshire senior officer standing nearby. It was not until the conclusion of the operation that I realised it was their assistant chief constable. He later wrote to our chief constable with regard to the BTP's assistance stating that Hampshire Police came close to breaking point without our assistance.

On 13 April 2002, a fight occurred at Maze Hill station in Greenwich, south-east London, between Charlton and Southampton fans, which left three men in hospital. The brief but violent fight happened on the platform of the station when about fifteen Southampton fans arrived off a train and clashed with about thirty Charlton fans.

The group of fans from Southampton, outnumbered and mostly younger and in their twenties, were left nursing injuries as they were showered with bottles by the more experienced Charlton gang, numbering some thirty individuals. They had arranged to meet at the station 1 hour before the kick-off of the Premier League fixture at Charlton's Valley Ground, and chose Maze Hill because it was two stops away from the station served by the ground and unlikely to be policed.

In common with many incidents of this type, the actual fight was over in minutes, and those responsible had all left the scene by the time the police had arrived. Their undoing was that the whole incident, which became known as 'The Battle of Maze Hill', was captured on CCTV and the British Transport Police commenced the methodical process of identifying suspects.

After the fight, both sides congratulated each other for a 'good day out' on the internet. Unwittingly, they were providing additional evidence of their wrongdoing for the police to put before the courts. One Charlton fan wrote, 'Fair play to the group that got off at Maze Hill. Don't worry about the result. At least you bothered to get off despite knowing there'd be no Old Bill about.'

Twenty people were arrested during dawn raids in October 2002 after warrants were executed at twenty-two addresses in Hampshire and London. More than 150 officers from the British Transport Police, Metropolitan Police and Hampshire Police took part in the raids, and computers and mobile phones were seized.

Fifteen men were originally charged with conspiracy to commit violent disorder, and a further four individuals were charged subsequently.

Analysis of computer email records provided evidence that the fight had been pre-arranged between members of the two groups.

At Kingston Crown Court, eighteen months later, seven football fans were jailed for conspiracy to commit violent disorder, and were all issued with six-year football banning orders. Ten other defendants had already received jail terms and banning orders, which resulted in overall sentencing of thirty-eight years in prison for the group as a whole.

In passing sentences of up to four years on the seven, Judge Fergus Mitchell said, 'passengers, including children, had fled in fear as the mob rampaged through the station throwing bottles.'

One of those arrested, a thirty-seven-year-old, was a married father and employed as a history schoolteacher in Birmingham. He used the pseudonym of Three Lions, a reference to the England teams badge, to converse with, and taunt, opposing fans online on a US-based internet site, as well as by mobile phone. He was not actually present at the fight but admitted organising it and was sentenced to two years and three months imprisonment, being described in court by the Judge as the 'Bedroom General.' A number of the defendants frequented England games and it was believed that they had been planning to attend the Euro 2004 Championships in Portugal. The banning orders played their part in preventing some from doing so.

Speaking after the sentencing, Superintendent Colum Price from the British Transport Police said,

> Our experience of football hooliganism over the last two years is that it has become more organised and the violence more intense. We have devoted increasing resources to policing football fans, and have a good record of pre-empting disorder through good intelligence, and the timely deployment of officers to escort trains and cover stations.

On 21 April 2002, Sheffield United hooligans, known as the Blades Business Crew, tried to ambush Wolverhampton supporters on Sheffield railway station and a number of arrests were made.

Peter McHugh recalls another match during his days at Cardiff,

> On 13 May 2002, the Welsh Cup final took place at Ninian Park between Cardiff and Swansea. The attendance was just over 6,000, so in terms of numbers you would not have expected there to be trouble, but hooliganism was not about numbers, it was about behaviour. Cardiff and Swansea fans shared an intense dislike of each other, which routinely led to incidents of violence. Cardiff shared this dislike with Bristol City fans and violence also often occurred when so-called Severnside Derbies took place.
>
> At the end of the game the two sets of fans threw bricks and bottles at each other. I was a chief inspector at the time and deployed at Ninian Park Halt station, near to the ground, with a Public Order Unit in full riot gear. As I watched events unfold, with a police helicopter overhead, lighting up the area, I was conscious that there were mounted police officers everywhere. At this point I was struck on the head by a stone. Fortunately my helmet deflected the blow. Next day I had my promotion board for superintendent.

For the 2001/02 season, the National Criminal Intelligence Service recorded eighty-one serious football-related incidents as having occurred within the railway environment.

On Saturday 23 February 2003, a football fan, believed to be a Manchester United fan from Wigan, was left fighting for his life in the neurosurgical unit at the Royal Preston Hospital after a fight between football fans on Chorley railway station.

After initial surgery he was placed on a life support machine in the hospital's intensive care unit, where his condition was described as poor. The forty-six-year-old man suffered severe facial injuries, some of which later required reconstructive surgery, during the incident, which occurred at about 7 p.m. and involved up to ten people.

Sergeant Steve Murtagh told the media, 'There was a fight among a number of people who had been to the football match between Bolton Wanderers and Manchester United at the Reebok Stadium ...'

Two other men were taken to hospital after sustaining cuts and bruises, and required stitches after three men were knocked to the ground and kicked repeatedly.

Three men were initially arrested in connection with the attack and detained for questioning at police stations in Lancashire, and BTP Detective Chief Inspector Alistair Cumming took charge of the investigation. Five further arrests followed as CCTV images were released of a number of men climbing over a wall at the station into Clifford Street.

In a twist to the investigation, it was found that a key piece of CCTV evidence of the incident had been accidentally wiped when officers and rail staff were initially trying to view the material. Instead of pressing play, the record button on the video machine was pressed which overwrote the images. However, the tape and the video recorder were sent to the FBI Headquarters in Virginia, USA, where scientists were able to restore the images from what was effectively a blank tape.

Ten people subsequently pleaded guilty to violent disorder at Preston Crown Court following this incident, when Judge Michael Evans said, 'It is a tragic example of what can happen when otherwise respectable people have been inebriated by excessive amounts of alcohol and are carried away by herd instinct and pack mentality.' The main victim was still unable to walk without the aid of a walking stick, and needed extensive surgery to a damaged eye socket and torn ear.

On 26 February 2003, Bolton railway station was the scene of a large-scale fight when up to a hundred Bolton fans poured out of local pubs to confront sixty Manchester United fans. Rail staff cowered behind counters as the two groups charged at each other, and the station floors and walls were left spattered with blood. Twelve arrests were made, including one for possession of an offensive weapon, and one person was taken to hospital with a head injury.

Peter McHugh again recalls an incident at Cardiff on 2 March 2003,

> Manchester United were playing Liverpool and there were problems in St Mary Street and the city centre, as they mixed in with Cardiff fans on a Saturday evening. We had one Public Order Unit, which we had already been asked to deploy to support South Wales Police. We had another two PSUs travelling up from London to support an event on the Sunday. They had already worked a full day but on arrival the local police asked us to deploy them as well as things were so bad. Suddenly they found themselves policing Cardiff city centre.

On Saturday 5 April 2003, a 250-strong mob of Swansea fans, on their way home from a match at Shrewsbury, wrecked a train at Cardiff railway station and fought with police. Windows were smashed on the First Great Western train, which had to be taken out of service as damage valued at £10,000 was caused to two carriages. The trouble erupted when Swansea fans, arriving by train at Cardiff, caught sight of local fans on the platforms and tried to confront them. Two arrests for public order offences and criminal damage were made as several BTP officers suffered facial injuries after being attacked. Dog handlers and officers from South Wales Police were called in to back them up as order was finally restored.

Detective Inspector Malcolm McKinnon, from the BTP at Cardiff, set up an incident room staffed by eight officers under an operation code-named Thunderbird and CCTV footage was examined in detail in an effort to make further arrests. Ten football banning orders were subsequently obtained for periods of three to six years. The investigation was part-funded by the government-led initiative into football hooliganism leading up to Euro 2004 in Portugal.

In 2004, BTP had thirty-two active football banning orders in place in Wales with five cases pending.

Paul Nicholas QPM, retired assistant chief constable with BTP, reflects on his involvement in trying to address the problem known in BTP circles as 'football dumping'. Paul recalls,

In 2004 a complete re-write of the ACPO Public Order Manual of Guidance covering standards, tactics, and training took place. Published within it was a large section covering tactics for the railways, including the removal of demonstrators from trains, railway station clearance, carriage containment or diversion, violent persons on railways and the use of incapacitant spray on stations and trains. Reference was also made to the need to consider the guidance alongside individual force 'Rail Safety Agreements' and other Association of Chief Police Officers guidelines.

While liaison between BTP and local police forces relating to the movement of large groups of football supporters by train had been improving over a number of years, a growing problem in the 1990s, and early 2000s, known as 'football dumping', had become more and more prevalent.

Some of these occasions involved local police rounding up drunken or disorderly fans around the town centres, prior to the games kick-off, in order to take them to the railway station, with the intention of requiring them to leave the locality via next available train services. Notwithstanding their condition or behaviour, many hadn't even arrived by train in the first place, and had no valid tickets to travel, yet they were being presented to staff at the station with a police direction to allow them to travel, just to get rid of them as soon as possible.

Frequently, BTP had no prior knowledge, or were only present in small numbers to cope with this unplanned influx, facing the choice of either leaving their allocated duty in order to travel with the fans, in the interests of safety and convenience of other passengers, or to allow the train to leave unescorted due to a reluctance of the local police to permit their own officers to supplement the meagre resources of BTP at the time; a less than ideal situation.

This particular problem would also manifest itself at the end of matches as well, and was clearly illustrated to me on one occasion during a local derby game between Southampton and Portsmouth, which was played at Southampton. On this occasion the local police decided to kettle the Portsmouth fans and to take them en masse under the supervision of a Public Order Support Unit to Southampton Central station, whether or not they had intended to travel by train!

I can recall being the duty chief officer at the time and, being aware of the particular reputation for disorder that this derby game was renowned for, I decided to attend the return phase to observe things for myself.

The returning fans were forced onto Portsmouth-bound trains, some were rattling car keys or waving a bus ticket at the escorting officers, in an attempt to indicate that they hadn't used the trains to get to Southampton in the first place. Many didn't even want to travel in the direction of Portsmouth, and many had no valid train tickets at all. On this occasion, however, I was able to make representations resulting in significant numbers of local police officers being permitted to supplement the police escort with officers in every carriage to deter unruly behaviour.

In London, during this period, very similar events were taking place, particularly around London Underground stations that directly served some of the nearby football stadia. I can recall Superintendent Micky Joyce regularly taking a very tough stance with his Metropolitan Police counterparts, directing the closure of these stations until agreement was reached for their orderly access to the station under joint police escorting arrangements.

Similar reports were coming in at the time from other parts of the country too, so clearly something more formal needed to be put into place on a national basis to resolve this issue. Fortunately, at the time I was a member of the ACPO Public Order Sub Committee, and was able to raise concerns and to put examples on the table at one of our regular meetings. All present agreed that improvements needed to be made in respect of joint planning for football fixtures that involved large numbers of supporters converging at railway stations.

Richard Jones, who was a chief inspector in the BTP special constabulary at Cardiff, recalls an incident he was present at where eight BTP officers, led by Sergeant Dave Carter, formed a line between fifty hardcore Cardiff hooligans and Wolverhampton fans, and stood their ground.

Richard worked on a number of football-related duties and recalls another incident,

We were taking Cardiff City to Wembley for one of the FA Cup play-offs. On the return journey we were on a special train and I was in First Class. Now this train was something else, it must have been one of the first 125 demonstrator carriages, it was 70s plush with wood and mirrors.

Halfway through the journey I could smell burning and saw smoke in the middle of the carriage where I found four drunken City fans fast asleep with the paper on their table well alight, where someone had dropped a cigarette. I went up to the fire, shouted at these guys to wake up, and grabbed their unopened cans of Carling. I shook them and sprayed them over the flames – result, fire out and made the guys clean up the mess!

11

2005–2009 –
NED SAVES THE DAY

On 30 April 2005, BTP launched a 'Day of Action' against football hooligans, as fifteen problem games were targeted and ten arrests made. In one incident, twenty fans, wielding bottles and other weapons, clashed at Clapham Junction station in south London.

Following the FA Cup Final in 2005 at the Millennium Stadium, between Manchester United and Arsenal, a thirty-two-year-old football fan was assaulted on a train at Newport and was left unconscious. A description from the victim's brother quickly led to the arrest of a thirty-nine-year-old Arsenal fan on the station platform. As the victim, and his brother, lived in the Republic of Ireland, the offender was later identified by way of a video line-up and the case was committed to Gwent Crown Court for trial. Prior to the case being heard the victim's brother started to receive threatening phone calls, as a result of which he reluctantly declined to appear in court to give evidence.

In an unusual step, BTP made an application to the courts for his evidence to be presented as hearsay evidence without the need for him to personally attend, as well as presenting evidence of the defendant's previous bad character. This was accepted and the offender was duly convicted of inflicting grievous bodily harm.

On Saturday 29 October 2005, a group of thirty unruly Hereford fans confronted police officers on Worcester Foregate Street station. They were making their way to a game with Kidderminster Harriers and, while no arrests were made, one police officer felt it necessary to deploy his CS spray to contain the crowd. On the return journey, BTP officers prevented Hereford fans from alighting early at Droitwich station as they feared that they would cause trouble in the town.

On 5 November 2005, eight Liverpool fans were ejected from a train at Wolverhampton railway station after being abusive to passengers, and on the same day officers attended Stafford railway station to deal with a group of thirty Liverpool supporters, and an opposing group of Manchester United fans, who were throwing bottles and beer cans at each other.

On Saturday 26 November 2005, the British Transport Police targeted hooligan elements travelling to nineteen fixtures, including five Premier League games where trouble was anticipated. In the previous three months there had been more than a hundred football-related incidents on the network alone. Up to 500 officers were deployed as Andy Trotter, then deputy chief constable, said,

> Rowdy football fans can be a nightmare for other passengers. Even when they are only being boisterous, in the confines of a train, or in large groups on stations, they can be very intimidating. Active policing of travelling fans is a 'must do' for us. If we get it wrong, people get hurt.

Officers focussed on the Hull game against Queens Park Rangers, at Loftus Road in west London, following a previous match between the two clubs where Hull fans hurled taunts about the 7/7 bombings. With a history of violent rivalry, the game between Leeds and Millwall was also earmarked for additional attention. In the previous season Leeds had been ranked as the most troublesome club, and this season was fourth placed, while Millwall shared the dubious title of being fifth.

The force highlighted their commitment to tackling football violence and badged it as their 'Second Day of Action'. PCSOs handed out leaflets and cards saying 'Don't let the hooligans win,' and 'Keep football for the fans.' With 125 English and Scottish clubs to monitor each week, in the Championship and First and Second Divisions the reality was, and indeed still is, that BTP could not possibly be everywhere and must reach out to the vast majority of law-abiding fans for support.

On 7 January 2006, the three London areas of BTP were involved in a large-scale policing operation to cope with the demands of the FA Cup third round. More than 400 officers were involved, with travelling serials of officers provided from every area except Scotland. Superintendent Alex Carson was the appointed BTP Silver Commander for the operation, which required close working with the Metropolitan Police and City of London Police.

Policing football within the capital is normally a seamless process, with officers from all three forces operating in the streets and stations, and even underground on occasions. At Highbury, Arsenal were set to play Cardiff City and, with 6,000 tickets sold to their fans, all the morning trains from Wales arrived full and standing. A substantial risk element also travelled and 700 were subsequently met at Paddington and escorted to the Holloway Road area.

At the same time, a group of 200 risk supporters from Everton were met at Euston station and searched, using powers under Section 60 of the Criminal Justice and Public Order Act 1994, before being escorted to London Bridge on their way to Millwall. A fifty-strong group of Huddersfield Town supporters set themselves up in a pub opposite Baker Street station, and smaller risk groups from Northampton Town and Charlton Athletic were also located by football intelligence officers, including PC Nick Keighley, from BTP London North. The Huddersfield fans were later escorted to Fulham Broadway for the game with Chelsea, without incident.

After the games finished Cardiff City fans made determined efforts at confronting opposing fans, and several skirmishes took place at railway stations in London, with officers deployed in full riot gear, arrests made, and offensive weapons including Stanley knives and metal batons recovered.

200 Everton fans were put on a train at South Bermondsey station. A group of 150 Millwall fans were put on the train behind, but both trains subsequently arrived at London Bridge railway station at the same time and a confrontation took place, with the BTP once again finding themselves as the meat between the sandwich. A post-incident investigation into violent disorder

was subsequently launched. After order was restored, the Everton group was escorted to Euston station where they were put on a train. Two supporters only made it as far as Milton Keynes station, where they were arrested for racial chanting and abuse.

As the Everton fans departed, a group of Huddersfield fans required firm policing in Euston Road as BTP officers continued policing football fans hours after the final whistles had blown at the matches themselves.

On Saturday 4 February 2006, Sunderland fans travelling back on two GNER train services from Kings Cross railway station, after playing West Ham, made their presence felt with antisocial behaviour. Drunken fans terrified other passengers and three were removed from one of the trains when it arrived at Peterborough. Another two were subsequently removed from a train at Doncaster. Their behaviour was a rerun of a match at the end of 2005, where, following a game with Arsenal, twenty Sunderland fans were removed from a train for fighting and indecently exposing themselves.

On 4 June 2006 a BTP team, all wearing matching civilian jackets and ties and led by Chief Inspector Bob Kenwrick, flew out to Frankfurt from Heathrow Airport for the start of the 2006 World Cup. Sergeant Nick Cross was BTP's intelligence liaison officer at the German police intelligence cell in Kassel, while the majority of officers were deployed operationally in Germany alongside police officers from sixteen other countries. In fact, the BTP provided twenty-eight of the forty-four British Police uniformed patrol officers patrolling trains and stations in the vicinity of different venues. The officers engaged in joint patrols with German police and were afforded full police powers, which they used effectively on four occasions with arrests for public order, drink, drugs and a robbery. They also intervened in several public order situations before returning to the UK on 5 July 2006 after England's quarter-final defeat by Portugal.

Running in parallel to the operation in Germany, BTP officers, headed by ACC Alan Pacey and co-ordinated by PC Lee Garrett, London South's football intelligence officer, set up Operation Jardon, a ports operation based at Waterloo and Ashford International stations. During a four-week operation, 1,815 stop checks were carried out and five men detained under the Football Disorder Act. Of those, three were given two-year football banning orders, and two people were arrested who were wanted on warrant for serious offences. Ports operations were to become a regular feature of BTP's tactics in policing supporters travelling to European games via Eurostar.

In August 2006, the BTP football intelligence officer in the north east, PC John Stubbs, highlighted the fact that in any one season they covered the movements of travelling fans for up to 2,000 games in the north east, which was home to sixteen Football League and three Premier League teams. Announcing a crackdown on bad behaviour for the beginning of the new season, he added that in the previous season fifty-seven football-related arrests had been made, and eighteen football banning orders obtained, while in the adjoining North West area sixty arrests had been made in the 2005/06 season, as the use of 'head cam' cameras by patrolling officers commenced.

Nationally, arrests rose to a total of 331, while serious disorder incidents fell from sixty-two the previous year to fifty-six, and recorded instances of football-related antisocial behaviour were marginally down from 266 to 260.

By the time the Premier League kicked off on 19 August 2006, the BTP had already recorded half a dozen incidents of serious disorder as so-called friendly games set the tone for fans' behaviour. At a meeting held with train operating companies in Birmingham with BTP, Paula Durrans, then Head of Security and Revenue Protection with Virgin Trains, said, 'Regrettably we have noticed a recent trend of increasing disorder and antisocial behaviour among a minority of football fans who travel on our trains.'

On Saturday 2 September 2006, a mini riot broke out on Preston railway station between Blackpool fans returning from their match at Millwall and local fans returning from an England match in Manchester. Bottles, cans and signs were hurled and two BTP officers were injured as they tried to control the disturbances.

On Wednesday 6 September 2006, Detective Superintendent Layton, then Director of Intelligence with the British Transport Police, held a meeting in London to discuss what pro-active measures headquarters CID could take in combatting the problem of football violence on a UK-wide basis. At that time the force was using metal detector arches commonly known as shields, similar to those in use at airports, in an effort to detect people unlawfully in possession of knives.

A strategy was developed, which included the use of these arches, the use of a mixture of plain clothes and uniform officers, and the deployment of drugs sniffer dogs. There was plenty of evidence to suggest that a sizeable minority of football hooligans were taking Class B drugs, such as cannabis, and others were taking cocaine and amphetamines. The cost of some drugs was little more than the price of a couple of pints, so many opted for the quick fix and this gave BTP another opportunity to disrupt hooligan behaviour.

Borrowing the name from his former life in the West Midlands Police, Detective Superintendent Layton announced the formation of BTP's own Operation Red Card, and in the following weeks a number of limited operations took place in London and the Midlands.

On Saturday 18 November 2006, Birmingham were at home to Wolverhampton and another BTP Operation Red Card was set up at New Street station, using a combination of plain clothes and uniform officers, some with metal detector arches. Detective Superintendent Michael Layton briefed his managers and let them get on with it, although he stayed on the ground with them.

Retired Inspector Kevin Thompson tells the rest of the story,

> There was a heavy presence in and around Birmingham New Street station for Wolves away to Birmingham. My team had had an early start at Birmingham Snow Hill, where intelligence had led us to believe we would get trouble. No joy: a quiet morning. The same for the afternoon at Birmingham New Street.
>
> Ciaron Dermody, a great man, led the intercept officers. He was one of the hardest workers I have ever met and committed to policing, being well on the pathway to detective inspector. Another inspector led the uniforms. We moved the shield around several locations on Birmingham New Street but it was very difficult to capture a decent flow of people passing through. Wolves fans are notorious for circumventing police interest and that Saturday proved a point. Until, of course, the final whistle.

There was a rethink on strategy and Mike Layton directed fluidity of BTP movement, 'eyes about' and see what came off.

On this day, about 100 fans were 'bubbled' outside the ramp entrance to Birmingham New Street station and held for about an hour in order to calm them down. WMP planned to usher these fans onto Birmingham New Street at which point they would be within our jurisdiction – over to you BTP!

Meanwhile, I had spotted a likely lad literally bouncing around the main concourse of the station focusing on the sloped exit, high on something. Now it is not difficult to observe someone on a station on a busy Saturday afternoon. Lots of people are waiting for friends, waiting for trains and using the copious amounts of bars, restaurants and shops. But these people don't generally look like troublemakers. It takes a copper's sense to hone in on something that is not right. I was aware that Mike Layton was close by too. The magic of Mike was that his presence almost always resulted in a decent 'knock off' for the team.

We had our own kick-off as there were sporadic outbursts of tribal chants or singing by opposing fans, goading and the usual pre-fight disorder. One could only have experienced this through following football week-in week-out. The bouncing likely lad with glazed eyes was still about, arms tensed at the side, loosely dressed in fight attire – T shirt and jeans, no colours. He was clearly looking for a fight. I saw him for thirty minutes. He knew, probably from mobile telephone, that the Wolves fans would be let loose and he wanted blood.

I spoke with Ciaron and told him, 'He is trouble – get him stopped' and Ciaron did the deed. I grabbed another Birmingham City fan and rotated him accidentally into a photo booth. My baton was out discretely and Mike Layton was face-to-face with another fan. Uniform officers were doing their best to contain sporadic disorder outbursts. I glimpsed at Ciaron and saw our likely lad was handcuffed. Ciaron held up a glinting Bowie-type knife. We had averted a murder that day without doubt. This was an insidious Birmingham City FC fan who was a violent offender and he was subsequently sentenced to twelve months in prison for his behaviour and weaponry that day.

The buzz I got from that duty was immense. I quietly reflected on a great day's work and the excellent negotiation skills of the uniform inspector who had prevented a complaint about false imprisonment in a photo booth. I didn't have clue what he was talking about! The adrenaline rush stayed with me for a good few days. We had all come as close as you can get to the nastiest side of football policing.

Kevin went on to recall Operation Moonlight, which was picked up in the Force Intelligence Bureau and adopted by the BTP Operation Red Card team at the end of November 2006,

Paddington railway station can claim to have had its fair share of gatherings of violent football battles, sometimes when least expected. For some reason a simple allegation of threatening behaviour by a Torquay fan, against a Brentford fan, landed on the desk of DC Craig 'Nobbie' Naylor in late November 2006. A fortnight-or-so later, CCTV of the fight at Paddington, which started as fans came up and out of the underground station escalators onto the main concourse, ended up in the hands of the Football Intelligence Unit.

There were chair legs, chairs and other metal implements being rained upon Brentford supporters and guess who happened to be coordinating the violence? None other than Nobbie's threatening behaviour victim! This was a man quietly residing in his simple Torquay existence, unaware of the maelstrom which would soon hit this quiet seaside town.

D.C. Mike Evans was one of the finest detectives I had ever worked with in my whole career and remains so, God rest his soul. He was deaf in one ear, and with a bad back, and had twenty-eight years of service. He was in the process of passing the police promotion exam and eventually came a fantastic eighth in the country. He made it to detective sergeant before his untimely death in 2012.

Mike Evans, PC Kay Clifforth, and DC Graham Naughton MBE began putting together intelligence packages on around nine key Torquay offenders who were suspected of being involved in hooliganism. Brentford fans were none too good either, but that is another story.

My team and I hit Torquay en masse on Wednesday 6 December 2006. We made the nine arrests and Mike and Kay in particular were determined to find their targets as we made our presence felt in Torquay from 6 a.m. in the morning. I felt like the Pied Piper. I had absolute trust in my team and I have never before held a briefing discretely in a facility as austere as the Grand Hotel Torquay, while being waited on by the finest traditional silver service staff.

By this time, BTP's Operation Red Card had chalked up forty-seven arrests to its credit.

On Saturday 16 December 2006, Shrewsbury played Hereford at home and another BTP Red Card operation was put in place at Shrewsbury railway station. It was also a national BTP day of action against football-related violence.

Detective Superintendent Layton travelled up to Shrewsbury during the morning, but Kevin Thompson again put things in place prior to his arrival and recalls,

I travelled up on the Friday. Four hours door-to-door by train. Another hotel room, another bed – a bit like the *Crossroads* motel, I noted. Pouring with rain, I called home, had a couple of beers and went to bed apprehensive about the unknown entity. How nasty will this lower-league battle turn out to be?

This Saturday was a cold day so I got out in the morning on another hearty breakfast. Shrewsbury is a beautiful town and our presence was met positively by the Christmas shoppers heading into Birmingham for the day. Local media were in attendance and the design of the station allowed us to put a total shield arch block on the station with a mix of plain clothes spotters and local uniformed officers.

Because of the planning, media briefings, and reception of the local people, all too aware of Hereford's hardcore but small group of 'fans', the day passed generally without event. There were the usual drugs stops, followed by one arrest, and local criminals out for the day, but nothing too untoward.

However, as well as one key nominal, a stocky Hereford fan who bit off more that he could chew with the local West Mercia and

BTP officers, the event threw up only one positive hit by the shield for possession of a bladed article.

This polite Shrewsbury fan, of university age, had had a heavy Friday night in his local tandoori and pocketed a lemon segment squeezer of the type seen in one of the more upmarket restaurants. En route to follow his team the shield had lit up. He gladly accepted a swiftly administered caution at Shrewsbury police station and made it to the ground on time to see a dull lifeless match. I never did discover if the caution was for possessing a blade article or for theft, but I was later informed he was gracious and grateful for the service he got.

I travelled home to Essex much later that day with a sense of pride of how reassured my public, my bosses, and my team were. It is amazing what a metal detecting arch can reveal and I seemed to think our work that day happened just as Mike Layton was passing our location!

Kevin recalls his funniest football policing moment during this period of his service as follows,

One event, which must have been Cardiff coming up to the Smoke for a Millwall game, resulted in probably one of the funniest arrests ever made in my career. Again, I was in plain clothes leading a spotting team as a detective inspector. For the first time, shields filtered with uniform staff and Metropolitan Police dogs. One particular German Shepherd stuck his nose straight into the crotch of this small guy. I grabbed him and detained him for a drugs search. A willing tutor constable, Joe Prouse, brought over his brand-new probationer and off we went for the search, to be carried out discretely in the BTP office at Paddington.

By now this guy was shaking even more. After having had five stone of German Shepherd nuzzling him, eighteen stone of me inviting him to be searched, and now finally a fresh out of the tin probationer going through his pockets it simply was not his day. I took hold of a small Aerial washbag, of the type used to place wash balls into a washing machine, gently pulled it out and stopped at the whine 'No – please!'

It contained a mixture of cannabis, amphetamine and cocaine and I seem to recall he went to prison for twelve weeks the following Monday morning.

In December 2006, a twenty-year-old was detained on his way to a Chelsea *v*. Newcastle game when he was arrested for hurling racist and sexist abuse at passengers. When he was finally dealt with at court in the New Year he was banned from travelling on trains to matches.

On Saturday 23 December 2006, Operation Red Card was mounted at Manchester for a game between Manchester United and Aston Villa, resulting in seven arrests in Manchester and two arrests as Villa fans returned home to Birmingham.

On Saturday 13 January 2007, a further BTP Operation Red Card netted two football-related arrests at Sheffield railway station. Another operation at Leicester railway station, on 17 February 2007, resulted in six arrests for drugs possession, bringing the tally to seventy-two arrests.

In a six-month period prior to February 2007, Manchester United fans headed the transport disruption league after being involved in sixteen incidents, on trains and tubes, which were reported to BTP. They were followed by Coventry (twelve incidents), Aston Villa (nine incidents), Chelsea (nine incidents), Liverpool (nine incidents), Cardiff (eight incidents), Leeds (eight incidents), Millwall (seven incidents), Birmingham City (six incidents), and West Ham (five incidents).

On Thursday 22 February 2007, BTP in Scotland launched its biggest ever operation on the fifteen stations making up the Glasgow Subway, as preparations were made for a UEFA Cup game between Glasgow Rangers and Hapoel Tel Aviv. Specialist BTP public order teams were drafted in from London, and an officer placed in the networks' Broomloan CCTV control room.

At the beginning of March 2007, PC Robert Bowley from BTP was on duty at Derby railway station when, together with other officers, he intervened in a fight between two rival sets of fans. He was surrounded and violently assaulted but managed to hold onto his attacker until assistance arrived. The person responsible was later sent to prison for twelve months for affray and given a six-year football banning order.

Two weeks later, PCs Craig Farrell and Kirk Taylor responded to a call that a fight was taking place at Cardiff Central railway station. When they arrived they found Cardiff and Sunderland fans, on opposite platforms, hurling abuse at each other. A group of ten men were actually on the tracks fighting.

One officer went down onto the tracks, while the other attempted to restore order on the platform they were on. Both officers were forced to use their batons and deployed their Captor sprays. It was 10 minutes before assistance arrived but, despite receiving an arm injury, PC Farrell was still able to make two arrests and hang onto them until help arrived.

At 8.10 p.m. on Saturday 31 March 2007, a group of up to seventeen Ipswich fans were involved in a pre-arranged fight at Ipswich railway station with a number of Norwich fans. Several people were assaulted, including railway staff, as families with young children ran for cover. One train was forced to make an emergency stop as some of those involved tried to climb through the train windows as it started to move from the station. BTP Sergeant Bob Munn said, 'Such disgraceful behaviour will not be tolerated,' and the following month ten Ipswich Town supporters were arrested in co-ordinated raids by twenty-five BTP officers, supported by local police. They were arrested for conspiracy to commit violent disorder.

On Sunday 1 April 2007, a BTP Operation Red Card was mounted at Bristol railway station, and four drugs arrests made, as Bristol fans arrived to travel by train to Cardiff.

Two weeks later, on Saturday 14 April 2007, a similar operation at Birmingham focussed on the arrival of Manchester United fans. On this date six people were detained in possession of drugs, and a seventh had sufficient quantity in his possession to be charged with 'possession with intent to supply.'

To finish off a good month, on Saturday 28 April 2007 another operation mounted at Paddington railway station, for a fixture between Millwall and Bristol, resulted in no fewer than sixteen arrests for possession of Class A and Class B drugs.

On Saturday 5 May 2007, an eighteen-year-old West Ham fan subjected BTP officers to a stream of abuse at Upton Park Tube station following a game against Bolton Wanderers. Two officers were returning home after a shift and were on board a District line train when he confronted them and started shouting and swearing. He was arrested and subsequently received a three-year football banning order as well as being banned from the rail and Tube networks on days that his team, or England, were playing.

The following day, on Sunday 6 May 2007, another Red Card operation was mounted at Derby railway station for a fixture with Leeds, and five arrests for drugs possession followed. The hooligan elements hated being the subject of close attention, and the additional policing activity definitely moderated their behaviour.

A further, final, operation at Marylebone railway station led to six further arrests for drugs possession on Monday 28 May 2007. All in all, BTP's Operation Red Card led to 113 persons being dealt with.

In May 2007, Wembley Stadium reopened its doors again, after seven years of major redevelopment, for the FA Cup final between Chelsea and Manchester United. More than 500 BTP officers were on duty to monitor the 90,000 fans as 85 per cent of them used the Underground to get to the venue. Some of those officers worked in plain clothes at Wembley Park station, to deal with pickpockets and other antisocial elements in the crowds, and a Police Support Unit consisting of twenty-five officers was on standby to deploy to trouble spots. Just four arrests were made by BTP in a relatively trouble-free day. This consisted of two for public order offences, one for common assault, and one person for being drunk and disorderly.

In the same month, at the other end of the UK, another major event for BTP passed off peacefully in Glasgow as supporters of Sevilla and Espanyol arrived in the city for the UEFA Cup final at Hampden Park. Eighty BTP officers were deployed, including a Police Support Unit from the Midlands area, but despite the presence of 51,000 supporters a carnival atmosphere prevailed and no arrests were made.

For the reporting year 2006/07, the British Transport Police recorded eighty serious football-related incidents, as opposed to fewer than sixty the previous year, and less serious incidents increased significantly to more than 300, with some passengers describing 'the journey from hell surrounded by chanting, drunken, swearing football fans.'

On 7 July 2007, Liverpool played Wrexham in a preseason friendly at the Racecourse stadium. After the match, fighting broke out on an Arriva Trains service from Wrexham to Chester, and two men from Wrexham were repeatedly punched and kicked by Liverpool fans and suffered facial injuries. Two officers on the train observed a seventeen-year-old, who was the ringleader of a group, singing racially abusive songs that related to the racist murder of Anthony Walker in Liverpool and the Heysel Stadium disaster. Despite the fact that there was more than a hundred rowdy fans on the train, they managed to arrest him in extremely intimidating circumstances as the train arrived at a station.

Following a post-incident investigation, and examination of CCTV evidence, at 8 a.m. on 9 November 2007 some eighty BTP and Merseyside officers conducted raids across Merseyside and made ten arrests on suspicion of violent disorder. The operation was led by Detective Inspector Steve Lewis from BTP who said, 'Members of the public have a right to travel in safety.' Nine of them subsequently received three-year football banning orders, while a tenth was sent to prison for five months and given a six-year ban.

At 2.20 p.m. on Saturday 1 September 2007, some thirty to forty Crystal Palace fans boarded a train at Sydenham, in south-east London. As the train arrived at the platform they banged on train windows and threw bottles. They boarded the first two carriages, which contained Charlton fans on their way to a game with Crystal Palace as well as members of the travelling public. A roar went up as they chanted 'Kill them' and 'Get off our Manor.'

The Crystal Palace group then proceeded to attack people randomly, with one twenty-four-year-old Charlton fan receiving a broken nose, while women, children and elderly victims were head-butted, punched and kicked, in what was described by one witness as a 'one-sided riot.'

The attackers fled at Penge East station but police, who responded to a number of 999 calls, detained some at the scene and identified more from CCTV footage.

Seventeen arrests of persons aged between nineteen and forty-six years were subsequently made, many in coordinated raids involving up to 150 officers, with the vast majority of those charged receiving custodial sentences and football banning orders. Their conduct was described in court as 'mob conduct at its worst' by Judge Robbins.

Detective Inspector Keith Bennett from the BTP, who led the post-incident investigation, code-named Operation Dispatch, said,

> CCTV footage of the incident clearly shows the terror that ordinary members of the public were subjected to. No-one was safe from this motley crew. They arrived en masse and had only one objective, and that was to assault and cause violence to innocent members of the public. The footage showed parents trying to shield their children from flying punches, alcoholic drinks were thrown at women, and elderly people cowered as this group rampaged like caged animals through the train carriage.

At 12.30 p.m. on Monday 3 September 2007, Detective Superintendent Michael Layton attended a meeting chaired by Assistant Chief Constable Alan Pacey to discuss the next steps to be taken to tackle football violence, and a full-scale seminar involving rail industry partners quickly followed on Thursday 4 October 2007.

From these discussions, Operation ERA was born, which was to be led by the Force Operations Department but would involve an increased use of covert options. There had been some friendly rivalry between headquarters departments over who should have the operational lead on these pro-active operations, and these moves were designed to still the waters, as well as engaging with the FA and supporters clubs.

On Saturday 20 October 2007, a uniform escort travelling back from Manchester to Birmingham had to deal with a number of unruly supporters. Disorder had taken place in Manchester involving Birmingham City fans, who were escorted back to Manchester Piccadilly railway station by a Greater Manchester Police Public Order Unit. Some 300–400 were put onto a train which left full and standing.

One particularly troublesome group positioned themselves in the buffet bar area, which had been closed, and proceeded to spend the journey eyeball to eyeball with some of the BTP officers, including PC Marcos Dominguez who was personally threatened by one individual.

Unbeknown to them, and the fans themselves, Detective Superintendent Layton had briefed a number of officers who were deployed covertly on the train, and with the risks involved he anxiously awaited their safe return on the platform at Birmingham New Street. Officers on the train asked for assistance on arrival and indicated that a number of tactical arrests would be made.

A reception committee was arranged and as the train pulled into Birmingham New Street a number of arrests were made on the platform. One of those arrested struggled violently, even when handcuffed, and it took several officers to restrain him on the ground. A young boy in the crowd became momentarily split up from his mother and became distressed at the unfolding scene, as a second person in custody also resisted arrest. The remaining fans were contained by weight of police numbers in a cordon and thought better about intervening. This was not always the case.

Also on 20 October 2007, a violent incident occurred on a York-bound train between Middlesbrough and Thornaby, following the Middlesbrough *v.* Chelsea match, which left a number of passengers injured. Four Middlesbrough fans were filmed on the on-board CCTV as they approached six well-behaved Chelsea fans on the train and initially engaged in some seemingly friendly banter.

This then developed into a confrontation as the Middlesbrough fans began to punch and kick the other group, while women passengers cried hysterically. One woman had her glasses knocked off, which were then stamped on by one of the offenders. The violence only stopped after the lone train manager courageously stepped in between them.

Four men later pleaded guilty to affray and received a combination of fines and suspended prison sentences, as well as receiving five-year football banning orders.

After the court case, BTP Chief Inspector Jane Townsley said, 'These people are not football fans. They are criminals and will be dealt with as criminals. The clubs don't want it, we don't want it, and we are not going to put up with it.'

In the same month, a forty-three-year-old Leicester City supporter was sent to prison for five months and received a football banning order for six years for an unprovoked attack on an elderly couple. The man had been on a train with a mixed group of Leicester and Sheffield Wednesday fans who were rowdy, singing and chanting. As the train approached Kettering railway station an elderly lady asked him to moderate his language, at which point he became aggressive, assaulting both her and her partner.

On Saturday 3 November 2007, Operation ERA was mounted at Birmingham New Street station for a game between Derby and Aston Villa. One person was dealt with for possession of cannabis and one for threatening behaviour. As more than forty stop and searches were carried out, two knives, which had been hastily abandoned, were recovered from the floor of the station.

On Saturday 10 November 2007, a pre-arranged fight took place outside Tamebridge Parkway railway station in Wednesbury between Walsall and Shrewsbury hooligans. Sergeant Dan Gregory was quickly on the scene with five other BTP officers, and video images of the violence were captured by the officers as traffic was forced to stop and fighting spilled out into the roadways. A post-incident investigation commenced, which was supported by the Force Intelligence Bureau, on the direction of Detective Superintendent Layton.

Throughout November 2007, raids were carried out across London, Kent, Sussex and Merseyside, resulting in twenty-four people being charged with football-related offences.

Also in November 2007, Blackpool fans arriving at Preston railway station went through airport-style security scanners to check for potential weapons.

On Sunday 2 December 2007, Operation ERA was conducted at Fulham Broadway in London, leading to five arrests, and on Saturday 8 December 2007 a similar operation at Manchester, where Derby were the visitors, resulted in twenty-five people being detained.

Also in December 2007, BTP officers were deployed for the first time on the new high-speed trains operating on the Channel Tunnel link for a major sporting event. Tottenham Hotspurs' UEFA Cup tie with Anderlecht saw Belgian and BTP officers travelling together on trains.

On 5 January 2008, the BTP deployed 100 officers at Birmingham New Street station between 11 a.m. and 11 p.m., with all rest days cancelled, as Cardiff, Manchester United and Millwall fans visited the Midlands for FA Cup matches. The BTP football intelligence officer for the area outlined the fact that 15 per cent of the Villa ground had been allocated to Manchester United fans, who would be coming from all parts of the country, and that New Street station would be a focal point. PC Rentell said, 'If anyone steps out of line they will cop it!'

On 5 and 6 January 2008, the BTP deployed 790 officers to ensure the safety of travelling supporters during the FA Cup third round under the auspices of Operation ERA, in an operation which was coordinated by Superintendent Andy Ball.

By close of play on 5 January, a total of twenty-five arrests were made, and the following day there were an additional fourteen arrests. The majority were made for public order and drugs offences, with several for possession of bladed articles. No significant football-related incidents occurred and ACC Alan Pacey went out on patrol with a reporter from Sky Sports to highlight the challenges that BTP routinely faced.

On Tuesday 8 January 2008, fifty BTP officers conducted early morning raids under the code name Operation Highway in the Shrewsbury area, resulting in the arrest of eleven suspects believed to have been involved in the violence at Tamebridge. Another suspect later gave himself up, and a further individual indicated that he would do so later in the day. A total of fifteen people were subsequently dealt with by the courts and received football banning orders.

On Saturday 16 January 2008, up to fifty Eastleigh FC and Crawley Town FC fans clashed at Crawley railway station. Planks of wood were used as weapons, and fighting eventually spilled over onto the track, which also had a live rail. Women and children were left cowering in fear. Four Eastleigh fans were arrested as police converged on the station, and trains were brought to a halt for safety reasons. A further seventeen were escorted by BTP back to Eastleigh.

On Saturday 19 January 2008, officers were deployed again to Operation ERA, resulting in sixteen arrests throughout the day.

On Saturday 26 January 2008, arches were deployed for Operation ERA at Coventry railway station, together with a drugs dog, for the arrival of Millwall fans. A tense atmosphere developed as arriving Millwall fans tested the resilience of the ERA team to hold them at the ticket barrier prior to being monitored through.

Detective Superintendent Layton was on duty at the station that day, and, following a somewhat urgent plea from officers, the drugs dog was replaced with a general purpose dog. German Shepherds have far bigger teeth than Cocker Spaniels and the swap had the desired effect on the belligerent fans.

Two arrests were made for possession of drugs, one for being drunk and disorderly, one for threatening behaviour, and one person dealt with for trespass. Not a bad day's work, and more operations followed with thirteen arrests in Birmingham for the arrival of Leeds on Saturday 16 February 2008.

On Saturday 1 March 2008, six uniform officers and six officers in plain clothes set up Operation ERA at Cardiff railway station for arriving Leicester fans. Two arrests for possession of drugs were made; one person was arrested for assaulting two people, and one arrest was made for being in possession of a bladed article.

On Saturday 8 March 2008, a similar operation was mounted at Leicester for a game with Bristol City. Three arrests were made for threatening behaviour at Nuneaton railway station, and three others ejected from a train.

On Saturday 15 March 2008, fifteen BTP officers were called to a train at Chelmsford railway station following a disturbance involving Charlton fans. That same day, at three other high-profile venues and under the banner of Operation ERA, two arrests were made for theft, one for threatening behaviour, one for possession of drugs and one for forgery.

On Saturday 29 March 2008, at 6 p.m., a group of fifteen Queens Park Rangers fans got off a train at Manningtree railway station and burst into the station buffet bar shouting 'We are QPR'. They set about attacking a group of Ipswich Town supporters, some as young as eight years of age, and a pensioner. Three people were injured as the QPR fans threw punches, smashed bottles, a window and three bar stools. They jumped back on the train but the National Express service was held at the station while local police made four arrests and handed them over to the BTP.

Retired BTP dog handler Andy Fidgett recalls his involvement in the incident,

> On 29 March 2008, Ipswich Town played Queens Park Rangers at Portman Road, Ipswich's ground. Before the game started some QPR fans were either not allowed in, or got put out very early in the match. They started to go back to London, however the first station in the London direction after Ipswich is Manningtree, which is part of Constable Country and very popular with walkers and tourists, and they got off there. The buffet bar on the station is famous for its beer and this particular group stayed for several hours drinking.
>
> After the match, which finished 0-0, another group of QPR fans started making their way home, but also stopped off at Maningtree on the way, and for some reason never known to me they initially started fighting with each other.
>
> As the only dog handler on duty, I had been sent to Colchester, just before the game had ended, to monitor fans through the station. I was immediately sent to Manningtree on a Grade 1 call, however, as often happens in these situations when busy, and information becomes a bit blurred, I was redirected a couple of times before finally making it to Manningtree.
>
> By the time I got there a train had arrived containing Ipswich fans, who would usually go on the Harwich Branch line, and a violent fight had taken place between them and the QPR fans in the buffet, with a table or chair being thrown through the buffet window. On my arrival there were five police cars and two ambulances at the station, something of chaos was occurring, with reports of someone running down the line, another report of a sexual assault, and a head injury all being talked about.
>
> Lucky for me an Essex Police dog handler, who I knew, arrived and we decided to put a break into the crowd. With my German Shepherd Ned, and the Essex officer, we charged the crowd hoping they would not fall onto the track, although we had been told that all trains were at a stop, it was not a good place to be.
>
> We successfully divided the crowd into two halves and stood back to back for about twenty minutes pushing the crowds back

using drawn batons and the dogs. We eventually managed to get the Ipswich fans away on a train. Some of the Ipswich fans knew me and I reassured them that they would not be followed by QPR fans.

Eventually it was decided that a train to London should leave, as the main Norwich to Liverpool Street line had been blocked for forty-five minutes. Unfortunately, at this point this left just me and the Essex officer as the only two officers on the station with the remaining QPR fans, until we eventually got them onto another London-bound train.

I believe that five fans were arrested and at least one went to prison, sentenced at Chelmsford Crown Court. The case was dealt with by DC Alan Reed, who is still in the force at Colchester today.

My old police dog Ned was a lion of an animal, who didn't know fear. There are lots of staff and public who were safer because of his sterling work and service to the Crown. Unfortunately he died on 26 November 2012, his spleen ruptured during the night and he was dead when I got up in the morning. His last duty was an Ipswich Town *versus* Peterborough game again at Ipswich railway station.

On Saturday 19 April 2008, 300 BTP officers were deployed to Operation ERA in a day of action against football violence on the network. Forty-two fixtures were monitored and thirty-two arrests were made throughout the day. The Leeds *v.* Millwall fixture in London was particularly busy, with twenty-three arrests at stations across London. A group of 120 risk Leeds fans were escorted from central London to South Bermondsey, and after the match twelve people were arrested at London Bridge railway station, a key cross-over point for transport in London and a favoured place for hooligans to carry out ambushes on visitors to London.

In the north west, two arrests were made of fans travelling to the Blackburn *v.* Manchester United fixture, one for public order and one for possession of a Class A drug. Five other people were given street warnings for possession of cannabis following the deployment of BTP sniffer dogs.

During this period one member of the public, who had been to a football match at Blackburn with Everton, praised the work of the BTP in the north west as she found herself on a train back to Liverpool and watched fans 'guzzling out of Jack Daniels and Vodka bottles.'

In the north-east area, one arrest was made relating to the West Ham *v*. Derby fixture, and a Nottingham Forest fan was arrested at the station for common assault. Two others were arrested for violent disorder on a train at Doncaster, which involved four men, and two arrests were made at Sheffield railway station, along with one at Middlesbrough, for public order offences.

On Sunday 20 April 2008, one person was arrested at Newcastle Central station following clashes between Newcastle and Sunderland fans who crossed the tracks to get at their opponents and had to be driven back using police dogs. Commenting at the end of the weekend's activities, Superintendent Andy Ball from BTP said that they would be looking to apply for football banning orders in all cases.

On 14 May 2008, serious disorder took place in Manchester on the day of the 2008 UEFA Cup final. Thousands of Glasgow Rangers fans converged on the city centre, with up to 25,000 supporters travelling by train into Manchester over a 48-hour period. Some 7,000 of these supporters travelled into Manchester from Blackpool, and the sheer numbers tested both the police and the industry severely.

A riot started following the failure of a large video screen constructed in Piccadilly Gardens. The local police were put under extreme pressure, with numerous injuries and arrests, and sporadic outbreaks of violence took place throughout the day at Manchester Piccadilly, Oxford Road and Deansgate railway stations, leaving the BTP severely stretched.

At one stage Manchester Piccadilly railway station was closed temporarily for health and safety reasons, as staff struggled to cope with the crowds and a small number of arrests were made by BTP. The temporary chief superintendent at the time, Peter Holden, later paid tribute to his officers.

On 17 May 2008, a thirty-eight-year-old Cardiff fan punched a Portsmouth fan in the face at Harrow on the Hill station. The attacker was sent to prison for four weeks and banned from attending matches for six years. PC Vick Ackerman from the BTP said that the victim was attacked purely because he was wearing a Portsmouth FC shirt.

From 1 June 2008, London's mayor announced the start of a drinking ban on Tubes, buses, trams and Docklands Light Railway, providing further policing challenges for the BTP.

In July 2008, two Glasgow Rangers fans were arrested on the subway system singing sectarian songs before the Champions League qualifier with Lithuanian side FC Kaunas.

On 15 August 2008, Superintendent Andy Ball, in charge of BTP's Event Planning and Coordination Unit, highlighted in the media the growing problems the force was facing from 'youth groups, aged between sixteen years to twenty-two years, who had less respect for authority and were more inclined to drink heavily.'

He went on to stress that highly paid football players had a key responsibility to act as role models, following the conviction of a Newcastle United player who had been jailed following a street fight.

Incidents on trains heading to matches had increased by 10 per cent and Detective Constable Graham Naughton, a BTP force football intelligence officer, commented,

> The core hooligans we are used to dealing with had some sort of code of conduct when they met to fight each other. For example they would never attack what they classed to be 'normal' fans, and they knew that if they bashed a policeman then they would be in deep trouble. These younger groups do not respect that.

Sadly, it was not a code that was always followed.

On 16 August 2008, local police invoked powers under Section 27 of the Violent Crime Reduction Act when a group of Swindon fans arrived at Cheltenham railway station. Fearing trouble from the group, who had been drinking heavily, they were put back on the first train to Swindon and escorted home.

In September 2008, figures released by the British Transport Police highlighted that the north-east area had seen an increase in incidents and arrests. A total of 601 arrests had been recorded by the force for the previous season. BTP Assistant Chief Constable (Operations) Alan Pacey said, 'Alcohol-fuelled disorder was the most prevalent problem, with an increase from 305 to 337 less serious incidents nationally. We also had twenty-five police officers assaulted during the 2007/08 season – the highest number ever recorded by BTP.'

For the 2007/08 season, BTP figures revealed that for the eighth season running football-related arrests had increased, and in the same period 122 football banning orders were obtained. Less serious incidents increased from 305 incidents to 337 incidents, while more serious incidents decreased from eighty-three incidents in the previous season to sixty-three incidents. For the first time football banning orders were imposed in Scotland, with two St Johnstone fans being banned from every football ground in the country, as well as being banned from travelling abroad to support Scotland.

In response to the figures, the BTP launched Operation Scorpion at the end of September 2008 and each territorial area was tasked with planning coordinated operations at key risk fixtures.

On 30 September 2008, PCs Mark Dickens, Paul Morse and Steven Lawrence were commended by ACC Alan Pacey for their bravery during a serious football-related public order incident at Cardiff Central railway station.

On 18 October 2008, a twenty-strong group of Aldershot fans gathered at Ash Vale railway station, in Surrey, to confront Brentford supporters. Eleven of them were arrested and six charged with public order offences.

On 1 November 2008, a confrontation occurred on a Northern Rail service train when Middlesbrough fans started taunting West Ham fans travelling on the service. A fight broke out near Eaglescliffe railway station, which was witnessed by an off-duty police officer and a club steward, who provided witness evidence to the BTP. Four Middlesbrough fans were arrested and charged with affray. In addition to receiving football banning orders, they were also banned by their own club for life.

In November 2008, five Manchester United fans, all members of the same family, clashed with two Millwall fans at Euston station. As their train pulled in, the Manchester group were chanting football songs and swearing before engaging in a confrontation with the Millwall fans. One man was kicked as he lay on the platform. All seven were arrested, and in subsequently sentencing the men to 60 hours' unpaid community work, the judge at Southwark Crown Court said the men were in 'football fan mode'.

On Saturday 8 November 2008, a forty-eight-year-old Cardiff City football fan pushed a police officer at Wood Lane Tube station in London and made several Nazi salutes towards police before a game with Queens Park Rangers. He was charged with racially aggravated threatening behaviour and subsequently received a three-year football banning order.

On Saturday 20 December 2008, a twenty-three-year-old West Ham fan was arrested at Upton Park Tube station for public order offences. PC Vic Ackerman from BTP told the media,

> This man was part of a group making their way into Upton Park Tube station, after a match which West Ham lost 1–0. As he walked past two uniformed officers he looked at one of them, swore at him, and asked him what he was looking at. He was warned about his language and refused permission to travel. After ignoring further warnings he was arrested and became violent, repeatedly shoving the officer and continuing to use foul and abusive language, before being restrained and handcuffed.

He subsequently received a three-year football banning order.

Meanwhile, north of the border, on the same date, a pre-arranged fight took place on Queen Street station in Glasgow between Glasgow Rangers fans and Hibernian fans. A Rangers fan who was arrested subsequently went to jail for five months and received the maximum ten-year ban on attending football matches.

Sixty-three football-related arrests had been made by BTP in the previous season across Scotland. Reports of his conviction attracted 144 responses on the Rangers Media Forum alone.

Across the force area as a whole, scores of organised crime groups, specifically engaged in football violence on the networks, were identified as a result of structured intelligence gathering. Each of them had a ranking score, which enabled BTP to target resources on the most troublesome.

On 11 January 2009, Superintendent Layton commenced a new role, in uniform, as the BTP operations superintendent on the Wales and Western area, based in Birmingham. He was finally back home in the location where he first started his police career, and was looking forward to taking on responsibility for football policing on the rail network in an area that covered Wales, the South West and large parts of the Midlands.

On the evening of Saturday 17 January 2009, Shrewsbury fans travelled by train between Crewe and Shrewsbury following a match at Port Vale. During the journey one of them made a lewd comment to a female BTP officer, who was part of an escort serial, after she asked him to stop swearing. Three others among the group became aggressive and one started shouting 'Kill the Bill'.

Superintendent Layton directed officers by radio, including PC Marcos Dominguez, to meet the train in at Shrewsbury as it was clear that there was going to be a confrontation on arrival, and the local police were also alerted.

On arrival at Shrewsbury railway station, all four, who were drunk, were arrested after a violent struggle on the station platforms and pandemonium broke out for several minutes. The officers involved were from BTP's Operational Support Units in Birmingham, who were highly effective in dealing with antisocial behaviour and didn't tolerate nonsense from anyone. During the course of policing football on this date, twelve persons were dealt with for public order offences, including two West Bromwich Albion fans, under the auspices of the specific football operation code-named Scorpion.

On the same date, a group of ten Wigan fans went to the Sports Bar at Manchester Piccadilly railway station and initially engaged in some friendly banter with a group of Oldham fans who were already there. Later, the mood changed and one of the Wigan fans was attacked and received minor injuries. Another was arrested for criminal damage.

On Friday 23 January 2009, Nottingham Forest played Derby in an evening game, and a BTP Public Order Support Unit was deployed to deal with travelling fans, while Superintendent Layton was in the BTP control room as Silver Commander. As one service train, crammed full of noisy fans, pulled into Long Eaton station, officers were obliged to hold the train as seven arrests were made for public order offences.

A message had been received from rail staff that the train was being damaged, and as it pulled onto the platform they started smashing the lights and goaded officers to try and enter one of the carriages. Eventually PC Marcos Dominguez, together with another officer, entered and tried to make an arrest. As punches were exchanged the officer received a kick to the testicles, and it took five officers to remove the prisoner. Abuse was hurled at the officers as more prisoners were restrained on the floor of the platform before being handcuffed and marched off to waiting police vehicles, while the officer was bent double being violently sick.

On the evening of Wednesday 4 February 2009, a further match was played between Derby and Nottingham, which resulted in eleven persons being dealt with for public order offences.

On Saturday 7 February 2009, a drugs operation was put in place at Birmingham New Street station for games between Birmingham City and Burnley, and Newcastle and Coventry. The station acted as a cross-over point for visiting fans and fifteen persons were detained in possession of controlled drugs.

On Saturday 14 February 2009, ten Plymouth Argyle fans were detained by BTP following complaints of disorder, and the following day two arrests were made for being drunk and disorderly following a game between Aston Villa and Everton.

On Saturday 21 February 2009, during yet another clash between Nottingham Forest and Derby, a further eleven arrests were made at Nottingham railway station following disturbances.

On Saturday 28 February 2009, six arrests followed a game between Shrewsbury and Macclesfield.

Also on Saturday 28 February 2009, large numbers of Cardiff City football supporters travelled back to Cardiff after a match at Southampton. They gathered at Salisbury railway station to catch either the 18.41 or 19.41 service trains, both of which were escorted by BTP officers. Many of them were already in a drunken state prior to departures, and while the first train travelled back relatively unscathed, the second train was plagued by antisocial behaviour, with fans smoking, shouting, and dancing in the aisles. In at least one incident, a fan stripped off completely naked and climbed into a luggage rack – not a pretty sight on the CCTV!

The escorting officers on the second train made a number of arrests and took them off the service at Bristol, where other officers joined them. All of the activity was captured on good-quality CCTV cameras, and the message went out from Superintendent Michael Layton, who signalled to staff that positive action should be taken against anyone where offences were disclosed.

This was later highlighted on the internet when a Cardiff fan using the name 'Aberdare Ska' posted on a forum,

> I spoke to one of the transport police to ask what the problem was and he said that there was a new boss of the transport police and there was to be zero tolerance of antisocial behaviour on trains by footy fans (not just city). He showed me a booklet they had and it contained pictures of about forty Cardiff City fans with whom they wanted a word – from what he told me a shot would be fired across the bow of those identified and gave the impression that it was high jinks that got over the top, nothing too serious to suggest that dawn raids would follow.

A post-incident investigation was set up, under the operational name Crusader, which was led by Detective Inspector Mark Cleland and Sergeant Guy Ellis, and almost thirty suspects were identified on video for a variety of offences. More than twenty of them were subsequently dealt with by the courts and received heavy fines. Sergeant Guy said, 'Anti-social behaviour of any kind involving sports fans will not be tolerated.' Next season, Cardiff fans did not travel in any numbers on the rail network – they had got the message.

During March 2009, a further twelve football-related arrests were made on the Wales and Western area, bringing the tally in the first three months of the year to 152.

In April 2009 there were a further ten arrests, and in May 2009 seven arrests in one day alone, Villa fans being those involved.

Robin Edwards was an inspector in the north-east area of the force who retired in June 2014, having transferred to BTP from Nottinghamshire Police in 2004. He was an experienced officer who was trained in public order tactics and operations. As such, he had dealt with a significant amount of disorder during his career.

Robin had also dealt with many football policing duties for BTP and had escorted football fans all over the country. One particular incident in 2009 sticks in his mind, and the following is an account of that incident in his own words,

On Saturday 4 April 2009, I was Bronze Commander for the North East area travelling football serials that were tasked to escort football fans home from London during the evening.

The day was nothing out of the ordinary in terms of football escorts ,with my officers and I making our way to London for mid-afternoon in preparation for the return journey, following the completion of the relevant matches. I was aware that Sunderland were one of the teams that we would be required to monitor and, as I had previous experience of their behaviour when travelling to and from matches, I was aware we might encounter some problems later in the day.

The day passed uneventfully and just after 5 p.m. I prepared my officers in advance of the fans returning to Kings Cross station. It was normal for officers from BTP to suffer the misfortune of being the thinnest blue line when it came to escorting fans on the return journey. We regularly found ourselves taking over from large numbers of local police officers, who would hand the fans over to a much smaller number of us. Sometimes the fact that the local police had large numbers would allow them to take a firm hand, and all too frequently we would receive large groups of fans who were very agitated and angry due to their perception of the way they had been treated.

This would lead to five or six BTP cops, if we were lucky, having to escort some wound-up fans on a train for several hours with little opportunity to call for back-up. We were used to this situation and worked very hard to lower any tension by engaging with the fans in a friendly manner wherever possible. On many occasions this worked, but on this particular day I'm afraid it did not!

The fans started to return to Kings Cross and it was obvious some of them were from the main risk group, who we would categorise as Category C fans at that time. I then had to make a decision in terms of how I would deploy my resources on the trains travelling north. One of my options was to send half of my officers, which amounted to four PCs, on an early train with the first risk group, and if problems developed later elsewhere I could drop them off their northbound service and meet them en route. On the basis of the behaviour of some of the fans already at Kings Cross, this was the decision I decided to take.

Unfortunately, there were very few London BTP officers at Kings Cross on this day as they had several of their own commitments. Officers from the northern areas of the force, like me, often felt that the cops from London did not pay football enough attention and I certainly felt like that on this particular day. This meant that my serials also had to take the extra responsibility of policing Kings Cross station as well as policing the trains travelling north.

At some stage, around 7 p.m., I had a conversation with the Silver Commander, Superintendent Terry Nicholson, who was deployed in the control room in Birmingham. From there, Terry was required to command the entire football operation for the force, with the exception of London and the south east, and pay particular attention to fans that were travelling to cities across the country on their way back from the capital.

I briefed Terry on the current situation and told him that I had decided to split the escort so I could ensure the majority of risk fans were escorted across a couple of trains. In principle this sounds quite easy, which I'm afraid is a long way from the reality of the situation I faced. These situations are always very fluid; intelligence can be patchy or inaccurate, and fans change their minds and don't always do what you expect them to do. Making the right decision in these circumstances can be a real challenge and is often based on experience and gut feeling. I was convinced, however, that I made the best decision I could in the circumstances.

The first group of Sunderland risk fans boarded an East Coast Train heading north and I deployed half of my officers to escort them home. I waited for the second group, who had allegedly been subdued by the Metropolitan Police and were on their way back to Kings Cross station. Although I can't recall exactly what time they arrived back at the station, it was clear that this group was much larger than I had anticipated, however they did appear to be compliant and in relatively good spirits.

They boarded the first available National Express Train service heading north and myself, a sergeant, and two constables joined them. To add a further complication to the situation, the service had a team of railway enforcement officers (REOs) on board. At this time I was seconded to National Express and I was heading up the Revenue Protection Department with specific responsibility for leading the franchise commitments of East Coast Trains, one of which was the development, recruitment, training, and management of the REO project. This was their first football escort and I had to support them as part of my responsibility to National Express, and each of them as individuals. While these individuals were enforcement officers, it was never intended for them to become involved in violent situations or serious disorder.

As we pulled out of Kings Cross station, I called Silver and gave him a full briefing on the situation and that, although the fans were predominately risk, they did appear to be in good spirits. At this stage it was around 8.30 p.m. and he informed me he would make his way back to our home station in Leeds and call me when he arrived.

As we left London the atmosphere immediately changed, and we discovered that we had around seventy risk fans in the rear coach who very quickly realised there were only four officers escorting them. We did our best to contain them in the carriage, but within ten minutes it was clear the fans were getting out of hand and we were in a very difficult and dangerous situation.

We quietly moved all the non-risk fans and other passengers out of the carriage and, with the help of the REOs, who could not be exposed to potential conflict, moved them up the train. We tried to create a sterile area between the risk group and the other passengers as they became more and more aggressive towards us. It was clear that one of them was the 'head man', and he was geeing up the rest of the group and seriously aggravating the situation.

The journey from London to Peterborough lasts about fifty-five minutes, and I can say with all honesty it was one of the longest train journeys I have had the misfortune to experience. Passengers on the train, which included children, were very frightened, as were the staff on board who acted with complete professionalism in the face of such adversity. The risk group was shouting, swearing and drinking, which I could do very little about, and throwing items around the carriage.

I was concerned that they would turn on us and in advance of our arrival at Peterborough I requested local officers join us as we were expecting the situation to blow up at any moment. About ten minutes before arriving at Peterborough, the situation did blow up and we had to step in to prevent the train being smashed up.

The REOs were instructed to keep the passengers away from the back of the train and keep everyone on as we pulled into the station. We moved into the carriage and tried to remove the ringleader, who was completely out of control and taking the rest of the group with him. As we moved in they turned on us and our situation changed from arresting the suspect to fighting for our survival.

We couldn't get out of the carriage and faced one of the worst situations I had experienced in my police career. Probably no more than a couple of minutes later, although it seemed much longer, we pulled into Peterborough station and to my relief I saw about twenty officers with a couple of dogs on the station. We were actually fighting with the group and I suspect we were very lucky not to be injured. The last thing I wanted was for any of us to end up on the floor being kicked by a pack of fans that were in a frenzy.

As soon as the train stopped the doors opened and the group surged off the train with us still fighting in the middle of them. PC Kevin Andrews showed great courage by hanging onto the ringleader as we all exploded out of the train onto the platform. What I can only describe as a mass brawl commenced on the platform as we tried to regain control of the situation with the help of the Cambridgeshire Police officers. At this stage the rail network conspired against us and unfortunately, at this exact moment, Cardiff and Sheffield fans also arrived at the station on a different train and started fighting each other, and the Sunderland risk group.

A group of these new individuals ran onto the train and started fighting with the remaining Sunderland risk group who were still in the carriage. I remember seeing a fire extinguisher going off inside the train, which was shortly afterwards thrown as a weapon. It was a highly volatile situation that we managed to bring under control with the help of a number of police dogs with very sharp teeth, which eventually resulted in nine arrests.

There possibly should have been more arrests, but we still had a large number of supporters to escort back to Sunderland and I could not afford to lose all of the officers on my serial to a custody suite to deal with prisoners. We did, however, get the main ringleaders into custody, which was good news!

We were able to contain the remainder of the risk group, who hadn't been arrested, on the train and were supported by other BTP officers who joined the escort. It is easy to say they shouldn't have been allowed back on the train, but, in reality, what was I supposed to do? If I left them in Peterborough they would have caused more problems and eventually would have made their way onto a different train that didn't have an escort.

Once the remaining fans realised that a group of their friends had been arrested and after I pointed out that the next stop was Doncaster, where the cops were less welcoming than the ones at Peterborough, they thankfully calmed down.

As things settled, I made my way through the train to check on the passengers, staff and the rail enforcement officers. I came across families who been out for the day, old people, and genuine football supporters. I saw children crying with fear, and very upset and frightened parents and passengers who had never experienced or seen anything like it before. It was disgraceful and inexcusable behaviour from a group of men who were mostly in their forties and fifties and should have grown up a long time ago.

The ringleader was charged with a football-related offence, but because of the nature of such incidents it became very difficult to secure a conviction. As I recall, he was not even the subject of a banning order, or convicted of anything other than a minor public order offence. This was one of the worst football-related incidents I was involved in during my police career and I can say without any hesitation that the three officers who were with me acted with courage, and professionalism, and we definitely put our own safety at serious risk to protect the passengers and staff on that train. The serial consisted of me, Inspector Rob Edwards, Sergeant Matt Popple, Constable Kevin Andrews and Constable Nick Storey.

I subsequently found out that the ringleader who was arrested, and who had travelled all over the world following football, later committed suicide by jumping off the cliffs on the north-east coast a couple of years after the incident.

Terry Nicholson, who retired as a chief superintendent with the BTP and covered the north-east area, reaffirms the difficulties they faced when policing fans returning north after fixtures in London,

If Leeds, for instance, started to give us the run around, we had to deploy additional resources to cover the routes Carlisle, Manchester, Leeds & Carlisle, Newcastle, York, Leeds & Doncaster. We often had to deploy officers at Doncaster to provide some cover for the late trains out of Kings Cross, as well as sending escorts to Kings Cross itself to bring fans from clubs in the north back.

It just demonstrates the game of chess we played and the flexibility of our officers in managing difficult situations over long distances. On other occasions we escorted EDL supporters, some of whom were football fans, especially from the Bolton area. I believe that they used the EDL as an excuse to go out and play when there were no matches.

On Saturday 11 April 2009, a number of Wolverhampton and Telford fans clashed on one of the platforms at Telford Central railway station. The violent disorder left members of the travelling public shocked and distressed. Three arrests were made in a joint operation between West Mercia Police and BTP, and the offenders subsequently received three-year football banning orders.

On 27 June 2009, at 7.45 p.m., up to fifteen Plymouth Argyle and Exeter fans confronted each other at Exeter St Thomas railway station. There was no match that day and the indications were that the fight had been prearranged. Bottles were thrown during the melee, and one person was left unconscious.

In a follow-up operation code-named Operation Incisor, which was overseen by Superintendent Michael Layton, forty BTP and Devon and Cornwall police officers made eleven arrests in connection with the incident. Much of the evidence relied on a photograph taken by a member of the public at the time of the fight, and the Crown Prosecution Service later decided not to proceed due to identification issues.

Sometimes such decisions could be frustrating, but that is the system.

On 11 July 2009, a group of drunken Sheffield Wednesday supporters were caught by on-board CCTV cameras attacking a group of Leeds United fans returning from a stag party at the races at York. The Leeds fans had the misfortune of sitting near to the ringleader of the Sheffield group, who had been out drinking in bars in York, and started talking about their team. Absolute pandemonium then broke out on the York to Manchester TransPennine Service, with fighting that lasted for 10 long minutes.

Parents were forced to shield their children while the attackers punched, kicked and stamped on their rivals on the train. A member of rail staff, who tried to block the aisle with his food trolley, was pushed aside as the conductor locked the train doors to try to contain the violence.

Eventually, however, the attackers used the emergency levers to force open the train doors, and escaped close to Garforth station in West Yorkshire. Three of them were quickly identified from CCTV images, and nine further arrests followed.

Judge Paul Hoffman described it as the worst case of mob violence he had ever seen, commenting, 'This is quite the worst and ugliest incident of mob violence on a train that I've personally ever had to deal with. I find it hard to imagine a more violent disorder on a train of ferocity and persistence of violence.' He jailed the defendants for a total of twenty-seven years imprisonment when they appeared at Leeds Crown Court.

At the end of the court proceedings, BTP Detective Sergeant Granville Sellers said,

This was an appalling unprovoked attack on a group of young men who were simply returning from an enjoyable day at the races. It was also a terrifying ordeal for the large numbers of passengers and staff who were travelling on this train and who genuinely feared for their safety.

At 6 p.m. on Tuesday 25 August 2009, hundreds of West Ham and Millwall supporters confronted each other outside Upton Park Underground station prior to a Carling Cup match. Fifty police officers in riot gear struggled to keep the two sides apart as bricks and bottles were thrown, just 600 yards from the ground. Before the game, Tube trains did not stop at West Ham station as fans toured the platforms looking for likely targets.

On 26 August 2009, 150 Bristol Rovers fans were escorted to Cardiff railway station in coaches after they had made efforts to have a pre-arranged fight with Cardiff supporters. As they were being escorted onto the platforms, by a mixture of BTP officers and South Wales Police, they spotted some Cardiff risk fans and made efforts to reach them while chanting 'GSH', which stands for Gas Hit Squad, loudly.

The Bristol fans initially refused to board the 10 p.m. service and started trying to push police officers down some steps leading to a subway. Officers were forced to draw batons to drive them back. For a few desperate moments the police were at a disadvantage as the hooligans made a stand at the top of the steps, but a determined push forced them back. Five arrests were made as a number of flailing bodies were restrained and handcuffed on the floor of the platform.

Three of the group, all of whom had previous convictions for football-related violence, were later convicted of public order offences and received football banning orders for three years. The BTP Silver Commander for that evening, Superintendent Michael Layton, briefed the media, 'Those guilty of taking part in football-related disorder will be dealt with severely by the courts, and football banning orders applied for. Behaviour such as that witnessed at Cardiff Central station will not be tolerated.'

Further south on the same day, a Carling Cup game was being held between West Ham and Millwall. Hundreds of Milwall fans, mostly young and dressed in casual clothing, flooded onto the District line at West Ham station. As some fans urinated in the carriages, the emergency cord was pulled at Upton Park station and there was a mass exodus out onto the streets and the waiting police cordons.

Just to illustrate how little some things had changed over the years, on 27 August 2009 'Clint Iguana' posted the following comments online during a debate on football violence set up by 'Urban 75',

> Never been involved, although travelling regularly by train in the 80s I saw an awful lot of it close up. I have to confess I did get a buzz out of being around it, but it was quite easy to stay out of it. I always felt quite safe being among Cardiff fans because when it kicked off they usually had the upper hand. The only time I did get a little worried (rephrase that, shit myself) was in Birmingham New Street station when the Zulu Warriors boarded our train with knives going mad before we had even set foot on the platform.

In September 2009, BTP announced that a total of 838 people had been arrested for football-related violence by the end of the previous season, and eighty-one football banning orders had been obtained. This represented a 40 per cent increase on the 601 arrests recorded for the same period in the previous season.

By the end of the 2008/09 football season, BTP had obtained eighty-three football banning orders and increased arrests by 49 per cent on the previous year. Throughout the season, problems had occurred with Middlesbrough, Sunderland and Newcastle United fans on the east coast mainline route into London, and plans were put in place to deter their antisocial behaviour for the new season by reinforcing ticket gate lines and introducing dry trains where the possession of alcohol was prohibited.

Also in September 2009, BTP Scottish Area Commander, Chief Superintendent Martyn Ripley, highlighted an increase in sectarian and racist chants among supporters, for example Aberdeen fans making Nazi salutes in one instance. He said, 'We are seeing an increase in sectarian breaches, and the resurgence of mob violence. For example we recently had to deal with a large fight that broke out among a number of fans in Stonehaven, in Aberdeenshire.' He also highlighted that clubs in Edinburgh were normally pretty well behaved, while pointing towards the fact that Glasgow clubs accounted for two thirds of the arrests on the rail network in Scotland, with sixty-two arrests in total taking place during the previous season.

On 26 September 2009, Chesterfield fans travelled to Bradford and provided details of their train travel to their rivals in advance. Predictably, they were met by a number of Bradford fans and during a confrontation missiles, including bottles, were thrown and one man suffered a head injury.

Also on Saturday 26 September 2009, Superintendent Michael Layton was Silver Commander in the BTP control room at Birmingham, overseeing a number of movements of fans across the country. He recalls,

We became aware that a group of Northampton fans had boarded a train, after arriving by coach in Wellington looking for Telford fans. There were issues on the train to Shrewsbury and three of them were arrested on arrival. This group were then escorted by BTP officers, and West Mercia Police, to Wolverhampton railway station.

Prior to their arrival a telephone call was received in the control room from a senior West Midlands Police officer, based in Wolverhampton, who started to dictate to one of the staff what would happen to the supporters when they arrived. He insisted that they would not be allowed to leave the station, and should be put on a train to Birmingham.

I took over the call midway and he was somewhat surprised to find himself being referred to in first name terms by a former colleague. We had never been close and a battle of wills went on for a few minutes where I made it clear that we had jurisdiction and that we would not be putting them on a train to Birmingham. For his part, he didn't want them in Wolverhampton town centre. It was all familiar territory, but fortunately we had made contact with the original coach driver, who was making good progress to Wolverhampton to pick them up. Clearly unhappy at being usurped, the telephone call was terminated but I was not expecting a Christmas card anyway from him.

On arrival, the troublesome, and by now very vocal, group were corralled and eventually placed onto the coach as soon as it arrived. They were then escorted to the motorway by West Midlands Police and left to their own devices. Somewhat surprisingly, a number of them later turned up in the bar at

Birmingham New Street before getting onto an evening train service.

They were monitored through Coventry and Rugby, but by the time they arrived at Northampton it was evident that some of them had behaved in a disorderly manner, and one individual had been captured on CCTV spraying a fire extinguisher at people in one of the coaches. I arranged for a post-incident investigation to take place under the operational name Leather, and members of the Birmingham-based OSU teams subsequently identified, and dealt with, a number of these individuals who received the statutory knock at the door. Once these two teams got their teeth into an enquiry they rarely failed to deliver and were at the forefront of my approach to policing football in my area.

At 11 p.m. on 28 October 2009, following a match between Barnsley and Manchester United, two arrests were made at Barnsley railway station as fans jumped onto the track in an effort to stop a train to Sheffield before it started moving.

In December 2009, BTP pointed out that over five million journeys were made every year on the rail network by football fans alone. Nationally, a total of sixty-eight serious football-related incidents were recorded by the BTP in 2009, which put some context into the scale of the problems, albeit any offences recorded were one too many.

12

2010–2014 –
OPERATION SKYLARK

On 23 January 2010, Superintendent Layton acted as the Silver North football commander for a number of matches, as well as monitoring an EDL march in Stoke-on-Trent. During the course of the events five arrests were made by BTP officers for assault, affray and threatening behaviour.

At 7.10 p.m. on 30 January 2010, a fight took place on a First Great Western service from Paddington to Swansea between a Cardiff fan and a Swansea fan, who were travelling with others. As the train pulled into Bridgend railway station the Cardiff fans alighted, but at the same time pulled a Swansea fan out of the train and a brawl developed with up to nine people, as other Swansea fans got involved on platform 5.

DI Mark Cleland from the BTP released images of seven men that they were looking for. There was intense rivalry between these two sets of fans and violent confrontations were almost inevitable.

On the evening of Saturday 6 February 2010, at around 9.10 p.m., a group of Sheffield Wednesday and Nottingham Forest fans became involved in fighting on the platforms of Nottingham railway station. A female PCSO from BTP who attended the incident was punched twice in the head and received minor facial injuries. Five people were arrested by BTP at the time, and a further three following a post-incident investigation, and dealt with by the courts.

At 7.45 p.m. on Sunday 28 February 2010, two men and a woman travelled back from Wembley Central and were standing on a platform at Northampton railway station when they were approached by a group of five men, believed to be Aston Villa supporters returning from the Carling Cup final.

For no apparent reason, the three victims were then attacked, leaving one of the men with two broken ribs and severe bruising, while the other received swelling to the eye.

On Saturday 6 March 2010, Superintendent Michael Layton launched Operation Reactor after disorder on a train involving Newport fans, and recalls,

On this date I was again the BTP Silver North commander for football, based in the control room at Birmingham. Newport played away at Weymouth that day and after the game some ninety Newport fans boarded the 17.30 hours service from Weymouth to Bristol Temple Meads. Dorset police escorted the train from Weymouth to Dorchester.

During the journey from Dorchester to Yeovil, public order offences were committed, the on board CCTV was tampered with, people were smoking in contravention of byelaws, and the communication cord was pulled twice, as the female train manager struggled bravely to keep genuine passengers safe. BTP officers, led by Chief Inspector Kevin Marshall, intercepted the train at Westbury and escorted it into Bristol, where on arrival four arrests were made of men aged twenty years, twenty-six years, thirty-seven years and forty-seven years after threats were made against the officers. As other fans confronted them officers were obliged to draw their batons, and Captor sprays, on the platform to defend themselves.

Detective Inspector Mick Southerton was put in charge of a post-incident investigation and nine CCTV images were released of further suspects, all of whom were identified and dealt with.

Also on 6 March 2010, the media reported on the scene at Bolton railway station as a mob of a hundred men punched the air in unison and shouted 'Muslim bombers off our streets.' Hardened football hooligans from Cardiff City's Soul Crew, Bolton Wanderers' Cuckoo Boys and Luton Town's Men in Gear stood side by side, some waving St George's cross flags. Normally they would be fighting each other on a match day. Today they stood together on their way to an English Defence League march.

At 7 p.m. on 24 April 2010, a pre-arranged fight took place outside Chesterfield railway station between supporters from Chesterfield and Bradford City. It was a grudge attack relating to earlier violence in the season between the two sets of supporters. Sticks were brandished and, as police intervened, several arrests were made and ten people subsequently appeared in court charged with public order offences.

On 15 May 2010, a twenty-seven-year-old Chelsea fan was arrested at Peterborough railway station for hurling racist abuse at passengers after travelling back on a train from London. He was extremely drunk and aggressive towards passengers, chanting and making racist comments before doing a Nazi salute. He later received a three-year football banning order.

In the preceding football season, fifteen football-related incidents had occurred at the station as local BTP officers pledged a clampdown.

On Saturday 22 May 2010, Cardiff City played Blackpool at Wembley for the play-off final. At Cardiff railway station, BTP Superintendent Michael Layton and Chief Inspector Sandra England set up a coordinated drugs and alcohol operation as fans arrived for the trip to Paddington station in London. The policy of keeping trains dry from alcohol was enforced, and a number of sniffer dogs, including one handled by PC Paul Morse, identified some twenty-five persons in possession of controlled drugs. To a degree it was like fishing in a barrel as, one after the other, the dogs gave positive indications.

The additional activity had the effect of calming the travelling fans behaviour. In the BTP's 2009/10 annual report, they listed sixty-eight serious football-related incidents as having taken place within the reporting period, with 582 less serious incidents recorded. Twenty-one BTP officers were assaulted during football-related incidents.

On Tuesday 22 June 2010, as a precursor to the coming season Superintendent Layton attended a meeting to discuss action plans that were being created to combat what were perceived to be the seven most troublesome clubs at that time.

On Saturday 31 July 2010, in a sign of things to come, seven persons were dealt with for football-related incidents in so-called friendly matches in the BTP's Wales and Western area. The reality was that for the police there was often very little to be regarded as friendly in terms of the fans' behaviour.

At 8.30 p.m. on Saturday 28 August 2010, a West Ham supporter was attacked on a train at Manchester Piccadilly station by five men, believed to be Stoke City fans, and punched in the head more than twenty times. The forty-year-old from London was left with cuts and bruises to the face. BTP subsequently circulated CCTV images of the suspects.

At 7.40 p.m. on Saturday 18 September 2010, a fight took place at Derby railway station between Derby County and Crewe Alexander supporters. After initially exchanging friendly banter the mood turned ugly, with punches being exchanged and glasses thrown. Three arrests were made.

On Saturday 25 September 2010, a forty-one-year-old woman, who was travelling on a train with her husband and five-year-old son, was so incensed by the behaviour of a group of football fans that she took the unusual step of standing in front of the train until the police were called. She was travelling on an Arriva service from Cardiff when she intervened when a group of Cardiff fans started to verbally abuse another female. As a result they turned their unwanted attention onto her, and as the train progressed, despite asking the driver to call the police, the harassment continued.

As the train arrived at Ystrad Mynach station, after again failing to get staff to call for the police, she stood on the track in front of the train and refused to move until they were called. Detective Inspector Mark Cleland was put in charge of a post-incident investigation and released CCTV images of ten men that BTP wanted to speak to in connection with the incidents.

In October 2010, BTP reported a 49 per cent increase in football-related arrests on trains.

On Saturday 27 November 2010, Superintendent Michael Layton acted as BTP Silver Commander for an EDL demonstration at Nuneaton. Once again, the Birmingham-based Operations Support Units and dog handlers were at the forefront of activity. A complete block was put in place on the station as EDL supporters arrived, and a large number of people were dealt with for being in possession of controlled drugs, as the passive drugs dogs made numerous indications. At the end of the event, a fight broke out on the station as BTP officers were confronted, and further arrests took place, leading to a tally of eighteen persons being processed in total.

On 9 January 2011, a thirty-six-year-old Manchester United fan from Stoke-on-Trent was drinking with friends in a bar at Manchester Piccadilly station when they got into a conversation with a number of Liverpool fans. The discussions about football turned violent and fighting erupted. The thirty-six-year-old was hit with a chair and received stitches to a head injury. For his troubles he was later convicted of affray and, together with a second person, was sent to prison for six months and banned from attending games for six years.

On 25 January 2011, two Arsenal fans became involved in an argument with another passenger as they made their way home from Finsbury Park to Peterborough following Arsenal's Carling Cup semi-final game against Ipswich Town. They turned violent and head-butted and punched their victim repeatedly, leaving him with cuts and bruises. They were arrested by BTP at Stevenage railway station and, following conviction, received three-year football banning orders.

On 30 April 2011, violence erupted at Sheffield railway station as members of Sheffield United's Blades Business Crew attacked Barnsley fans that were waiting for their trains. The group picked up ballast stones and threw them at the opposition, resulting in a sixty-year-old man suffering a serious cut to his head, which required hospital treatment. Three men were later identified from CCTV footage and jailed, as well as being banned from football matches for seven years for affray.

BTP Football Intelligence Officer PC Wayne Mitchell said, 'The actions of these three men put the safety of a host of people at Sheffield railway station at risk … they sullied the name of Sheffield United.'

In May 2011, after the FA Cup final, two Chelsea fans travelling on a Tube train from Wembley Park to Harrow on Hill got into an argument with a Portsmouth fan who was attacked, punched and kicked. He received a torn ear, as well as cuts and bruising to his face. The two offenders subsequently got suspended prison sentences and community service orders after being convicted of inflicting grievous bodily harm.

In the BTP annual report for 2010/11, a total of 1,054 football-related offences were recorded as detected in the reporting period, resulting from 760 arrests. Some fifty-two serious football-related incidents were recorded, as well as 724 less serious incidents. Fifteen BTP officers were assaulted during football commitments, and sixty-seven football banning orders obtained.

The Wales and Western area alone accounted for 279 of those arrested.

On 3 August 2011, a number of Villa fans seriously vandalised a carriage on a Cross Country service train taking them back to Birmingham from a friendly game with Derby County. Tray tables were ripped from the back of seats, seat coverings damaged, and lights smashed, resulting in the train being taken out of service for 24 hours.

On Saturday 6 August 2011, fighting among football fans at Reading station led to seven arrests after the first matches of the season. Millwall drew 2-2 at Reading and Leeds lost at Southampton. Three Millwall fans and two Leeds fans started fighting at about 8 p.m. on platform 5, and they were arrested and charged with affray. At 6.40 p.m. another Millwall fan was arrested for a racially aggravated public order offence, assaulting police and possession of cannabis after an incident on a Waterloo-bound train. Just 15 minutes later, yet another Millwall fan was detained for another racially aggravated offence and assaulting police following an incident outside the Three Guineas pub.

On Saturday 13 August 2011, the EDL held a static protest in Wellington town centre, near to the railway station. As demonstrators arrived by train at the station, at least two arrests were made for public order offences by BTP officers. Ordinarily they were believed to be Walsall football supporters.

In September 2011, a twenty-year-old Leeds fan from Gloucestershire, who breached his football banning order three times, was sent to a Young Offenders Institute after an investigation by BTP.

On 10 September 2011, four Hearts fans were arrested on their way back to Edinburgh after making sexually abusive chants to a woman on a train, purely because she had the courage to ask them to moderate their behaviour. They also sang racially offensive songs and were later given substantial fines, as well as receiving three-year football banning orders.

On Saturday 7 January 2012, a nineteen-year-old Bolton Wanderers fan was at Macclesfield railway station with the intention of attending the FA Cup game between Macclesfield and Bolton Wanderers. After a man he was travelling with was arrested, he became aggressive towards BTP officers and made as if to punch one of the officers. He was duly arrested and subsequently banned from attending football matches for four years.

On 7 January 2012, police were called by passengers on board a train from Putney to Waterloo after Charlton Athletic fans, who were returning from an FA Cup match with Fulham, started being rowdy, making sexual comments and singing racist songs.

In a pre-planned operation some two weeks later, BTP officers made nine arrests in the Bexley, Greenwich, Lewisham and Bromley areas. The suspects were aged between twenty-one years and thirty years of age, and the case involved a group of men singing and chanting racist abuse in praise of the convicted murderers of Stephen Lawrence.

Six men subsequently received prison sentences, and eight-year football banning orders, at Blackfriars Crown Court, while a seventh received a suspended sentence.

On Saturday 16 January 2012, four men in their twenties, who were believed to be Celtic fans, attacked a sixteen-year-old boy on the 16.42 hours train service from Glasgow Central to Kilmarnock after he asked them to stop singing sectarian songs. He was punched in the head and body several times, sustaining cuts to his head and face, and a bottle was smashed on the floor. His attackers got off the train at Barrhead railway station.

At 7.17 p.m. on Saturday 10 March 2012, horrified women and children looked on as violence erupted at Glasgow Central station after a Scottish cup tie at Somerset Park between Ayr United and Hibernian. It was to transpire later that an organised fight had been organised via text messages between hooligans with links to the two clubs and Chelsea hooligans. The fight started as Hibernian fans got off a train at the station and were confronted by an opposing group at the Hope Street entrance, just as five innocent women were passing through.

In keeping with incidents of this nature, both sets of hooligans 'faced off' each other, looking for potential weak points before moving into close-quarters fighting, punching, kicking and throwing bottles. At least one of them was dragged to the floor and punched and kicked mercilessly until he lay spread-eagled on the floor unconscious.

Two of the first officers on the scene, one male and one female, were simply overwhelmed by the scale of the violence and numbers involved, and struggled to keep the two sides apart as they were forced to draw their asps. Despite the fact that people were engaged in violent acts around them, however, none of it seemed to be directed towards them. At one point the female officer looked dangerously isolated until two others came running through the crowds with asps raised, closely followed by five other officers.

At one point up to seventy people were involved in the fighting, which surged backwards and forwards at the entrance, with some thirty subsequently being identified from CCTV images captured on several cameras within the station complex. A few remembered to pull their hoods up to avoid identification, but for the main part they were lost in the moment of the adrenalin-fuelled frenzy, which lasted for just 5 minutes.

Suspects were arrested by the BTP working under the operational name Skylark. A number claimed to have been innocently caught up in the mass brawl, which resulted in one Hibernian fan having the upper two thirds of his left ear bitten off, with the perpetrator literally clinging on to his target as he bit through the skin and bone. The severed ear was later found on the floor of the station concourse, but despite the best efforts of doctors they were unable to sew it back on.

Six men, aged between twenty-four and forty-eight years, were arrested at the time of the incident, and British Transport Police, supported by officers from Lothian and Borders Police, later arrested a further five men aged between twenty-two years and forty-five years, all from the Edinburgh area. Fans involved in this act of senseless violence were subsequently banned for a total of forty-three years from attending football matches.

Detective Inspector Grant Cathcart of BTP said after the convictions, 'Those involved and convicted of this pre-planned violence on a busy Saturday evening showed scant regard for members of the public.'

Footage of the CCTV images of the fight, uploaded to the internet by the Capital City Service (CCS), a hooligan group linked to Hibernian, has received nearly 68,000 views.

At the end of March 2012, BTP officers arrested two Glasgow Rangers fans at Ibrox Subway station for singing sectarian songs before their game with Aberdeen.

At 4.20 p.m. on Saturday 19 May 2012, more than a dozen men started fighting in the foyer of Huddersfield railway station in what was believed to be a pre-arranged fight between a mixture of Leeds United, Bradford City and Huddersfield Town supporters. A glass screen was smashed as they hurled large barriers and shopping trolleys at each other, before a number of them jumped onto the rail tracks and started throwing stones.

As they ran off down the tracks, massive disruption was caused as all trains were brought to a standstill and a police helicopter was deployed. BTP later confirmed that they had made eight arrests as trains were halted until 5.13 p.m., with sixty-one trains delayed. One tweeter at the scene commented, 'Love having my train delayed cos of some Green Street style fans at Huddersfield', making reference to a well-known hooligan film.

Still images of a further eight suspects were later released to the media.

The BTP annual report for 2011/12 highlighted the fact that 562 arrests had been made in the reporting year, with fifty-nine serious football-related incidents recorded and 649 less serious incidents. Thirty-three football banning orders were obtained, and the force gave evidence to the Scottish Parliament's Justice Committee, which was looking at how to eliminate sectarianism from Scottish football.

At the beginning of August 2012, a friendly game between Leicester City and Lincoln City was called off after police received intelligence that disorder was planned in Lincoln town centre. This did not stop fans from Leicester travelling and a steward on one train was assaulted. BTP officers attended Lincoln railway station after the communication cord was pulled on a train and a female train guard was assaulted. Police lined the tracks as the train was moved into the station, with damaged brakes, and eighty Leicester fans were escorted onto another service. One fan was arrested for being drunk and disorderly.

Just after 7 p.m. on Saturday 18 August 2012, a fight broke out on platform 13 at Leeds railway station between fans from Leeds and Middlesbrough. Glasses and bottles were thrown during the fight and a number of people injured. Three arrests were made at the time, and a further four were arrested following the release of some CCTV images. They were all charged with violent disorder.

At 10.40 p.m. on Saturday 18 August 2012, a fight broke out between Sunderland and Manchester United fans as a train service they were both on pulled into Northallerton railway station. As the United fans left the train, one of them threw a beer bottle that hit a Sunderland fan on the head. The Sunderland group also then disembarked and disturbances took place throughout the station.

On Saturday 25 August 2012, BTP officers were on duty at Shrewsbury railway station when their attention was drawn to a group of fifteen Tranmere fans who had spent the day drinking in the town centre and were drunk and noisy, not having even bothered to go to the local game. As officers spoke to them at 5.10 p.m. they became aggressive towards them, and one forty-year-old man threatened to bite the face off an officer and to rip the head off another. He was so violent that when arrested he had to be placed in leg restraints, and on arrival at the police custody suite he assaulted an officer. He was subsequently sentenced to eighteen weeks in prison and banned from attending football matches for ten years.

On 10 November 2012, Crystal Palace and Brighton & Hove Albion fans clashed outside Kings Cross railway station as they hurled bottles, glasses, sandwich boards and road bollards at each other. The fight took place outside the Flying Scotsman pub in Caledonian Road, where Crystal Palace fans were celebrating their win against Peterborough United. Brighton fans had been to a game in Wolverhampton and after getting off a train at Euston headed straight for Kings Cross.

Just two police officers were initially on duty at the location as they tried in vain to contain the mass brawl. Nine people were subsequently convicted of violent disorder, in an incident which left members of the public terrified.

At 11.10 p.m., on Saturday 22 December 2012, a forty-eight-year-old West Ham fan was returning home from a 24-hour binge drinking session in London after watching West Ham *v*. Everton on big-screen TV in a pub. While on a Paddington to Bristol Temple Meads service he started abusing passengers, and then turned his attention to the train manager. He was arrested at Reading railway station and was eventually jailed for twenty weeks and made the subject of a football banning order.

On 29 December 2012, after a game between Aberdeen and Dundee, an Aberdeen fan was attacked as he walked to Dundee railway station and punched and knocked to the ground, where he was kicked repeatedly. A second fan was attacked and punched in the head on the station itself. Both incidents were captured on CCTV and the two offenders were arrested and received custodial sentences.

In 2012, BTP recorded a total of 650 football-related offences.

At 10.15 p.m. on Friday 4 January 2013, a fifty-six-year-old Portsmouth fan was on Walsall railway station with his wife. They had been to the match and were on the station to pick up their car when they were approached by a group of Walsall fans. One of them grabbed his wife's bobble hat and as the victim chased after them to retrieve it he was punched and kicked.

As he collapsed against a wall one of his attackers then kicked him in the jaw, which was broken. He was taken to hospital, where metal plates were inserted, and for a while he could only eat baby food. CCTV pictures of the attackers were subsequently released to the media by DC Simon Taylor, BTP, and arrests followed. Three men were subsequently banned from football matches for a total of fourteen years and one of them was sent to prison for two years.

On Saturday 5 January 2013 at 9 p.m., a thirty-one-year-old man wearing a Manchester United scarf was singled out for abuse on a train to Chorley by a group of Manchester City fans. One of the group tried to punch him but he managed to escape.

In February 2013, commuters were forced to scatter as fighting broke out among fans at Earls Court station following an FA Cup tie at Stamford Bridge between Chelsea and Brentford.

On 16 February 2013, a London-based BTP Police Support Unit formed a thin blue line to escort massed ranks of supporters to a game between Luton and Millwall during a fifth round FA Cup match at Kenilworth Road, which ended with Millwall winning 3-0. It is a tribute to British policing that small numbers of highly trained officers can still exert influence over hundreds of people, some of whom had a propensity to commit disorder. Just seven arrests were made by police on the day.

In March 2013 four drunken Manchester United fans, who had been watching a game with Norwich, clashed with a group of men on a travellator at Manchester Piccadilly station. The other group were dressed as *Where's Wally?* characters and were on a stag do. Five of them were subsequently arrested for public order offences.

In April 2013 there were scuffles at Tube stations after trouble at the FA Cup semi-final between Millwall, and Wigan at Wembley.

On Saturday 13 April 2013, a large group of Watford fans were returning by train from Peterborough when they boarded an East Coast train heading for Kings Cross railway station. They moved into the First Class carriages while en route and started chanting and shouting abuse at rail staff. The train was met by the BTP at Kings Cross and twelve arrests were made, seven of whom were charged with public order offences and one with possession of drugs. Two of the group later received three-year football banning orders, which were applied for by one of BTP's football intelligence officers, PC Alvin Soomary.

During the weekend of 13 and 14 April 2013, BTP officers made thirty-six football-related arrests. In addition to the arrests relating to Watford fans, four Manchester United fans were detained at rail stations for racially aggravated public order offences, assaulting a train conductor and possession of drugs. Seven Chelsea fans were arrested for common assault and public order offences at Wembley Park, while three more were held at Milton Keynes on a late-night service. Six Millwall fans were arrested for affray, theft and being drunk and disorderly.

During the course of violent disturbances in Newcastle on the same day, three BTP officers were assaulted, and one of them, a female officer, was taken to hospital after being hit on the shoulder with a brick. Another officer suffered a black eye after being elbowed in the face, while the third officer, a sergeant, received facial and leg injuries after being hit by ballast stones as they stood between fighting Newcastle and Sunderland fans. Four Newcastle fans were arrested for violent disorder and being drunk and disorderly, as terrified rail workers tried to lock the station doors.

On 27 April 2013, Nottingham Forest fans were returning from an away fixture at Millwall and Doncaster Rovers were playing a league match at Brentford that saw them promoted to the Championship. An argument between two supporters at Kings Cross in London resulted in a Forest fan phoning for friends to meet the train at Newark in Nottinghamshire.

As the train pulled in, the Forest fans banged on the train windows before the two groups confronted each other in an exit lobby, as fighting then spilled out onto the platform. Members of rail staff and the public ran for safety as bottles were thrown and punches and kicks exchanged. One rail staff member was assaulted and threatened with being pushed under the train. One of the offenders was stabbed in the face with a broken bottle and received significant facial injuries.

After a post-incident investigation by BTP, fifteen people, from both groups, were charged with various offences and were later dealt with at Nottingham Crown Court. The eight Forest supporters, and seven Doncaster supporters, received a mixture of prison sentences, community service, and in one case a conditional discharge. All of them received football banning orders.

Detective Inspector Glen Alderson from BTP, who led the enquiry, said at the conclusion of the court proceedings, 'We simply will not tolerate this violent and barbaric behaviour.'

BTP launched an investigation after an incident at 7.40 p.m. on 15 May 2013, on the day of the Europa League final. A number of Chelsea fans were already on a Tube train when a Jewish man boarded the District line service travelling towards Wimbledon Underground station. A witness heard one of the Chelsea fans singing 'One man went to gas, went to gas a yiddo,' a song aimed at Tottenham Hotspur, which has a large Jewish fan base, and he refused to stop singing despite protestations about its anti-Semitic tone.

In July 2013, two twenty-year-old members of Dundee's Alliance Under Fives hooligan group were sentenced to detention for assaulting two Aberdeen fans at Dundee railway station.

On 3 August 2013, a train carrying Tranmere Rovers fans back to Birmingham from a game with Walsall was pelted with bricks and bottles. No-one was injured, but they were delayed on arrival at New Street station as Birmingham and Watford fans engaged in serious disorder at the entrance to the station.

On 23 August 2013, the BTP released figures to the media which indicated a leap of 38 per cent in football-related offences on the rail network and on London's Tube system. Less serious incidents for the reporting year 2012/13 stood at 812, and arrests nationwide stood at 780, as senior officers officer's pointed out that violence had moved away from stadiums due to the presence of CCTV and heavy policing.

BTP Assistant Chief Constable Steve Thomas urged rail staff to report incidents and not to accept that it was just part of the job. Twenty-two football banning orders were obtained, as it was highlighted that 26 per cent of all BTP command and control logs for football-related matters had an 'alcohol related' flag attached to them.

On 28 August 2013, Aston Villa fans, returning from a Capital One Cup clash with Rotherham, became involved in disturbances on New Street station at 11.30 p.m. One member of the public was so alarmed by events that he tweeted for help.

On Saturday 5 October 2013, a fight broke out on a train travelling between Bournemouth and Brockenhurst. Millwall had lost to Bournemouth that day with a score line of 5-2. Two men were subsequently found on the train with facial injuries, but nobody came forward with any complaints. BTP later released CCTV images of three men that they wanted to speak to.

On 22 October 2013, two BTP officers were deployed to Bridgetown railway station, in Glasgow, for the Champions League match between Celtic and Ajax at Celtic Park. While on patrol they heard shouting and were confronted by fifteen supporters engaged in a fight. Despite several warnings they refused to stop, and finally one of the officers sprayed them with his Captor spray, which dampened their appetite for further trouble.

At 6.45 p.m. on Saturday 12 April 2014, three men from Wrexham were involved in a football-related disturbance while their train was stationary on the platform of Rhyl railway station.

At 7.37 p.m. on Sunday 13 April 2014, a group of fifteen Liverpool and Manchester City fans confronted each other on Liverpool Lime Street railway station. Grown men jumped up and down, punching, pushing and jostling each other at the glass doors to one of the entrances, as innocent members of the public weaved their way through them. One individual belatedly remembered that his behaviour was likely to be captured on CCTV and pulled up his tracksuit hood over his head – rather pointlessly, as it happened.

As the violence moved onto the main concourse, one woman in a wheelchair, with a dog, made frantic efforts to get out of the way, while another woman with a pushchair became marooned among the milling morons.

The action came to an end as a number of BTP officers ran in and took one of the protagonists, a Manchester City fan, to the floor, while most of the combatants melted away. He was subsequently given a community order, together with a second Manchester City fan, and also ordered to pay compensation to one of the officers who he assaulted.

One thirty-two-year member of Liverpool's Urchin hooligan group headbutted an unknown Manchester City fan, who was left with blood streaming from his nose, while a forty-year-old member of the same group also displayed gratuitous violence. Both were subsequently identified from CCTV images and received suspended prison sentences and football banning orders for their part in the fight, in what the judge hearing the case described as 'disgraceful and quite shocking behaviour given their ages.'

On Sunday 11 May 2014, on the last day of the football season, a group of Arsenal and Tottenham fans started chanting at each other at the Hamilton Hall pub at Liverpool Street station in London. However, the situation quickly deteriorated as one thirty-seven-year-old Arsenal fan threw his beer over Spurs fans and started shouting racist remarks. In the ensuing fight, tables were pushed over and glasses smashed. The thirty-seven-year-old was arrested and subsequently received a three-year football banning order. PC Barry Vasselin from the BTP said, 'Football is a game for people to enjoy and be passionate about, however violence or criminal behaviour will not be tolerated on the rail network.'

On Saturday 9 August 2014, Sheffield Wednesday fans on their way back home after an away game with Brighton got involved in a fight with Chesterfield fans at about 10 p.m., as their train drew into Leicester railway station. Up to twenty people were involved in the disturbance, which resulted in a number of them suffering minor injuries, and the train was delayed for twenty minutes.

At 7.42 p.m. on Saturday 16 August 2014, a disturbance took place at Nuneaton railway station, in Warwickshire, as a group of Everton fans threw bottles and ran across the tracks before being corralled together by BTP and local officers.

At 5.30 p.m. on Saturday 30 August 2014, BTP were called to a fight on board a Surbiton to London Waterloo train. As the train stopped at Raynes Park station, on the way back from a game at Stevenage, fans confronted each other.

On the same date, BTP officers arrested a man for assault at Fratton railway station after violence broke out between Newport and Portsmouth supporters.

At 6 p.m. on Saturday 20 September 2014, police were called to control Barnsley fans, who had been to a game at Port Vale, as they clashed with Stoke City fans at Stoke railway station who had arrived on trains from an away game in London.

At 8 p.m. on Sunday 21 September 2014, three hooligans arrived at Harborough railway station to catch a train heading north towards Manchester. One proceeded to throw an advertising board on to the tracks and urinated on the platform. All three then proceeded to pull a pedal cycle apart, which had been in a cycle rack, and threw the pieces onto the line in an act of mindless insanity.

On Friday 12 December 2014, fighting occurred at Brighton's railway station as Millwall fans arrived for a match.

At 6.45 p.m. on Sunday 29 December 2014, a group of football supporters boarded a train from Perth following the St Johnstone *v.* Dundee United SPFL match. The fans shouted racist slogans and jumped up and down in the carriage, punching windows and the ceiling during the journey north. Several passengers, including children, were alarmed by their behaviour.

13

FROM POLICE CONSTABLE TO GOLD COMMANDER

Alan Pacey retired from the British Transport Police towards the end of 2014, having spent the whole of his police career with the force. These are his personal recollections of policing football, both at an operational level, and as a senior commander:

I joined the British Transport Police in June 1980 and within a few weeks went to the district training centre at Ashford in Kent to learn my trade. To be honest, it came as a bit of a shock when I arrived and was given a plastic beaker with a room key in it and a set of instructions that were pages long. I had to share a room with three other trainee police officers and iron and press my own uniform. I had been used to living at home, where my mum did all that sort of stuff; but I learned very quickly as the alternative was uniform parades at 9 p.m. with the drill sergeant or an equally friendly type of character!

After my initial dread I settled in to training school life very quickly. I found the constant marching and uniform parades completely boring and in my view unnecessary, but I thoroughly enjoyed learning the laws and procedures of policing as they were in 1980 and in the final law exams came third out of about 100 fellow trainee officers. It is fair to say a lot had changed by the time I retired in late 2014.

After ten weeks of bulling boots, pressing uniform and learning the law, I could not wait to get started and do some real police work! I was often asked at training school, why the BTP? The answer is simple: having applied to the Metropolitan Police, Kent Police (I had moved out of London and lived in Dartford at the time) and BTP, it was the Transport Police that responded and offered me a job first. After serving for nearly thirty-five years, I can honestly say how lucky and privileged I feel to have served in such a wonderful police force for all that time.

In the few weeks leading up to training school, I was posted to Lambeth North station in south London, where making tea for the patrolling officers on their meal break seemed to be my main function. Some of the experienced PCs, or at least those who would lower themselves to talk to a 'sprog', as new recruits were fondly called, had delighted in telling me how much fun it was policing football supporters travelling to and from games across the country.

They revelled in stories about rival sets of fans doing battle between Kings Cross and Euston stations every Saturday and how often so-called fans of the beautiful game needed to be arrested because of their behaviour. As an avid football supporter myself, it used to really aggravate me that a minority of football followers ruined it for the majority of us! So I was really looking forward to my first football duty in the 1980/81 season and was hoping to be posted to duty at one of the stations near the big London clubs like Arsenal, Tottenham Hotspur, or Chelsea.

I was eagerly awaiting the football roster to come out, and you can imagine how disappointed I was when I learned I had drawn the short straw and been allocated to Leytonstone London Underground station for a match between Leyton Orient and another less fashionable club that I cannot even remember.

Suffice to say my first football duty was one of the most tedious duties I ever experienced. At the very most 200 supporters came through the station in total, without so much as a raised voice or football chant. The sergeant I was with at the time thought it was great as we did not have to do anything and could get back to our home station early as he was on a day shift and might get an early dart. It made no difference to me as I was working a 10.30 to 22.30 twelve-hour shift, as was very common on Saturdays in the football season.

When I got back to my station at Mansion House I had to wait for the rest of my usual shift to come back from their allotted football duty to regroup before going out on the patch again. When they arrived back I had to endure one of my probationer colleagues telling me how much fun he had getting among rival sets of fans at King's Cross station and how he had made his first football arrest for 'threatening behaviour.' I thought at the time that he had exaggerated the whole experience as, according to him, he had saved lives and separated hundreds of fans who were intent on doing severe damage to each other in the name of football. Actually, it wasn't long before I experienced a similar situation myself!

Later in that season I was allocated to Fulham Broadway underground station, which isn't actually underground, for a Chelsea home match. This was more like it as, although Chelsea were in the second tier of English football at that time, they still drew big crowds and had a hardcore element that would cause trouble if they could. I also have to admit to a secret admiration for Chelsea due to watching the likes of Peter Osgood, Charlie Cooke, Alan Hudson and Peter Bonnetti as I was growing up. While they were not my team, I always looked out for their results and wanted them to do well.

Clearly this would not affect the way I carried out my duties and I have to say that the conduct of some Chelsea fans in the early 1980s soured my view of the club going forward. The main Chelsea crew were known as the Headhunters and were one of the most feared football groups at that time as a result of travelling up and down the country, dishing out violence and ruining the days out of many genuine football supporters.

I actually cannot remember who the match was against, although I remember it was not a London derby. It was also not one of the clubs that we thought would cause trouble so we had a fairly light serial on duty at the station on the day. This proved to be a big mistake! I remember that we were all surprised by the number and conduct of the away supporters that kept turning up at the station to take the short walk down to the ground. It has to be acknowledged that police intelligence structures in those days were not as sophisticated or effective as they are today, but even then we usually knew when trouble was likely.

The forward phase of the operation, as we called it in BTP, passed without incident, even though we realised we had a lot more fans than we expected and the mood of both sets of fans, as they moved through the station, was far from friendly. Our inspector did try to get more resources allocated to us but struggled due to a number of other higher profile fixtures that were taking place in London on that day, so we had to make do with what we had.

As was the norm, we were briefed at half time by the inspector and our plan for after the match, the return phase, was to keep the Chelsea fans at one end of the platform, as they entered via the main way in, and the away fans at the other end of the end of the platform. This was to be achieved by forcing the away fans to enter via the alleyway from the main road, which ran parallel to the platform with an entrance onto the platform that had some metal gates about halfway down. My small unit was to be deployed halfway along the platform to ensure that the two sets of fans were kept apart on the platform and on any train that they boarded. The plan seemed sensible but did not survive contact with the enemy!

About five minutes before the end of the match several fans began to trickle into the station as usual, and we managed to get rid of them quickly onto trains that were going into central London, but after about twenty minutes the main groups from both clubs started to turn up and rapidly started to fill the platform.

Thankfully it is only a minority of fans that are intent on causing trouble on most occasions, but on Fulham Broadway station that day we seemed to have a large group who were intent on doing serious injury to each other. I had, by now, policed enough football days to know when things were going to get ugly and this was one of them. To make matters worse, the tube service conspired against us and quite a gap between trains occurred. The inspector did consider holding the away fans by the metal gates halfway down the platform but considered that would be more dangerous than allowing them on to the platform and keeping them apart.

As a result of sheer numbers, my small unit were unable to keep the fans apart and vicious hand-to-hand fighting started to take place as the Chelsea fans broke through our cordon. In addition, some normal Saturday travellers were getting caught up in the situation, which for a couple of minutes was completely out of control. My unit was doing its utmost to restore order and truncheons were drawn, and used ferociously, in an attempt to regain some sort of order.

At one stage during the melee, I remember striking a very large Chelsea fan on the shoulder with my truncheon a number of times as he was trying to get to some away fans behind me. Sadly, this was having no impact and he got through me with a group of other Chelsea fans. This whole incident seemed to go on for ages, but I suspect in reality it was only a couple of minutes before enough further police assistance arrived to help us contain the situation. A few fans were arrested but, sadly, I had lost sight of the big Chelsea fan by the time we had regained control, he deserved to be taken into custody and there were now enough resources to make that possible.

I scoured the Chelsea group for him but to no avail: I made a vow, however, to reintroduce myself to him the next time I was policing Chelsea! With the assistance that turned up, we eventually got the away fans onto a train that finally turned up at the platform, after moving some normal members of the public out of two carriages in the centre of the train.

To ensure they did not just get off at the next station and wait for the Chelsea crew, we sent some hastily convened travelling serials with them. Those of us that were left contained the Chelsea crew on the platform and made them miss the next couple of trains to give the away fans plenty of time to get out of West London. This of course frustrated the Chelsea crew, and some genuine football supporters, immensely, but we felt it was the safest thing to do. To be frank, frustrating the hooligan group did not bother me at all.

I policed Chelsea many times after this incident but unfortunately never did see the Chelsea fan that I wanted to reacquaint myself with. Perhaps that was just as well!

While these type of incidents were exciting, I could never say that I enjoyed them as so many innocent football fans and members of the public had to witness and sometimes suffer as a result of these mindless minorities.

For some reason, Fulham Broadway station and Chelsea seemed to be a jinx to me as many of the more difficult football days

I endured occurred at that location or while escorting Chelsea fans. As I said earlier, I had a soft spot for Chelsea when I joined the police, but to be honest that wore off after a couple of years of policing the Headhunters.

'*Wem-ber-ley, Wem-ber-ley* –
We're the famous [insert whichever team it happened to be] *and we're going to Wem-ber-ley, Wem-ber-ley, Wem-ber-ley.*'

I have listened to this chant many times over the years when on duty for FA Cup finals in my early years, and semi-finals and play-off finals in my latter years. I even admit to singing the song myself when my club, Charlton Athletic, beat Ipswich Town to reach the First Division play-off final at Wembley in May 1998. On most occasions these were good football duties, with the vast majority of fans intent on having a good day out, and enough police on duty to quell any potential problems very quickly. In the main, I enjoyed my Wembley duties and even accepted the fact that I would have to listen to the unimaginative 'Wem-ber-ley' chant more than I would have liked.

I remember my last Wembley duty as a police constable as I made three separate arrests in the one day, which was pretty unusual. It was Saturday 19 May 1984 and Everton were due to play Watford in the FA Cup final. Two days later, on the Monday, I was due to start a plain clothes CID secondment, which led to a CID posting as a detective constable and a long spell in crime investigation.

Everton *versus* Watford was pretty benign in football terms and I was initially allocated to a serial at Baker Street Underground station, which was the main interchange from Central London up to Wembley and always very busy on these days.

I arrived at Baker Street around 11 a.m. and within a couple of minutes of being there, and prior to receiving my briefing, I couldn't believe my eyes. A small group of Everton fans, who were obviously already the worse for drink, came on to the station and one of them smashed a station light deliberately right in front of me. Well he had to go, and sure enough I arrested him for criminal damage and quickly arranged for transport so that we could go to the local police station for the offender to be dealt with.

Due to his drunken state, the sergeant in charge of custody decided that he would have to sober up before being processed, so no cup final for him! He missed the match and was eventually charged with criminal damage and received a small fine at Marylebone Magistrates Court some weeks later. Having booked the offender into custody and being unable to deal with him straight away due to his drunkenness, I made my way back to Baker Street and reported to the sergeant in charge of my serial. The next two or three hours were uneventful but busy in terms of the number of people using the station.

At about 2.30 p.m. a small but fairly rowdy group of around fifteen stragglers came onto Baker Street station obviously intending to take the short journey up to Wembley Park station. Myself and a colleague were detailed to travel with this group up to Wembley to make sure they did not cause any trouble. Most of this group were okay, but one in particular was pretty obnoxious and had to be warned several times about his language as general members of the public were also on the train. One of his colleagues did his best to quieten him down but this seemed to make him worse.

As we arrived at Wembley, about fifteen minutes after leaving Baker Street, I had already made up my mind to have a meaningful chat with this individual regarding his conduct. On the platform I separated him from his group and took him into an office at the station to have a quiet word. The rest of his group were torn between waiting for him or seeing the start of the match – the start of the match won.

On asking for this gentleman's name, address and date of birth for a Police National Computer check, he immediately became evasive and was nowhere near as vociferous now that he was on his own, which was par for the course for a lot of rowdy fans who were generally happier to be in the company of their particular pack. This caused me to undertake a more thorough interest and, sure enough, on checking his possessions I found credit cards in two separate names for which he could not give me a reasonable explanation.

So another one had to go, and off we went to one of the designated charging centres as per the operational order for the fixture. While it was good for me as an aspiring detective to have another 'body', as prisoners were referred to in those days, for a crime job, it meant that I missed the operational feeding that took place during the match as I was dealing with the offender. I cannot actually remember the outcome of this particular arrest, but it amazed me that a football fan who had a stolen credit card on him would be stupid enough to bring attention to himself by upsetting the police on a train to Wembley just before the cup final was about to start.

The return phase went without too much incident and, after most of the fans had started their journey home, London Underground Division officers like myself were stood down and directed back to home police stations. I was by now at Euston and needed to make my way back to Baker Street, a short two-stop journey from Euston Square station. I was with a colleague, who I would describe as long in the tooth and not the most proactive, which is a nice way of saying he was a bit lazy, particularly at the end of a shift near going home time!

I was still full of energy and extending shifts meant extra overtime to me in those days, so it was always going to be me who made the arrest when we got on the train and found two young men openly smoking a cannabis joint. I ended up working something like a fourteen-hour rest day working shift, at time and a half, which was a good earner and great for the bank balance.

I mentioned in the preceding paragraph that London Underground Division officers were usually stood down from duty as travelling fans started to leave London. That was not the case for my colleagues based around the country, who spent hours and hours of their careers escorting football fans the length and breadth of the country. These officers were often heavily outnumbered and had to use a wide range of policing skills to keep order and to keep safe on these escort duties.

Many others will have described the reality of this situation elsewhere in this book, but I have to express my utmost admiration for the BTP officers who regularly carry out these duties and retain their professionalism, good humour and patience with some of the people they have to deal with.

There were several other football policing incidents that I was involved in as a police constable in the first half of the 1980s.

They ranged from handbags at ten paces to violent confrontations on Tube trains and stations all over London. There were so many I cannot even remember the detail of most of them, other than that I worked nearly every Saturday in the football season and many Tuesday evenings as well. It was a sure bet that at around 5.30 to 6 p.m. on most Saturday afternoons you would find yourself at Kings Cross or Euston stations keeping rival sets of fans apart and making sure they started their journey home out of central London.

It became almost inevitable that certain fixtures would result in disorder and violence, and this definitely diminished my love for the game for quite a while afterwards. Of course nowadays it is not only Saturdays and one evening during the week that football occurs, but almost every day, which puts a massive strain on the resources of BTP even though the disorder is nowhere near as bad as it was back in the 1980s.

In mid-1984, I was attached to the Criminal Investigation Department and in the main left football policing behind for several years. I have to say that I found investigating and dealing with pickpockets, gang robberies and other major crime significantly more interesting and rewarding. I kept away from football even as a spectator for a good few years and it was quite a bit later, when my son started to be interested, that I resumed my love affair with the game, and my club Charlton Athletic.

Although, like most clubs, Charlton had an element of potential hooligans, they were not in the same league as some of the more infamous groups from the likes of Chelsea, West Ham United and Millwall to name just a few. Also, by the mid-1990s the violence had diminished considerably and we witnessed very few incidents at Charlton matches, either home or away.

In January 2003, after a considerable time predominately spent in CID and a good few promotions, I was posted to Birmingham as a chief superintendent in charge of the BTP Wales and Western area. The area I was in charge of covered the East and West Midlands, the whole of Wales, and the south-west of England.

It was great to be promoted to that rank, but it meant a move of home location from the south east, which at the time was a bit worrying. Choosing somewhere to live that enabled me to get to the far reaches of my enormous patch was a challenge and we eventually settled for the borders of the South Midlands and the south-west, which had good transport links to my base station at Birmingham and most of the cities that I needed to get to. It is also a fantastic place to live! This move also meant working as a uniform officer and being in overall charge of football policing for this massive part of the country.

To be honest, it was only then that I learned just how much of a challenge football policing was for BTP outside of London. For a start, I was responsible for an area that housed all of the East Midland clubs; Derby County; Leicester City and Nottingham Forest, the big West Midlands clubs; Birmingham City; Aston Villa; West Bromwich Albion and Wolverhampton Wanderers, and covered arguably the biggest interchange station in the country at Birmingham New Street.

Added to that, Cardiff City, who came with their own baggage and hooligan reputation, were also on my patch. Those who follow football will also remember that while Wembley Stadium was being refurbished, the Millennium Stadium in Cardiff housed all of the FA Cup Finals and other key fixtures that took place for quite a few years, including the period I was in charge.

I had been out of the fray of football policing for several years and needed to get up to speed with developments in public order and safety operations very quickly. Although this was all quite daunting, it was also very exciting and I couldn't wait to get started. The first thing to do was get trained in the command of such operations and events. I quickly did this and got myself up to speed with all the advances that had been made tactically and operationally while I had been swanning around in a suit and tie in CID. Command protocols had significantly changed and were much more professional than in the early 1980s. Intelligence structures had also changed, but thankfully I was well versed in these, as I had been involved in introducing the National Intelligence Model into BTP and regularly became involved with the intelligence function as a senior detective.

I very quickly realised that operating as a PC in the 1980s was going to be very different to that of being in charge of big national football operations for BTP in 2003. My deputy at that time was

Superintendent Peter McHugh, who thankfully had bags of football and events policing operations experience. I shadowed Peter a few times before letting myself loose on the travelling public as the overall commander of football operations across great swathes of the country.

I was amazed at the knowledge, and experience, of the football intelligence officers that worked on my area. Not only did they have an intimate knowledge of all of the key football groups across the area, they also seemed to know exactly how these groups would travel from A to B at any given time, with a real understanding of the rail network across the country. This allowed us to deploy our scant resources to the maximum effect, and on most occasions we got it absolutely right and generally were in the right place at the right time.

I only had 250 officers at my disposal for the entire area, which included detectives and some other functions that were not regularly able to be deployed as part of our football response. Careful preparation, planning and tactics became second nature, as did working very closely with local police forces and the rail industry.

For example, a cup final at the Millenium Stadium, involving a club from London and a club from the north-west, would require joint planning, intelligence sharing and operational protocols with several different partners. This would include meetings with the clubs involved, to establish ticket sales and numbers of fans travelling by official club transport, and supporters clubs, which would give us an idea of the numbers who might travel by train. Then would come meetings with the rail industry to ascertain advance travel sales, and to ensure that the force and the rail staff involved would be joined up in the planning and operation on the day.

Meetings with local forces would be required for intelligence sharing and identification of handover and pinch points that might occur during the event itself. Staff from different BTP areas would then need to be engaged with, to ensure that sufficient escort serials would be deployed to see that the travelling fans arrived home safely without causing any problems on their return journey. As one can imagine, this was quite a task and in most cases undertaken by officers on top of their day job.

Peter McHugh recalls working with Alan and the complexities of policing football at that time,

> Alan came to the area and after shadowing me for a couple of fixtures we soon fitted into the recognised command structure, whereby he would perform the role of Silver Commander and I did Bronze Commander, on the ground.
>
> Before Alan arrived we had got into a ridiculous situation where we needed routinely to ask for mutual aid from our own force, but couldn't get it without paying each officer three rest day workings, so that they could travel to Cardiff the day before and get paid for going home the day after the event. We simply couldn't afford this type of arrangement, so I put a report into the Police Committee asking for permission to approach Home Office forces, who I knew would be prepared to assist at half the cost.
>
> They eventually agreed and I developed something of a unique 'Service Level Agreement' for a number of forces to provide Police Support Units (PSUs), which would come under the command of the BTP while they were working with us. We used Dyfed Powys Police first, and then used Wiltshire Police a lot, and possibly even West Midlands Police on one occasion. It worked very well, the officers enjoyed working in a different environment, and to a degree it was one of the measures that brought BTP into mainstream policing.

Alan continues,

> As I have said, most of the time we got it absolutely right, but I remember two occasions when I made errors of judgement or mistakes.
>
> One incident was quite humorous looking back because it did not have an operational impact. In 2004, Millwall football club, from the second tier of English football, reached the FA Cup final to be played at the Millennium Stadium, Cardiff on 22 May 2004. This was a fantastic achievement for the club and obviously their supporters would all want a piece of the action. Their opponents would be Manchester United, who always took a large crowd wherever they went. It is regularly commented upon in football

supporting circles that as many Manchester United fans come from out of Manchester as from the city itself. This is definitely a fact in relation to Cockney Reds, and we knew that trains between Cardiff and London on the day would contain sets of fans from both clubs, which is never the best situation!

I was due to be the BTP Gold Commander for the event and duly arranged and chaired the first planning meeting in Cardiff, involving senior officials and members of several other organisations. After the usual introductions, the agenda for this type of meeting usually starts with the Gold Commander setting out their strategy for the event.

As a Charlton fan, Millwall are never going to be my favourite club, and they do of course come with their own reputation. Their supporters anthem of, 'We are Millwall, We are Millwall, no-one like us we don't care' is well known throughout football and is not without reason. As I said earlier, football violence had diminished considerably by 2004, but I was slightly anxious, particularly as we were gaining intelligence that supporters from local club Cardiff City were looking to spoil the Millwall party. The rivalry between Cardiff and Millwall was also well known in football circles and they were definitely not the best of friends.

I opened the meeting, which was being minuted by a very competent member of support staff, and started by saying some fairly non-complimentary, but in my mind light hearted, comments about Millwall supporters and said that our strategy for the day was merely 'to survive.' This all seemed pretty innocuous at the time and the meeting proceeded as planned. When I read the meeting minutes a couple of days later I was horrified; the comments I had made in humour, or so I thought, had been repeated in the minutes verbatim and did not look at all funny in print. I quickly contacted the minute taker and told her not to distribute them until I had made some changes. The problem was that, being so efficient, she had already sent them to the attendees with my less than wise comments in them! Suffice to say we spent a very uncomfortable time contacting colleagues and explaining that the minutes contained some errors and a corrected version would be sent out later that afternoon.

I learned two very valuable lessons that afternoon; do not make jokes at major event briefings particularly at the expense of those involved, and always check minutes before they are sent, however much you trust the minute taker. As it turned out, my anxiety around the event was completely unnecessary. It was one of the best events I commanded and we had almost no incidents of disorder at all on the rail system either before or after the game. The supporters from both clubs behaved impeccably, the train networks operated perfectly and we had tremendous support from all across the force, which enabled us to escort every train back to London after the event.

A good day was had by all and I was mightily relieved when I stood down the last of our officers at Cardiff late in the evening and had been advised that the last of the London trains had arrived back to the English capital without incident.

The second thing I got wrong was definitely not humorous, did have an operational impact, and I still feel bad about it, although the outcome could have been much worse.

On 25 September 2004, I was the senior officer for the football Saturday in the Wales and Western area. This was a duty I had undertaken many times and, as usual, we had planned for the day meticulously having considered all the fixtures taking place and the intelligence available to us. We were concerned with about seven fixtures that were predominately assessed as category A or B. Category A fixtures required little, if any, policing, whereas Category B fixtures were assessed as having the potential for spontaneous disorder. Category C matches were those where disorder was likely and required a significant police operation.

The match we were most focussed on was Wolverhampton Wanderers, who were hosting Cardiff City for a 3 p.m. kick-off. This was a category B match and quite a few Cardiff fans had travelled to Wolverhampton, including some of their potential trouble-causing element. We had therefore deployed a reasonably strong travelling serial from our Cardiff police station to escort them. The supporters were described as boisterous but under control on their journey from Cardiff across to Wolverhampton.

The day was going reasonably well elsewhere, but the match at Wolverhampton had caused some problems, both in the town centre and around the stadium before kick-off. I discussed the return phase with the football intelligence officers, and colleagues from West Midlands Police who stated that they would deploy a Police Support Unit, being a specially trained and equipped unit of an inspector, three sergeants and eighteen police constables, at Wolverhampton station after the match. This was to help us ensure that the rival sets of fans were kept apart at the station.

With this assurance in place, I decided to forward deploy some of our travelling serial to Shrewsbury station, as it was believed that the fans from Cardiff might travel there for a potential confrontation with Shrewsbury Town fans, who had been playing at home against Yeovil Town. Clearly I thought this was the correct decision at the time, but yet again the plan did not survive contact with the enemy!

The West Midlands Police Support Unit that we had been promised was at the last minute forced to redeploy to the town centre as a result of disorder, but by then our travelling serial were already en route to Shrewsbury. This left our remaining officers at Wolverhampton somewhat exposed if disorder was to occur. A few minutes later, with Cardiff City fans on the station but under control, around 200 Wolverhampton Wanderers fans approached the station with only one thing on their minds.

It was only the incredible bravery of the BTP officers, and some excellent work by a BTP dog handler, that prevented the disorder that took place from getting totally out of control. Despite their bravery by putting themselves between the fans, some fighting did take place and one or two of our officers received minor injuries. A couple of arrests were made, but many more would have been taken into custody had the resources been available.

I felt terrible for putting my officers in that position and apologised profusely to Tony Barrett, the inspector who was in charge at Wolverhampton station. While he listened to my explanation, and accepted the rationale for the decision I had made, I knew that he was frustrated with me and I completely understood his feelings.

That was the last time I ever relied on resources that were not under my own control during public order or football policing operations. This incident still makes me shudder at what could have happened to my officers, but thankfully it was nowhere near as bad as it could have been. The rest of the 2004/05 season passed off reasonably well and despite having to work many Saturdays we nearly always managed to frustrate the potential troublemakers.

In 2006 I was temporarily promoted to assistant chief constable operations and posted to the role permanently in July 2007. This was a real achievement and I was of course delighted. It also meant working back in London and, among many other things, being in charge of uniform operations for British Transport Police over the whole country, which brought a massive amount of responsibility with it. This of course included football policing.

In the two previous years, as a chief superintendent in Birmingham, I had occasionally been frustrated with my London-based area commander colleagues as I sometimes felt they could, and should, have provided more resources for travelling serials for their clubs when they came on to our patch. In fairness to them, my area did not suffer the level of general crime that theirs did, as they never stopped reminding me when I banged on about football! I was now, though, in a position to exert more influence across the whole force and I suspect that I probably drove my colleagues mad for a while, insisting that they upped their game in relation to football policing.

I used to look at the logs every Monday morning and get immensely frustrated at the number of football incidents recorded, albeit the majority of them were at the minor end of the scale. I felt that the force had to allocate more time and resource to this issue and gradually convinced others that this was the case. It was around this time that I began to work with my co-author Mike Layton, who was Director of Intelligence for the force at the time. It is fair to say that Mike shared my view that we had to do more to deal with the issue of football disorder that was definitely starting to raise its profile again.

One operation that we definitely got right and gave lots of attention to was the first FA Cup final back at Wembley on 19 May 2007. The stadium had been rebuilt and this fixture was definitely going to be a showcase event. The stadium is served by two Overground stations, Wembley Stadium and Wembley Central. In addition, Wembley Park London Underground station is only a few minute walk from the famous venue and is the station that the vast majority of fans use. Most attendees at Wembley use public transport for at least part of their journey, so we knew it was going to be a busy event for us and it was vital for London as a city to be able to manage such an event successfully.

There was also understandably a lot of political interest from Transport for London and the Mayor's office, as of course London had been allocated the Olympic Games for 2012 by this time, and hosting this event successfully would assist with confidence levels in the lead up to the Games. This was not an operation to get wrong.

I was very fortunate in that the lead operational commander working with me for this event was Paul Crowther, who was chief superintendent and area commander for our London Underground area at that time. Paul is, and was then, ruthlessly efficient and I knew that his operational planning would be spot on, so I felt pretty confident about being in overall charge of the event. He was also the area commander for our London Underground area and had direct access to a large number of resources, so that was something else that fell into place without any intervention needed from me.

Paul Crowther OBE is now the chief constable of the BTP.

The final was between Chelsea and Manchester United and had the potential for disorder but was not a Category C high-risk match. In planning for the event, Paul focussed predominately on the London end of the operation, and I paid more attention to ensuring that our North West area colleagues provided sufficient support in terms of escort serials for the supporters travelling down from Manchester. At one of the final pre-event meetings we went through the tactical and operational plans and it became clear that every eventuality that could be foreseen had been covered by the planning team. There is, however, always something that tests you in these operations and on the day of the event far more supporters than expected came in to Wembley from the north.

Stations such as Watford Junction and Stanmore were very busy, but this was quickly dealt with by the control room, who deployed some of our reserve resources to those areas. During the forward phase I visited Euston, Baker Street and all three Wembley stations and it was clear from talking to our officers that they were all well briefed and ready for whatever they would have to deal with.

While there were some potential flash points, and some supporters seeking out trouble, we always seemed to be one step ahead with our officers in the right place at the right time to prevent any disorder.

The event went very successfully and our Wembley event plan certainly stood up to the test. I was the Gold Commander for several Wembley events after this and each one could be considered as a success with relatively low amounts of disorder taking place.

The force's response to football was still taking up a lot of my time. While there were some serious incidents that took place, it was the amount of low-level disorder that was taking place on trains that was really annoying me. It seemed that some football fans, although definitely a small minority, still thought that using abusive, racist and sexist language and behaviour was acceptable. To me it definitely was not and several operations were put in place to combat that sort of behaviour right across the country.

I strengthened the Central Event Planning Unit at force headquarters and directed that they take a more proactive role in assessing the resourcing levels that our area planning teams were allocating to football. This occasionally led to a healthy debate and on a couple of occasions I was forced to directly order that resources were increased to a level that I thought acceptable.

I also made it clear that when we utilised travelling serials to escort fans, they had to be strong enough in numbers to be proactive and take strong action as necessary. This may sound simple and obvious, but resourcing stations and trains that were impacted by football all across the country was quite a challenge. In addition, the force also still had to cover all of its other commitments in relation to counter-terrorism, general crime, disruption and cable theft, which was becoming an increasing problem.

I remember checking the logs one Monday morning following a weekend that I had not worked and being anxious about the description of a particular football-related event. A female member of rail staff, who had been working the last train out of Kings Cross to Newcastle, had clearly had an awful time with a large group of Newcastle United supporters following their match in London. They had verbally and physically abused her and created an atmosphere of fear and intimidation throughout the journey north. It also appeared that BTP officers had not covered themselves in glory in the way that they had responded to her call for assistance.

The force had an officer seconded to the train operating company involved and I contacted this officer, Inspector Robin Edwards, to see if I could have a conversation with the lady concerned. This was arranged and I was shocked when she told me her story. She outlined how, if allocated the duty that covered the last train out of London to Newcastle on a Saturday night during the football season, she would immediately start to feel anxious and unwell. She hoped that BTP would deploy an escort serial, which made things better, but knew this did not always happen. It mattered not which team was travelling back to the north east, Newcastle United, Sunderland or Middlesbrough, as they were equally bad when in drink and in a crowd on the train.

Her description of the particular incident that had caused me to contact her was awful. A group of about thirty men calling themselves football fans had caused mayhem throughout a four-hour journey and she felt she just had to suffer what was taking place. This included extremely explicit sexual innuendos and crude abuse directly to her. All this had taken place in the sight and hearing of other passengers, who were so intimidated that they felt powerless to help her. In fairness, she did make it clear that this incident was the worst that she had ever encountered but I swore to myself this would not be allowed to happen again.

I immediately ensured that the last train out of Kings Cross to the north east would always be escorted if one of the three big clubs were playing in London. I also arranged for the member of staff to attend our Force Management Team meeting to tell her story as I wanted all of our senior officers to feel as angry about this as I did. When she did attend and tell her story you could have heard a pin drop. It was obvious that my colleagues felt the same as I did and we collectively agreed to resolve this type of situation and prevent it in the future.

I also arranged and hosted seminars with senior staff from the train operating companies as they also had a responsibility to support their staff and passengers on football Saturdays. It was all very well encouraging football fans on to their services, but measures had to be put in place to keep the trains free from antisocial behaviour and that was not only the domain of the police.

I engaged with the Football Association, Premier League and Football League in an effort to raise the issue of football disorder, particularly on train journeys after matches had taken place. To be fair, these bodies did engage with me and senior people from the rail industry, but they always held their stance that behaviour outside of stadia was not really their responsibility. These bodies had done a lot to eradicate problems within football grounds and I understood their position, albeit I did not agree. I am certain they were also concerned that they may end up having to fund some policing activity away from the grounds and that was definitely not what they wanted to do.

There is no doubt that football policing did become more of a priority to BTP between 2006 and around 2010, when my role changed to directly overseeing our areas in England and Wales and being responsible for our major crime and intelligence function. The good thing was that the football and public order portfolio was being taken over by my friend and colleague, Assistant Chief Constable Stephen Thomas, who was extremely experienced, and for several years had been the lead football policing officer for the Association of Chief Police Officers. I knew, and was confident, that Steve would be just as interested in dealing with football issues as I was and that proved to be the case with football policing continuing to improve under Steve's stewardship.

It is interesting, however, that as I write this piece in May 2015, the force is once again facing some difficult football policing issues after a period of relative calm.

I don't think the issue will ever go away completely, but there is no doubt that the professionalism and dedication of BTP officers all over the country help to keep people safe when travelling on trains with the very small minority element of football fans that want to cause trouble.

As a fellow former chief officer, Paul Nicholas echoed the same sentiments as Alan at the manner in which BTP, as a unique national police force, carried out its duties in relation to policing football, and commented how far the BTP had come,

> The College of Policing has more recently updated ACPO guidance around football policing within which the partnership between police forces, the football and local authorities, BTP and others is given a very high prominence. It includes a specific section dedicated to the British Transport Police, and the need for them to be part of the planning and resourcing process, particularly if police forces are considering using powers under Section 27 of the Violent Crime Reduction Act 2006, which deals with giving directions to individuals to 'leave a locality.' We have truly come a long way from the days of 'football dumping' and now work ever more closely with train operators and other forces to alleviate problems.

14

2015 – THE HOOLIGANS ARE STILL AMONG US

On Saturday 10 January 2015, a forty-one-year-old Nottingham fan was walking through Nottingham railway station after a game with Sheffield Wednesday when he became involved in a confrontation with a Sheffield fan on platform 1. This resulted in him punching his opponent several times in the head. A BTP officer on duty at the station witnessed the assault and arrested the offender, who was later made the subject of a six-year football banning order.

On Saturday 17 January 2015, Stoke City fans returning from Leicester intimidated rail staff and members of the public on two East Midland train services. The emergency cord was pulled on one train, bringing it to a standstill. Hundreds of fans caught the 6.01 p.m. and 6.30 p.m. services from Leicester to Derby and police officers were assaulted. Detective Inspector Gareth Davies from BTP announced an investigation.

On the same date, police were drafted in to tackle fighting involving up to 150 Birmingham City fans as they prepared to travel home from Wakefield West station after a match with Leeds. At 7.25 p.m. West Yorkshire police officers were called to the station as fights broke out and bottles thrown before they were placed on board a train escorted by BTP officers.

Also, on the same date, a seventeen-year-old youth from Bedford travelling with his family from the Watford *v.* Charlton Athletic match was attacked at Watford High Street railway station.

As they were waiting for a train, a group of males entered the station, chanting and shouting, and a fight soon broke out as a train pulled onto the platform. The victim, his brother and cousin jumped onto the train to escape but were chased and spat on before the victim was punched so hard in the face that his jaw was fractured in two places.

On Saturday 24 January 2015, a group of up to five men were on board a stationary train at Derby station following a match between Derby County FC and Chesterfield FC. One of the men exposed himself to a member of rail staff on the train, while some of the other men grabbed his underwear and ripped it off him, leaving passengers feeling distressed and upset by their behaviour.

On Saturday 31 January 2015, Wolverhampton fans travelled to the Macron Stadium for a match with Bolton Wanderers. After the game a number of them boarded a Northern Rail train for the journey home, but while the train was stationary on the platform, with the doors closed, they were goaded by a group of Bolton fans. For a while, just two BTP officers stood between the two factions and tempers became frayed. As the train eventually started to move off, someone inside the train applied an emergency brake, following which a window in one of the carriage's was smashed from the inside. Only the timely arrival of police reinforcements prevented the situation from escalating.

In February 2015, a group of West Ham fans burst into anti-Jewish chants on the London Underground when a group of Hasidic Jews boarded the service. In the same month, the *Jewish Chronicle* reported that Chelsea fans on their way to a cup game with Tottenham were using anti-Semitic chants, the lyrics of which made reference to Hitler's gassing of the Jews.

Again in February 2015, Chelsea fans hit the national headlines following an incident in France, which was captured on camera, when they were filmed preventing a black man from entering a Metro train, and chanting racist slogans, before a match with Paris Saint-Germain. A complaint was subsequently made to the BTP that Chelsea fans had engaged in similar chants at St Pancras International railway station.

On Wednesday 18 February 2015, complaints were made that 'abhorrent' chants were shouted by a number of men, believed to be Chelsea supporters returning home, as they marched through the station. Superintendent Gill Murray of BTP said, 'The racist chanting was reported by a member of the public who was disgusted by the behaviour of the men who had travelled on the 18.40 hours service from Paris Gard du Nord.'

CCTV images were subsequently released of seven men whom BTP wished to speak to, and as a result they came forward.

Five men were subsequently summonsed by the Metropolitan Police in relation to the Paris incident, with a view to progressing football banning orders, and two twenty-one-year-old men were summoned by the BTP to appear before Westminster Magistrates Court with regard to the racist chants at St Pancras.

In 2015, BTP announced that it had dealt with fifteen incidents of alleged racist behaviour involving Chelsea fans since 2012.

On Thursday 19 February 2015, sectarian singing began on the 23.36 hours service between Gleneagles and Perth, shortly after midnight. A number of those involved were believed to be returning from a Europa League match in Glasgow.

On Saturday 28 February 2015, trouble occurred on the day of the Premier League match between West Bromwich Albion and Southampton. At 2.45 p.m., as a train was arriving at the Hawthorns railway station, a fifty-two-year-old man was assaulted and received a cut to his head and a black eye. On the same train a large group of fans began singing offensive songs without any regard for members of the public. Minutes later, another fifty-two-year-old man was assaulted on the station's platform and received a double fracture to his jaw, which required corrective surgery. Following the match at 7.30 p.m., fans heading south caused trouble on a Leamington-bound train.

On Sunday 1 March 2015, at least four men were captured on CCTV throwing punches following a stand-off between Chelsea and Tottenham fans at Wembley Park Tube station after the Capital One Cup final. Fighting broke out after a man took a Chelsea flag from a female and threw it onto the train tracks. She responded by hitting him with another flag and shouts of 'Yid Army' came from the opposite platform – a reference to Tottenham's strong Jewish support. BTP moved in to break up the fighting as more people got involved, and jostled each other dangerously close to the platform edges. Two arrests were made at the time for assault and BTP released images of others involved.

At 10.30 p.m. on the same day, BTP officers were called to Stoke railway station to meet a London Euston service, travelling to Manchester Piccadilly, following yet more complaints of racist and abusive behaviour. Four men, believed to be Chelsea fans travelling back from watching Chelsea beat Tottenham in the Capital One Cup final were removed from the train, and four others left of their own accord.

BTP began investigating claims that someone was heard to chant 'Paris, Paris, Paris, that's the way I like it, a n***** on the door' on the Virgin service. At least one passenger, himself black, moved carriages to avoid the abuse, and two Asian girls were alleged to have been asked by the troublemakers why they were not wearing burkas, leaving them distressed and in tears.

On Saturday 7 March 2015, West Bromwich Albion played at Aston Villa's ground in Birmingham in the FA Cup quarter-finals. Before and after the match trouble broke out between rival sets of fans, and BTP officers found themselves supporting local police outside Witton railway station as a fight broke out. At Birmingham New Street station BTP officers dealt with confrontation involving Birmingham City supporters looking for trouble, and officers were assaulted as they made arrests.

On Saturday 21 March 2015, a train conductor was verbally abused and threatened on an Edinburgh to Dunblane service after he asked a group of men to stop chanting and shouting. The incident occurred on the 15.35 hours train from Waverley station, and was believed to involve fans returning from a match between Hibs and Rangers.

On Saturday 21 March 2015, fifty Oldham fans boarded a Virgin train service at Crewe carrying large amounts of alcohol. As they travelled between Crewe and Stockport they began abusing a family. As they started fighting among themselves, the train manager decided to hold the train at Stockport fearing for the safety of other passengers.

At the end of March 2015, figures provided by the BTP were released in the media in relation to football-related incidents on the rail networks for the 2012/13 football season and 2013/14 seasons. A total of 1,027 incidents were recorded.

With seventy-seven incidents over the two seasons, Championship side Leeds United's hooligans topped the list of the worst offenders.

In the Premier League the top ten worst clubs, in relation to recorded incidents, consisted of Manchester United (36), Manchester City (30), Sunderland (28), Newcastle United (27), Aston Villa (24), Chelsea (24), Stoke City (21), Everton (19), Arsenal (18) and Tottenham Hotspur (18).

In the Championship, the top ten worst clubs were Leeds United (77), Birmingham City (40), Nottingham Forest (35), Wolverhampton Wanderers (25), Sheffield Wednesday (19), Wigan Athletic (18), Derby County (17), Millwall (17), Blackburn Rovers (15) and Blackpool (13).

The worst cases listed involved four cases of wounding and four cases of inflicting grievous bodily harm. Glasgow Rangers also featured prominently in the figures released.

At 12.20 p.m. on Monday 6 April 2015, trouble erupted at Sheffield railway station prior to a match with Alfreton Town Football Club. Some 200 Grimsby fans were making their way to the match on Easter Bank Holiday when violence erupted and two BTP officers were punched and kicked as missiles flew through the air. As the fans were dispersed, leaving the officers injured, they chanted and smashed glasses in the roadway outside.

On Saturday 11 April 2015, a number of families travelling north with children were on the 6.46 p.m. London Euston to Stoke-on-Trent train when they were subjected to abuse and foul language by a group of twelve football supporters. They shouted abuse at a boy in a wheelchair, as well as abusing a woman travelling with two daughters who left the train early at Nuneaton after fearing for their safety.

On Friday 17 April 2015, the current chief constable of the British Transport Police, Paul Crowther, chaired a national summit meeting to address rising concerns in relation to football hooligan-related incidents. The event was attended by football authorities, clubs, victims, the police and members of the rail industry. It received extensive media coverage and was deliberately timed to take place before the weekend's FA Cup semi-finals, when BTP would be deploying 400 officers.

Paul Crowther commented,

> Recently the media has highlighted cases of innocent bystanders who have been made victims of racial hatred – sadly they are not isolated cases. We must all accept that the behaviour of a sizeable minority of fans, and the processes in place to deal with them, is not acceptable, and is well below the standards we accept. Football hooligans are terrorising train passengers with casual thuggery every week.

He went on to say that serious organised gang violence was on the decline, but that 'thuggish behaviour' was on the increase, with a total of 630 incidents reported on the rail network so far this season (2014/15) alone, at the time of the writing, many of which were racist and hate crimes.

To reinforce this message, a forty-three-year-old head teacher, Dawn Preston, had described how her family endured a terrifying journey between London and Rugby after a day out with her family in London. It began at Euston station when she witnessed a skirmish and was allowed by rail staff to sit in First Class on the train for safety after her eight-year-old daughter burst into tears terrified. The coach was then invaded by up to forty football supporters, believed to be Everton fans, carrying cans of lager and bottles of vodka. They continually swore loudly and when two BTP officers tried to remove them from the carriage they simply ignored them initially and then started chanting 'Kill the Bill' as tension rose. Unable to endure the journey any further, the family got off at Rugby.

Only a week before, the chairman of Cambridge United Football Club, Dave Doggett, highlighted the dangers of an older generation of men who were trying to relive their heydays of the 1980s by trying to encourage younger fans to get involved in pre-arranged fights.

During the period between Friday 24 April 2015 and Sunday 26 April 2015, BTP officers made thirteen arrests across the rail networks in the UK during the course of twenty-one football-related incidents. The arrests were made for violence, racial abuse and drunken behaviour on trains and stations.

On Saturday 25 April 2015, shortly after 2 p.m., a woman boarded a Northern Rail service train travelling between Leeds and Bradford Forster Square, together with a four-year-old child. After sitting down in a carriage in the centre of the train, a group of men entered and immediately started chanting, singing football songs and using abusive language. Racist language was then directed at the child and, as the woman tried to remonstrate with the men, she was met with further abuse until she decided to leave the train at Shipley. BTP subsequently released CCTV pictures of eight men they were seeking to trace in connection with the incident.

Also on the same day, two men who had been refused entry to a football match earlier in the day were arrested for making racist comments towards two other men on a Kings Cross to Doncaster train. Both were charged with racial harassment.

Meanwhile, at Milton Keynes a sixteen-year-old boy from Bedford was punched by a forty-eight-year-old man on one of the platforms, in a football-related incident. The offender was duly arrested and charged with assault occasioning actual bodily harm.

In Scotland, Aberdeen fans were subjected to alcohol restrictions on Scot Rail trains for journeys to watch a match in Inverness.

On Saturday 15 May 2015, BTP officers made three arrests – two for affray, and one on suspicion of causing grievous bodily harm – after a fight broke out at 6.40 p.m. near to Kings Cross railway station, involving fans believed to be from Everton, Newcastle United and Hull City. Bottles and glasses were thrown indiscriminately, despite the presence of children, as people were randomly punched and kicked. One person sustained head injuries and was hospitalised, while others nursed black eyes and cuts and bruises, and the roadway was left covered in broken glass.

The conclusion of the football season at the end of May 2015 provided a brief period of respite for the BTP, the rail industry and the travelling public. It also provided an opportunity for reflection, in the knowledge that within six weeks a programme of so-called friendly games would start the whole process off all over again. Expectations had been raised by the force that standards of behaviour among fans would be moderated, but only time would tell if their efforts will succeed.

At that moment, it seemed that football violence on the network was still alive and well.

EPILOGUE

In 2011, during the last few months of his police service, Mike Layton, the operations superintendent with the British Transport Police in Birmingham, stood on New Street station. It had been a long journey from his first day as a police cadet with BTP on 1 September 1968, and on through service with the West Midlands Police and elsewhere. Today was to be a day of nostalgia as Birmingham City were due to play Aston Villa once again.

Standing next to him, in very familiar territory, was 'James', the officer who had worked with him as an undercover officer in 1987. Dotted around the station concourse were groups of traditional bluenoses, mixed in with some of the older generation of Zulu Warriors and the usual hangers on. These games were always massive grudge games and the Zulus were out to show that they were still a force to be reckoned with.

Superintendent Layton travelled with James and a police escort on the short train journey to Witton, which was just next to the Villa ground. The hardened hooligans kept their mouths shut, they knew better than to expose themselves, and watched mildly amused while a drunken fan tried to engage the officers.

Policing football fans on trains is entirely different to policing fans on the streets. Immediate assistance is simply not there and you have to learn how to survive and choose your moments. The drunk quickly got the message however and went quiet. While the officers were all crammed in together, a few among many, they nevertheless had confidence in each other and had no fear of the hooligan element.

The train arrived at Witton and the fans massed on the platform, ready for the short march to the ground. As they left the station, the BTP officers remained behind – their job done for that moment. For Mike Layton it was a moment for quiet reflection, tinged with some sadness, but a fitting finish to his career.

Alan Pacey reflects on his final moments in the job,

It was during the period that I was not in overall charge of football policing that I made the journey from my home town to Bolton to watch my team Charlton Athletic. It was Saturday 21 December and I was due to meet my friend, who was a Bolton fan and also a fellow BTP officer, and my son at Bolton station. I caught the train in the morning to Manchester Piccadilly, where I was due to change trains.

I started to read the newspaper and realised that Aston Villa were playing Stoke City that day, so it came as no surprise when about thirty Aston Villa fans boarded the train I was on at Birmingham New Street. The problem was that a number of them sat in seats that had been reserved by other passengers and refused to budge when asked by the train manager.

The situation was getting a little heated so I had no choice but to get involved! I quickly spoke to the most vociferous of them and immediately let them know I was a football fan, as well as a British Transport Police officer, and that I was going to a match myself. After taking some abuse, which was fairly light-hearted, I told them that if their conduct delayed me as a result of having to deal with them, it was likely that they might also miss their match, and obviously this was the last thing I wanted. To be honest, I was slightly anxious as there were quite a few of them and I was not exactly sure how this was going to pan out.

Thankfully, the thought of being delayed and missing their match won the day and they moved out of the reserved seats. We ended up having a good chat about football until they got off the train at Stoke, although I have to admit I was quite relieved when the train moved off with them on the platform.

Epilogue

Although my own role as an assistant chief constable had changed, I made sure that I continued to undertake my share of Gold Command football duties. I thoroughly enjoyed them and was always impressed by our officers and how they dealt with these operations. My last event before retiring was the FA Cup final in 2014.

During the planning processes, and while I visited our officers on the ground that day, I considered how much had changed since I had started in 1980. We had excellent planning processes in place, and sophisticated intelligence structures that kept us very well informed. Our tactical and operational commanders were experienced, and extremely well trained, and our officers on the ground were in my view some of the most professional in the country. I felt very proud to have played some part in the success of our football policing efforts.

Readers of this book could be forgiven for thinking that every time there is a football match the tube and rail networks turn into the Wild West. That is far from the truth and most of the time BTP officers keep football supporters and the travelling public very safe.

ACKNOWLEDGEMENTS

A very big thank you to the British Transport Police History Group.

Cartoonist 'PARK' – Retired BTP Sergeant Thomas Park (Nottingham).

The BTPHG Journal Digitalisation Group.

British Transport Police Retired Officers Association.

Glyn Hellam – British Transport Police (Press Desk Manager).

Constable On The Track – social media group.

Paul Robb QPM – Retired BTP Assistant Chief Constable (Crime).

Martyn Ripley OBE – retired BTP Chief Superintendent (North West and Scotland).

Ed Thompson – Retired BTP Sergeant (London Underground).

Bill Rogerson MBE – Retired BTP Sergeant (Bangor).

Kevin B. Thompson – Retired BTP Inspector (LU London).

Alistair Cumming – Retired BTP Detective Chief Inspector (Force Headquarters).

Robert C. Davison – Retired BTP Chief Inspector (Waterloo).

Paul Majster – Retired BTP Detective Constable (Birmingham).

Viv Head – Retired BTP Detective Inspector (Midlands Area HQ).

Ian Murray – Retired Inspector BTP (Scotland).

Andrew Fidgett – Retired BTP Dog Handler (London North) and Police Dog Ned.

Keith Feaviour – Retired BTP Constable (London North Crime Desk Kings Cross).

Christopher Hall – Retired BTP Sergeant (Liverpool Street).

Brian Preece – Retired BTP Detective Constable (Crime Management Unit Birmingham).

David Farrelly – Retired BTP Superintendent (London).

Keith Fleetwood – Retired BTP Inspector (Waterloo).

'Steve' – Retired BTP Sergeant (Birmingham).

Kevin Shanahan – Retired BTP Detective Chief Inspector (LU Area Crime Unit Commander).

Dennis Temporal MBE – Retired BTP Inspector (Force Football Intelligence Unit).

Walt Girdley – Retired BTP Sergeant (Heysham Harbour).

Stan Wade – Retired BTP Sergeant (Stranraer Port).

John Owen – Retired BTP Inspector (London North Area HQ) Kings Cross.

Keith Groves – Retired BTP Chief Inspector (North East Area Operations).

Cheryl Birbeck – Retired BTP Constable (Manchester Piccadilly).

Michael Barry – Retired BTP Detective Inspector (London North).

Andy Stonebridge and his late father Bert Stonebridge – retired BTP Constable (Park Royal).

Phil Trendall QPM – Retired BTP Superintendent (Force Headquarters Operations).

Richard Jones – Former BTP Special Constabulary Chief Inspector (Cardiff).

Robin Edwards – Retired BTP Inspector (North East Area).

Neil Moffatt – Retired BTP Chief Inspector (North West Area – Manchester).

Geoff Lowe – Retired BTP Inspector (Force Headquarters – London).

Terry Nicholson – Retired BTP Chief Superintendent (North East Area – Leeds).

'Ginger' Ablard BEM – Retired BTP Sergeant (Force Headquarters Dog Section).

'James' – BTP Officer who worked on Operation Red Card in Birmingham.

Brian Gosden – Retired BTP Chief Inspector (Force Control Rooms).

Paul Nicholas QPM – Retired BTP Assistant Chief Constable (Operations).

Willie Baker – Retired BTP Superintendent (Bramshill Programme Director SLDP).

Eamonn Carroll – Retired BTP Chief Superintendent (FHQ Territorial Policing).

Chris Jessup – Retired BTP Constable (Force Headquarters Dog Section).

Peter McHugh – Retired BTP Chief Superintendent (Area Commander Wales & Western).

Tony Thompson – Retired BTP Superintendent (Major Incident Support Unit FHQ).

'Joe' Duffy – Retired BTP Acting Police Sergeant (North West Area).

winning women's votes

1 WEEK LOAN

Re   to   of issue
F   er day

No renewal.